Decorating Cakes for Children's Parties

Polly Pinder studied graphics at Leeds Art College. She now is a lecturer in Graphic Design at Wakefield District College. Her first job was with a Yorkshire newspaper. She has four children and lives in Leeds where she has her own studio at the top of the house.

She has written a children's book *The Potato Man* (first published in Japan) and wrote and designed the *Home-Made* series which she successfully expanded in *Home-Made and at a fraction of the cost,* published in 1983. She also designed bed linen and wallpapers, and the graphics for a wallpaper book based upon newly discovered eighteenth century wallpapers. Her last book, *Decorating Cakes for Special Occasions* was published in 1985 and sells all over the world. She has just finished another book in which she breaks new ground: *A Whole New World of Chocolate* which is being published in 1988.

by the same author
HOME-MADE, AND AT A FRACTION OF THE COST.
DECORATING CAKES FOR CHILDREN'S PARTIES.
A WHOLE NEW WORLD OF CHOCOLATE.

Decorating Cakes

for Children's Parties

Polly Pinder

SEARCH PRESS LTD

First published 1984

Search Press Ltd.,
Wellwood, North Farm Road,
Tunbridge Wells, Kent. TN2 3DR

First published in paperback, 1985

Reprinted 1986, 1987

ISBN 0 85532 568 2

Printed in Spain by Elkar S. Coop, Bilbao-12

Contents

Introduction

I have to admit that, until being asked to write this book I had never iced a cake in my life . . . a fact which I hope will encourage those who feel that the art of cake decorating is beyond their capabilities. In fact, using fondant icing to decorate cakes is really just a tastier step-up from modelling with plasticine. When our four children were small, I used to spend hours with them at the kitchen table making plasticine cups, plates, fried eggs, animals and all sorts of little things. Fondant modelling gives even more enjoyment because the 'little things' can not only be looked at with delight, but also eaten!

There are thousands of women who relish the thought of their children's parties, the organising, the preparation and finally the big cake. This book is for them.

For those who have never used the fondant method of decorating before, the best way to approach it is with confidence and a sense of fun. If mistakes are made, they can always be covered up or hidden by a little something made from fondant or royal icing. When I was making the Superman cake (page 82) I did not allow him enough time to dry and as I picked him up to position him on the cake, his arm fell off! After sticking it back on, I made his cape swirl around the arm to cover most of the crack. These things frequently happen but they can usually be easily rectified.

None of the cakes in this book is difficult to decorate but some require more time and patience than others. It is important that you read the general notes first and then read through the step-by-step instructions, perhaps practising on a 'non-celebratory' cake to get used to working with fondant and using an icing bag.

General Notes

The cakes

All the cakes in the book are made from plain rice-cake mixture because, in my experience, children tend to prefer sponge to the rich fruit-cake recipe normally used for heavy decoration. For this reason the cakes ought to be eaten within a week of being made, because after much longer the sponge will become dry and begin to shrink. There is no reason however, why the sponge should not be replaced with a rich fruit mixture if you prefer. This book offers a chart, on page 9 which will give you the ingredients and quantities for the size of cake you require.

The plain sponge mixture can be varied in several ways: by adding glacé cherries, chopped walnuts, sultanas, chopped bananas or honey (as a rough guide, if the recipe requires 220g (8oz) of butter, add the same quantity of fruit or nuts); by substituting 1 tblsp of flour and 1 tblsp of ground rice for 2 tblsp of cocoa powder; or by adding essences – orange, lemon, raspberry, almond, vanilla, etc. The larger cakes can be split and filled with flavoured butter cream and/or jam. (If a cake has to be cut into different shapes it is better to add a flavouring rather than fruit or nuts.)

Method for baking

The method for baking the cakes is this: beat the sugar and butter until pale and fluffy (substitute margarine for butter if desired); gradually add alternate equal quantities of flour, ground rice and beaten egg and milk. The mixture should have a soft dropping consistency, a little more milk may be needed in some cases. The cakes are baked in the centre of the oven at 350°F (180°C), Gas Mark 4, and are ready when a firm, light-golden crust has formed and the cake has come slightly away from the sides of the tin. Allow to cool in the tin before removing, then leave overnight on a wire tray.

As well as the normal cake tins, food cans are also

used to give more variety to the shapes of the cakes. These should be washed, left to dry in a cool oven and then well greased. I cut out (to make releasing the cake easier) the bases and replace them with baking foil, then stand the cans on a baking sheet. They should be just over half filled with mixture and set on a shelf lower than the larger cakes. When the cake is baked, leave it until it is cold, remove the foil, turn a sharp knife around the cake and carefully push it out.

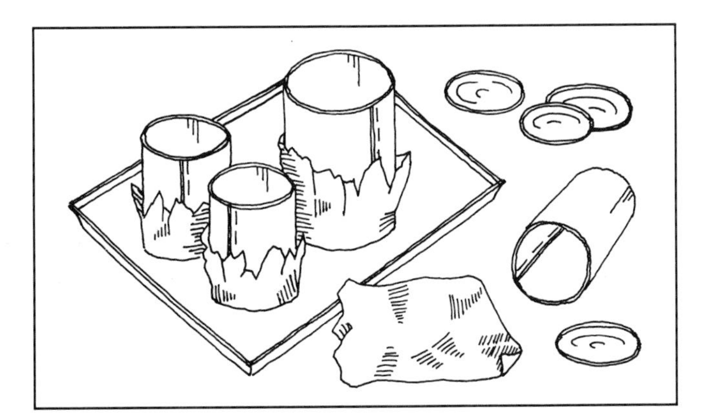

Apricot jam

This is used to coat the cakes before applying the fondant (apricot has the mildest flavour). It should be sieved, to remove skin and hard pieces, and gently heated just prior to brushing a thin film on to the cakes.

Fondant

This is an icing which has liquid glucose added to make it pliable and easy to model. To make 450g (1lb) drop the white of an egg into a basin and slowly mix in 450g (1lb) of sieved icing sugar and 2 tblsp of warmed liquid glucose. The quantities of icing sugar and egg white are not absolutely critical, more or less of one or the other may be needed to achieve the correct consistency, which should be easy and firm to work with – if it feels floppy, add some more sieved icing sugar; if it becomes difficult and hard to handle, add a little more egg white. Some recipes require one quarter of an egg white. As this is difficult to measure, make a rough guess, being generous rather than careful.

Fondant which is not needed immediately should be wrapped in greaseproof paper or cling film and kept in an airtight container at room temperature, not in the refrigerator.

Ready-made commercial fondant can be bought in 220g (½lb) blocks from cake-decorating specialists and some supermarkets. It is very convenient if you are short of time and it comes in a variety of flavours.

Flavour and colour is added to the fondant at the kneading stage, when all the icing sugar and glucose has been mixed in. I would suggest not flavouring the fondant if it has already been added to the cake mixture. If a pale fondant is required add the colour, drop by

drop, from a metal skewer. When a large piece of fondant needs to have a very deep colour, make a well in the centre, carefully pour in the colour, then give a liberal shake with the dredger (containing 50% icing sugar and 50% cornflour) and knead the fondant.

Gum tragacanth (powdered gum) is sometimes used as a hardening agent. Use 1 teaspoon to 220g (8oz) of icing sugar. It is very useful if the fondant is to remain flat, but problems start when you mould and shape round cakes, for it dries rapidly and fine cracks can appear on the surface. The secret is to work very quickly. The gum can be bought from most chemists. It is rather expensive but worth keeping if you intend to do more than one fondant cake.

Spacers

Spacers are used to ensure an even piece of flat fondant. They are placed at each side of the fondant so that the rolling pin rolls over them and the fondant at the same time.

Spacers can be bought from cake decorating specialists but it is cheaper to buy a packet of flat lolly sticks (LS) and make your own. These are usually about 2mm (1/10in) thick. Make four spacers (use clear cellotape to join the lolly sticks together) 4 LS long, the first pair 1 LS thick and the second pair 2 LS thick – see the illustration on this page. Sometimes a piece of fondant needs to be 3 or 4 LS thick. As these pieces are usually quite small the spacers do not have to be long – simply cellotape the required number together. Again, see the illustration.

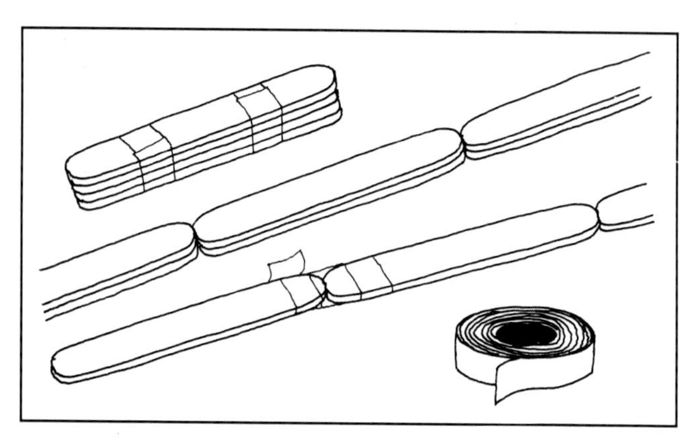

Royal Icing

To make 220g (8oz) of royal icing, drop one egg white into a very clean basin (with no traces of grease) and slowly mix in 220g (8oz) of sieved icing sugar. This can be done by hand or in the mixer, using a beater rather than a whisk, on the slowest speed.

Again, the quantities are not critical; you may need more or less of one or the other to obtain the correct consistency. Some recipes need only one-eighth of an egg white. As with the fondant, have a rough guess, erring on the side of generosity. The correct consistency can really only be judged after a little practice with the icing bag – it should not be too runny to lose its shape; or too stiff to flow easily from the bag.

As with the fondant, add colour, drop by drop, from a metal skewer. To obtain a shaded effect of piped work, drop a generous teaspoonful of two coloured icings, side by side, into the bag.

Royal icing can be stored in an airtight container and kept in the fridge for as long as three weeks, after which it will have to be gently beaten again before being used.

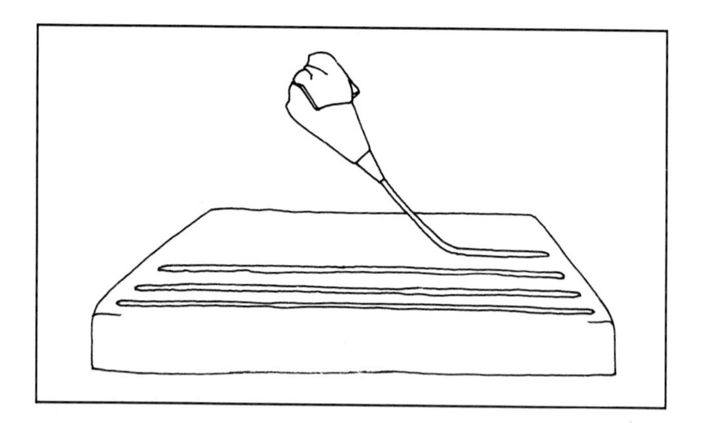

Icing bags and nozzles

I prefer to make my own disposable bags. They are more convenient and easier to use than the commercial tubes and bags, which one has to be continually washing when using different coloured icings.

Buy a packet of flat sheets of greaseproof paper (rather than a roll). Cut a strip off the sheet to make a square. See the illustration: fold the square into a triangle; fold point **A** to point **C**; then point **B** to point **D**; then point **C** to point **E**. Snip a small piece from point **X**. Open the bag, drop the nozzle in, making sure that half of it comes out at the bottom. Drop in a couple of teaspoons of royal icing, fold the flap over, fold the two corners **Y** and **Z** inwards, then pipe away! As the icing is used, fold the top of the bag over again.

Ateco icing nozzles have been used for all the pipe work on the cakes in this book, but if they are not available in your area you can use the equivalent in another make – where possible I have drawn the nozzles and the shape produced by each.

You can buy a small nozzle brush – which is extremely useful when you wash the nozzle – from cake-decorating specialists or kitchen equipment shops.

Piped writing

If you have not done piped writing before, it may be as well to practise on the table top.

To pipe on to the iced cake, first write the word on parchment paper, then attach the paper, with two dabs of royal icing, to the cake. Stick a pin at intervals through the pencil lines. Remove the paper. Use the pin marks as guides and the original drawn letters as reference.

To centre a word on the cake, using a tape measure or ruler, find the centre of the cake and mark with a pin. Find the centre of the word by measuring, mark with a pencil, then lay the pencil mark over the pin mark.

Colouring

The basic colours can be bought from most supermarkets. For unusual shades you will probably have to go to a cake-decorating specialist. The only *edible* gold and silver I have found comes in powdered form. There is a liquid form sold with other colours of the same brand, but this is labelled toxic and I suggest you do not use it.

Candles

There are candles called 'Magic Candles' which re-light after being blown out. They are fun, but can be dangerous. I used them for the Rocket (page 89) but we almost had to drown the cake in order to extinguish them.

Steel rule

This can be bought from cake-decorating specialists and some kitchen equipment shops. It is used to ensure a perfectly flat surface when covering a cake with royal icing – I use it as a straight-edge for cutting fondant.

Small paint brush

This is useful, not only for colour work on models, but for brushing the backs of pieces of fondant, which are then applied to the main cake.

Freezing

I have experimented with the cakes, but freezing is a 'hit and miss' way of trying to store them – some areas of the fondant dry, but others become soft and wet. All in all, I would not recommend it.

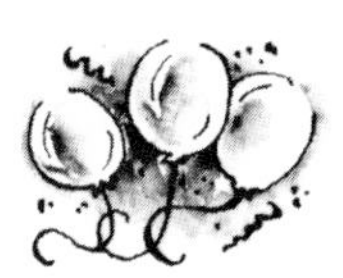

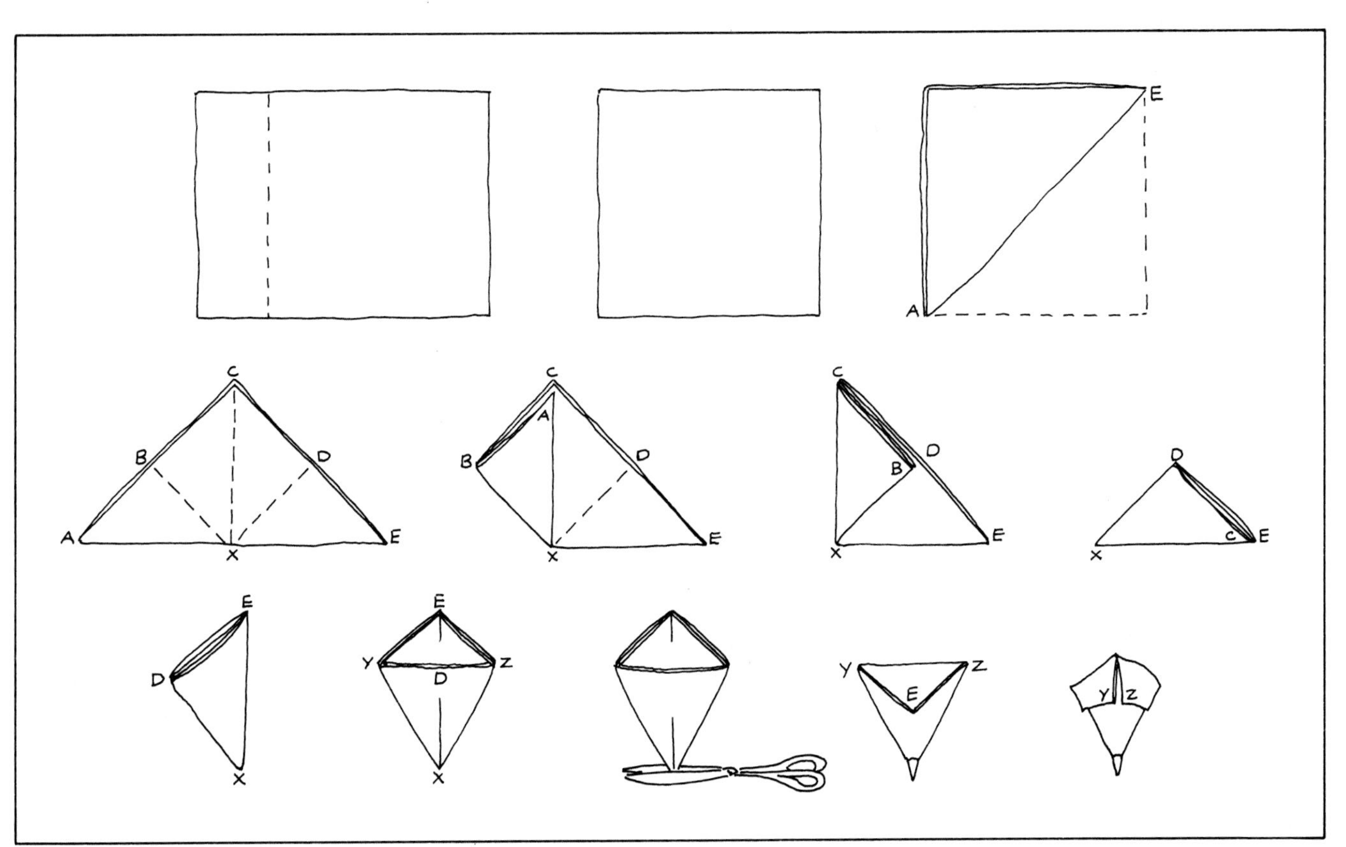

Rich fruit cake

	130mm (5in) square cake and 150mm (6in) round cake	150mm (6in) square cake and 180mm (7in) round cake	180mm (7in) square cake and 200mm (8in) round cake	200mm (8in) square cake and 230mm (9in) round cake	230mm (9in) square cake and 250mm (10in) round cake	250mm (10in) square cake and 280mm (11in) round cake	280mm (11in) square cake and 300mm (12in) round cake
Currants	110g (4oz)	170g (6oz)	280g (10oz)	360g (13oz)	500g (18oz)	670g (24oz)	900g (32oz)
Raisins	80g (3oz)	140g (5oz)	200g (7oz)	280g (10oz)	360g (13oz)	530g (19oz)	620g (22oz)
Sultanas	60g (2oz)	80g (3oz)	110g (4oz)	200g (7oz)	200g (7oz)	360g (13oz)	390g (14oz)
Chopped mixed peel	30g (1oz)	60g (2oz)	60g (2oz)	80g (3oz)	110g (4oz)	140g (5oz)	200g (7oz)
Glacé cherries	40g (1½oz)	70g (2½oz)	80g (3oz)	110g (4oz)	140g (5oz)	220g (8oz)	280g (10oz)
Chopped blanched almonds	30g (1oz)	60g (2oz)	60g (2oz)	80g (3oz)	110g (4oz)	140g (5oz)	200g (7oz)
Grated rind	½ lemon	½ lemon	¾ lemon	1 lemon	1 lemon	1 lemon	1½ lemons
Plain flour	100g (3½oz)	170g (6oz)	210g (7½oz)	340g (12oz)	390g (14oz)	590g (21oz)	670g (24oz)
Ground cinnamon	½ teasp	½ teasp	¾ teasp	1 teasp	1½ teasp	2 teasp	2½ teasp
Ground mixed spice	¼ teasp	¼ teasp	½ teasp	¾ teasp	1 teasp	1¼ teasp	1½ teasp
Butter	80g (3oz)	140g (5oz)	170g (6oz)	280g (10oz)	340g (12oz)	500g (18oz)	590g (21oz)
Soft brown sugar	80g (3oz)	140g (5oz)	170g (6oz)	280g (10oz)	340g (12oz)	500g (18oz)	590g (21oz)
Medium eggs	1½	2½	3	5	6	9	11
Black treacle	1 teasp	1 teasp	1 tblsp	1 tblsp	1 tblsp	2 tblsp	2 tblsp
Approx. cooking time	2 hours	2½ hours	2¾ hours	3¼ hours	3¾ hours	4¼ hours	5¼ hours

use first recipe for 900g (2lb) loaf cake

Mary, Mary, quite contrary

This is a pretty cake which will charm any little girl.

When buying the silver food colour for the bells, be sure to buy the edible sort (it comes in powdered form).

The basin I use as a base for Mary's dress is slightly smaller than the smallest pyrex mixing bowl. It holds just under 560ml (1pt) of water and has a diameter of 125mm (5in.).

The cake can be decorated in two days.

Please read the General Notes on pages 6 to 9 before starting to decorate the cake. Also read through the step-by-step instructions and check the ingredient and equipment lists.

Ingredients for cake

450g (16oz) butter
340g (12oz) caster sugar
560g (20oz) self-raising flour
200g (7oz) ground rice
220ml (8fl oz) milk beaten with 6 large eggs
filling (optional)

Make from this recipe:
1 × 180mm (7in.) round cake
1 pudding basin cake

Ingredients for fondant and royal icing

670g (1½lb) icing sugar, plus 170g (6oz)
1½ egg whites, plus ¾
3 tblsp liquid glucose
flavouring (optional)
Also: warm sieved apricot jam; 50/50 mixture of cornflour and icing sugar in a dusting dredger; green, pink, flesh, blue, yellow and silver food colouring; silver balls.

Equipment

Basins for mixing icings; sieve; spoons; rolling pin; steel rule; sharp-pointed knife; lolly sticks (LS) as spacers; pastry brush; small paint brush; greaseproof paper for icing bags; Ateco (or equivalent) icing nozzles 1, 2, 15, 66 and 82; 255mm (10in.) round silver board.

1. Leave the cakes overnight. Slice the tops until the surfaces are completely flat. Turn the round cake upside down and position it in the centre of the silver board.

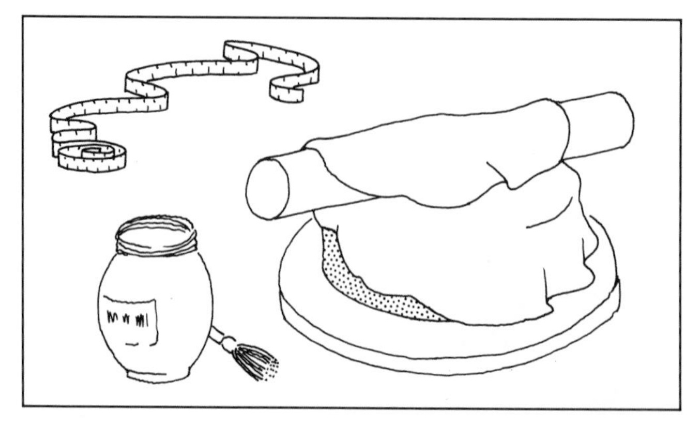

2. Make the fondant. Keep back 220g (8oz) and colour the remainder pale green. Measure across round cake. Roll fondant to 2 LS thick and cut a circle to cover cake. Brush cake with warm jam. With help of rolling pin apply fondant.

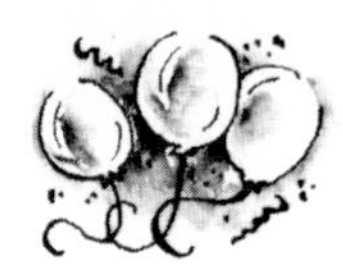

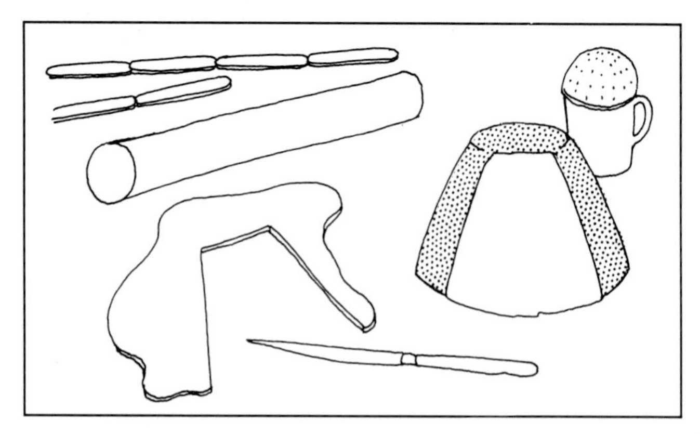

3. Break off a piece of white fondant. Roll to 1 LS thick. Measure depth of pudding cake. Cut a piece to fit – about 110mm (4¼in.) at widest part, as shown. Brush area to be covered with jam and apply fondant.

4. Brush top of pudding cake with jam. Take a piece of green fondant weighing about 80g (3oz). Model top of dress and body in two separate pieces, as shown.

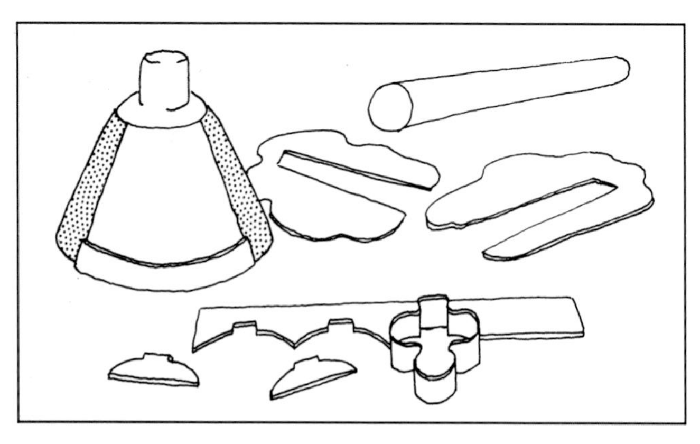

5. Take a piece of white fondant. Colour it bright pink. Roll to 1 LS thick and cut a strip 25mm (1in.) deep to fit bottom edge of panel. Apply with egg white, smoothing top edge of pink fondant into the white. Cut a white strip, same depth, to go above pink. Cut a fancy edge with cocktail cutter.

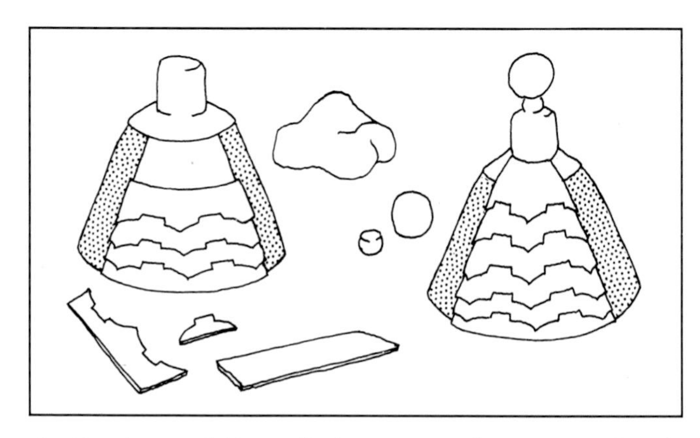

6. Continue adding a little more pink to strips. Work five fancy strips in all, then finish with a white one, deeper than the others, for the top of the dress.

Take some white fondant and add flesh colouring. Model a head and neck and attach to body with egg white. Leave both cakes to dry overnight.

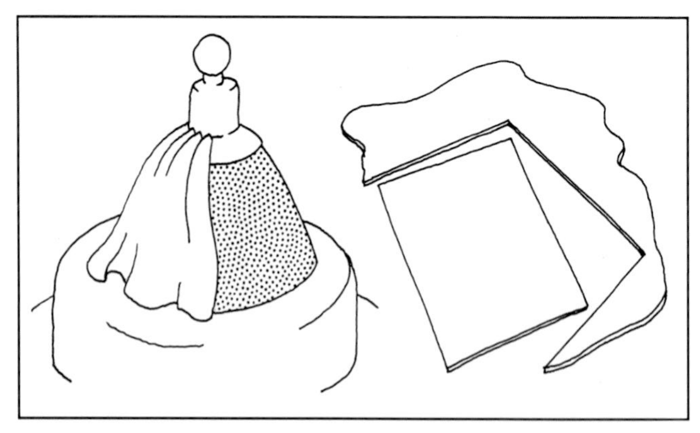

7. Position Mary on cake, towards back. Add a little blue to some white fondant. Roll to 1 LS thick. Make gathered part of dress in two pieces, as shown. Brush beneath waistline with egg white. Attach one rectangle of fondant, gathering into waist. Repeat with other piece – gathers will be smooth if fondant is soft.

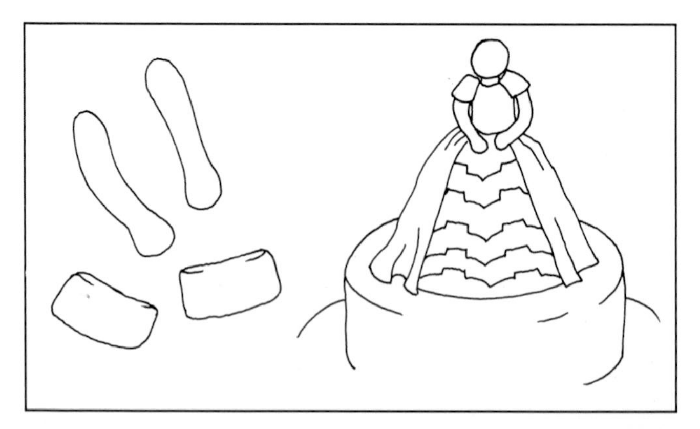

8. Take a little more white fondant and colour it flesh. Model two arms, attach them to body with egg white. Bend arms around slightly to support flowers. With a little green or blue fondant, model two small rectangles for sleeves. Attach around arm tops with egg white.

9. Take another small piece of fondant (any colour) and make into a roll. Lay across arm, securing with egg white. Model a little hat from a circle of remaining pink fondant. Attach to head with egg white.

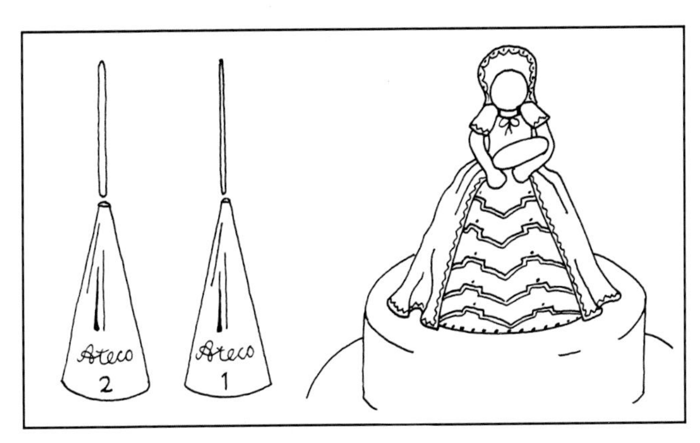

10. With *No. 2 nozzle* pipe white decoration around edge of bonnet. Pipe edging on layers of pink dress and a line of dots at bottom edge. With *No. 1 nozzle* and blue icing, pipe zigzag line around edge of blue dress and on sleeve edges. Pipe tiny dots underneath pink layers and on white icing of bonnet, as shown.

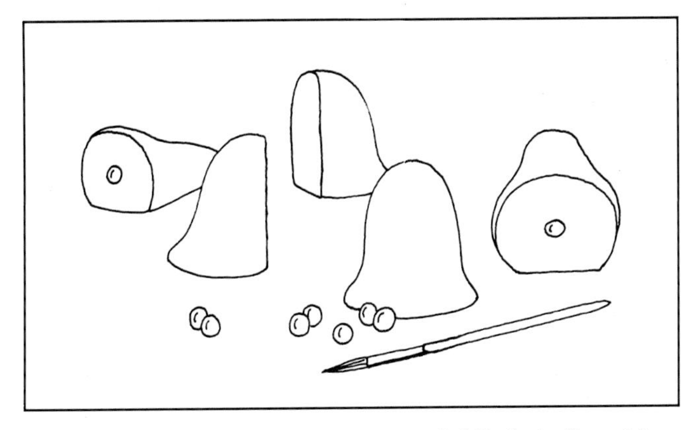

11. Using fondant trimmings, model little bells with a flat side to go against side of cake. Attach a silver ball underneath each, securing with egg white. Leave to dry for 20 minutes, then attach to sides of cake with a dab of icing. Paint with silver colouring.

12. Take a ball of white fondant, mix in silver to make grey. Roll into lengths about 80mm (3in.) long tapering at both ends. Curl around as shown. Leave to dry for 20 minutes then attach to sides of cake with a dab of icing.

13. With *nozzle No. 1* pipe pale yellow hair. Paint little blue eyes and red lips on the face. With *nozzle 82* pipe thick green stems for bells and shells. With darker green and *nozzle 2* pipe finer stems on sides of cake and over fondant in Mary's arms.

14. With dark green icing and *nozzle 66* pipe leaves coming up from base of cake. With very pale yellowy-green and *nozzle 15* pipe clusters of flowers at tops of finer stems and on stems in Mary's arms.

There was an old woman . . .

. . . who lived in a shoe, although it might be more accurate to say, 'There was an old woman who lived in a hiking boot'! I thought it might be better to have round cakes rather than the loaf cakes normally used for this subject – the finished shoe is not quite as I had intended, but the flat surfaces make it easier to decorate.

The food colouring used for the little children is 'Flesh'. This is not available from supermarkets but can be bought at cake-decorating specialists. If you have difficulty obtaining it, use pink with a drop of brown added.

The cake will take two days to decorate. All three components can be split and filled with butter cream.

Please read the General Notes on pages 6 to 9 before starting to decorate the cake. Also read through the step-by-step instructions and check the ingredient and equipment lists.

Ingredients for cake

280g (10oz) butter
220g (8oz) caster sugar
360g (13oz) self-raising flour
200g (7oz) ground rice
220ml (8fl oz) milk beaten with 4 large eggs
filling (optional)
Make from this recipe:
1 × 150mm (6in.) round cake
2 × 115mm (4½in.) round cakes

Ingredients for fondant and royal icing

790g (1¾lb) icing sugar, plus 110g (4oz)
1¾ egg whites, plus ½
almost 4 tblsp liquid glucose
flavouring (optional)
Also: warm sieved apricot jam; 50/50 mixture of cornflour and icing sugar in a dusting dredger; yellow, brown, blue, orange, black, and flesh food colouring.

Equipment

Basins for mixing icings: spoons; sieve; rolling pin; steel rule; sharp-pointed knife; lolly sticks (LS) as spacers; pastry brush; greaseproof paper for icing bag; Ateco (or equivalent) icing nozzles 1, 2 and 65; 300mm (12in.) round silver board.

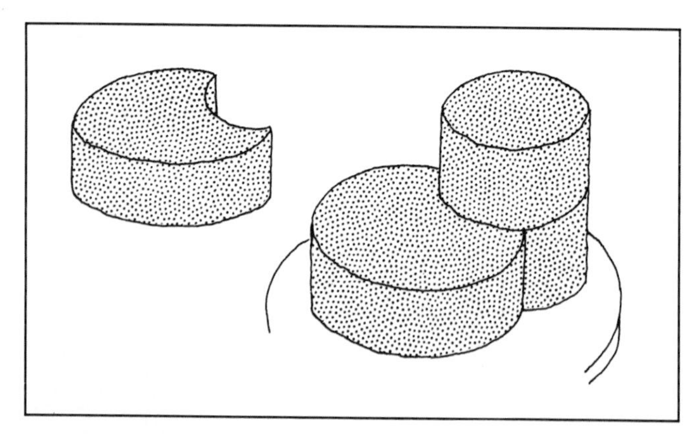

1. Having left the cakes overnight, slice the tops flat. Cut a curved piece out of the large cake, as shown, so that the small cake will fit flush. Sandwich the cakes together with butter icing and/or jam. Position in centre of silver board.

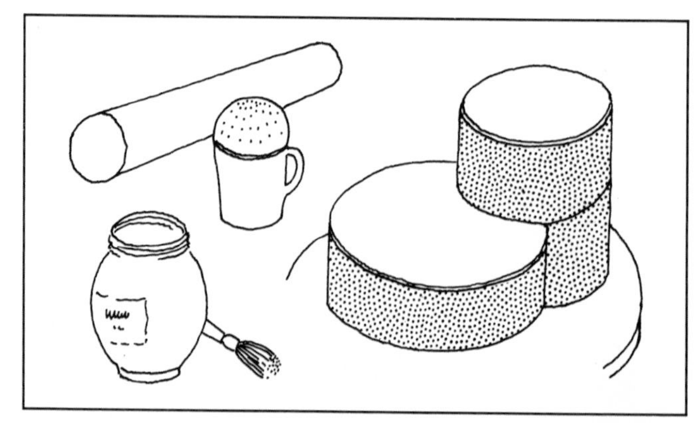

2. Make 790g (1¾lb) of fondant. Keep back 140g (5oz) and colour the remainder pale brown. Roll to 2 LS thick. Cut circles to fit tops of cakes (cut around baking tins). Brush sponge with warm jam and apply fondant.

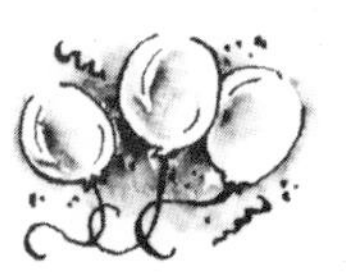

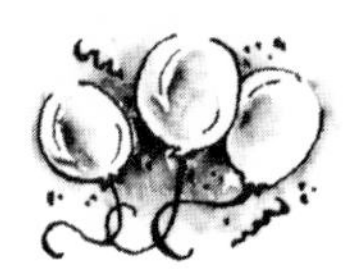

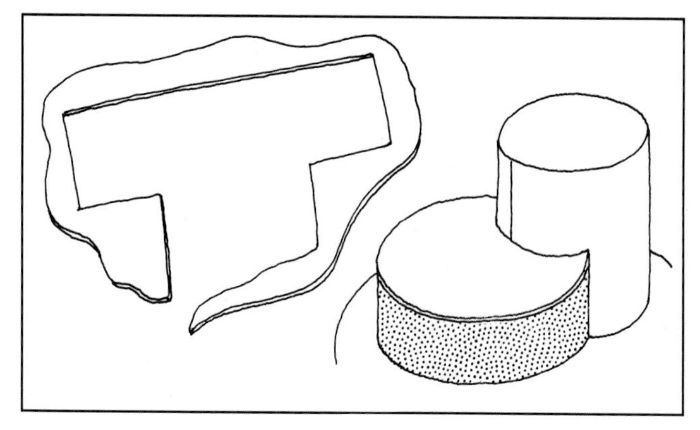

3. Measure around tall cake and cut fondant to fit. Apply as before. Measure around large cake and cut fondant to fit. Apply as before, then trim surplus if necessary.

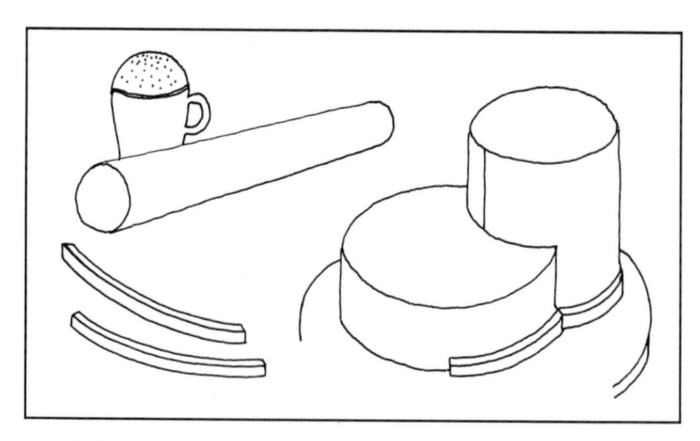

4. Colour the remaining fondant with more brown. Roll to 3 LS thick and cut a strip to go around base of shoe 10mm (⅜in.) wide (this can be cut in three or four sections). Mark tread with blunt edge of a knife.

5. Model remaining brown to form a tongue, as shown. Brush top and bottom (at back) with egg white and attach to shoe. Let it fall across the join of the cakes, i.e. do not push it into corner. Leave to dry overnight.

6. Break off some white fondant and colour it pale orange. Roll to 1 LS thick. Cut one round window and seven square – different sizes. Brush backs with egg white and apply to shoe walls.

7. Break off more white and colour pale blue. Model a square chimney. Score a deep line around top, and two lines down each side. Roll a small piece and attach to top. Attach chimney to shoe with egg white. Push candle-holder in while fondant is still soft.

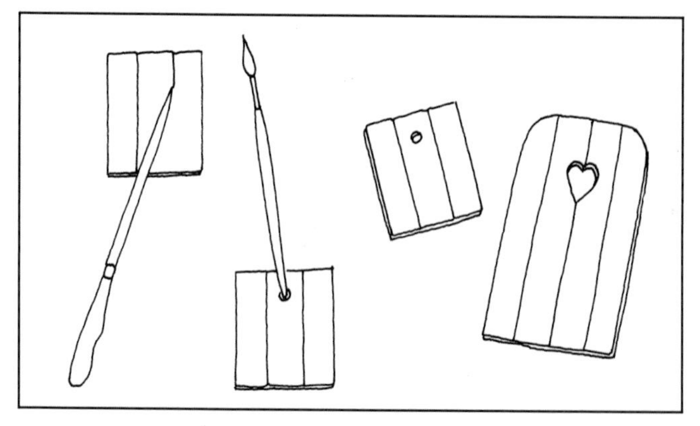

8. Roll blue fondant to 1 LS thick. Cut a door and shutters to fit the windows. Score vertical lines with knife, as shown. Brush backs with egg white and apply to shoe. Make small holes in shutters and cut a little heart in the centre of the door.

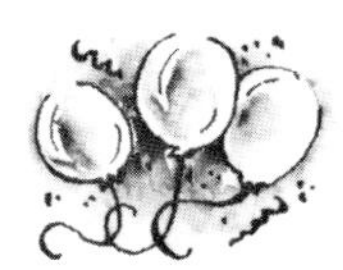

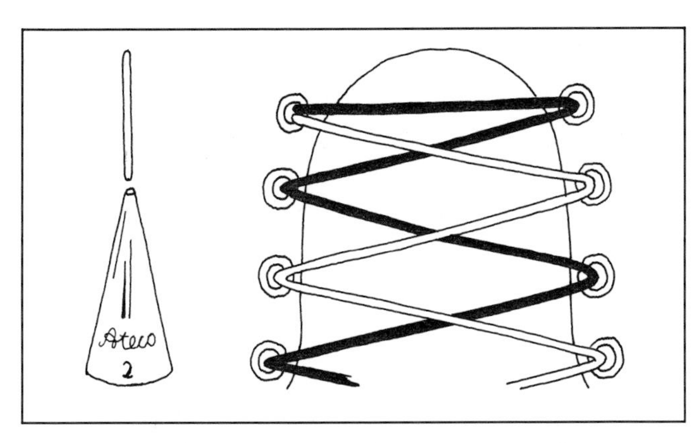

9. Make up the 110g (4oz) of royal icing. Colour some dark brown – add black to brown colouring. With icing *nozzle No. 2* pipe circles down each side of the tongue, then pipe laces, criss-cross, from and to each hole. Pipe cross-stitch around tops of shoe. Pipe a line of stitching above and below sole of shoe.

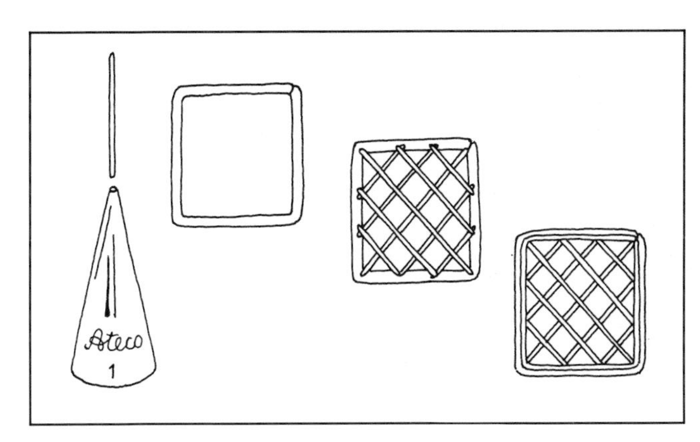

10. Colour some icing bright orange. With *No. 2 nozzle* pipe around each window. With *No. 1* pipe leading on windows, then pipe around each window again.

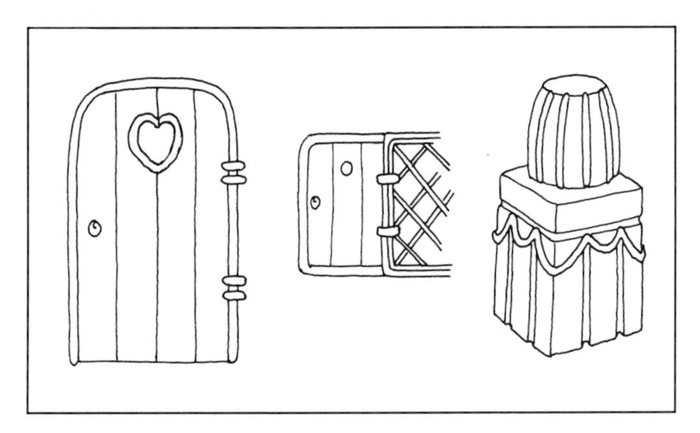

11. With *No. 2 nozzle* pipe blue around door and shutters. Pipe hinges and knobs, and decoration on chimney. Pipe round heart on door.

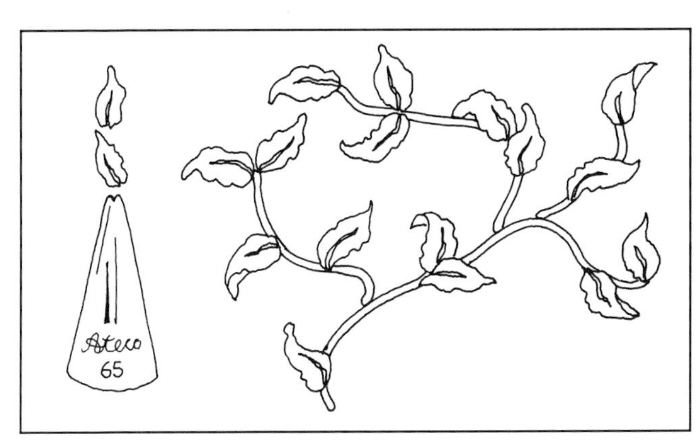

12. With *No. 2 nozzle* pipe green stems up the sides of the shoe. Using a different green and *No. 65* pipe leaves on stems.

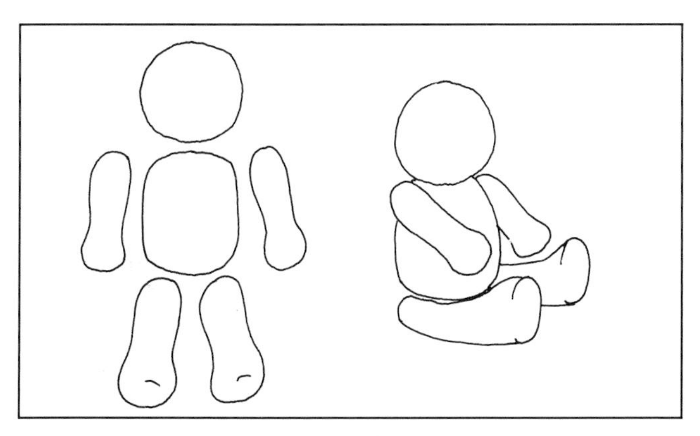

13. Colour the remaining white fondant flesh (or pink with a drop of brown added). Model little children as shown. Fix together with egg white while fondant is still fairly soft. Attach to shoe and silver board with egg white.

14. Using *No. 1 nozzle* pipe yellow crinkly hair on children. Put candle in candle-holder.

Happy Times!

Hickory Dickory Dock

The only problem with this cake is one of balance. You may notice from the photograph that the clock *leans* slightly – having done all within my power to make it upright, I have convinced myself that the 'leaning' adds to the charm, as with the Tower of Pisa!

The cake can be decorated in two days. A little practice on the kitchen table with the icing bag may be necessary if you have not piped before. The filigree can be drawn on to a piece of paper first, the pencil lines are then traced by pricking through them into the fondant, the pin marks being used as a guide. The same technique can be used for the clock numbers and lettering.

Please read the General Notes on pages 6 and 7 before starting to decorate the cake. Also read through the step-by-step instructions and check the ingredient and equipment lists.

Ingredients for cake

280g (10oz) butter
220g (8oz) caster sugar
360g (13oz) self-raising flour
200g (7oz) ground rice
220ml (8fl oz) milk beaten with 4 large eggs
butter cream and/or jam for filling
Make from this recipe: 3 × 450g (1lb) loaf cakes – loaf tins measure 75 × 150mm (3in. × 6in.)

Ingredients for fondant and royal icing

670g (1½lb) icing sugar, plus 60g (2oz)
1½ egg whites, plus ¼
3 tblsp liquid glucose
flavouring (optional)
Also: warm sieved apricot jam; 50/50 mixture of cornflour and icing sugar in a dusting dredger; yellow, blue and pink food colouring; silver balls for decoration.

Equipment

Basins for mixing icings; spoons; sieve; rolling pin; steel rule; sharp-pointed knife; lolly sticks (LS) as spacers; pastry brush; greaseproof paper for icing bags; Ateco (or equivalent) icing nozzles 1 and 15; 200mm (8in.) square silver board.

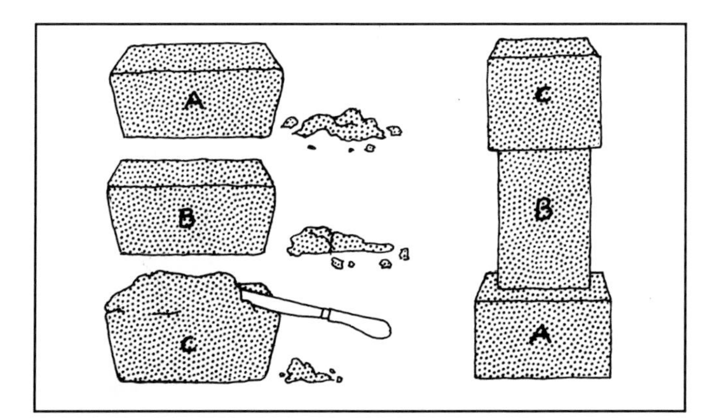

1. Having left the cakes overnight, slice the tops flat. Cut cake **A** to 100mm (4in.) wide – this will form the base of the clock. Turn cake **B** on its side with the underside facing. Cut cake **C** to 90mm (3½in.) wide, turn on its side with underside facing. Join all together with butter cream and/or jam.

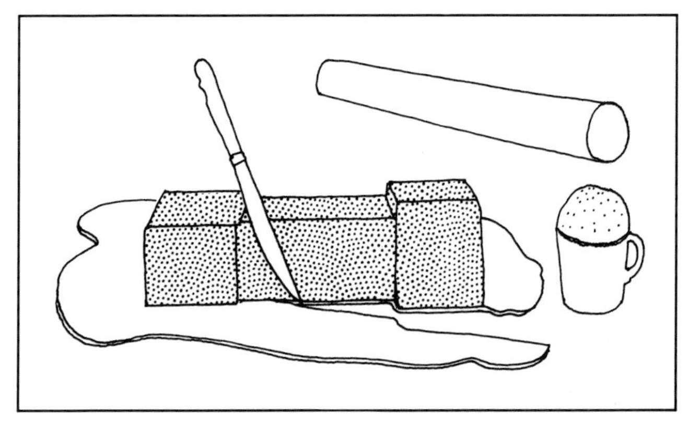

2. Make 670g (1½lb) of fondant. Break off 560g (1¼lb) and colour it pale blue. Roll to 2 LS thick. Measure back of clock. Cut fondant to fit. Brush sponge with warm jam and carefully apply fondant.

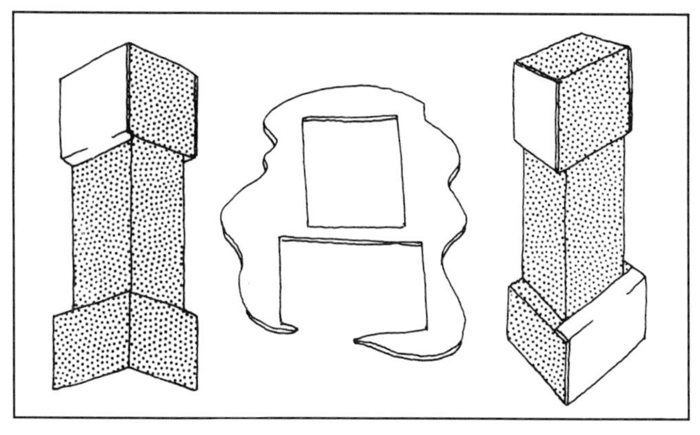

3. Keeping fondant at 2 LS thick, cut and fit all pieces (apply after brushing sponge with warm jam) in following order: top two sides, cutting them long enough to fit under lip; base front, again cutting long enough to fit over base ledge.

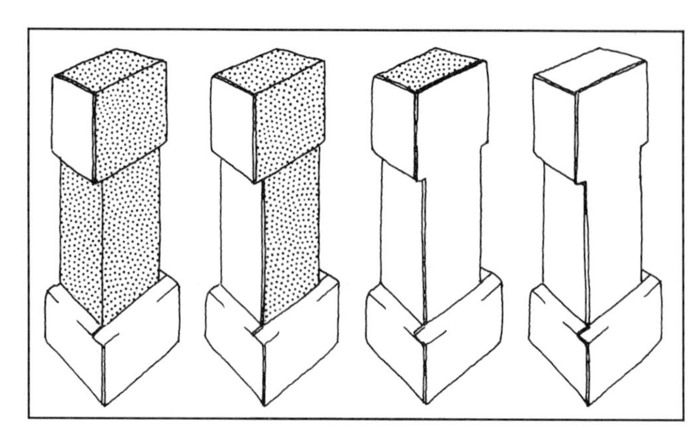

4. Cut base sides, as shown, to fit over ledge; cut and fit longest sides, then the front, and finally the top. Leave to dry overnight.

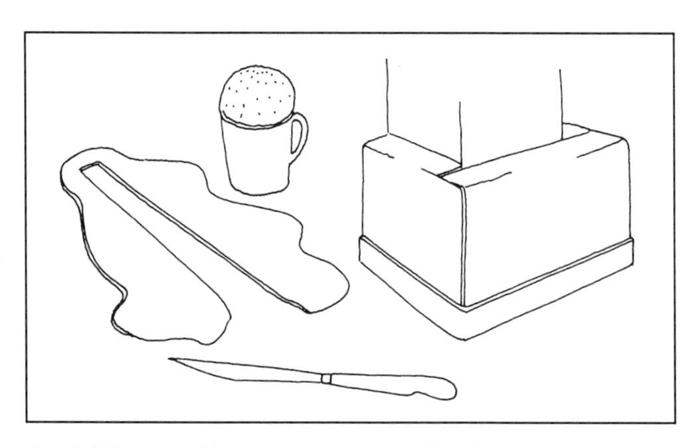

5. Add more blue to remaining fondant. Roll to 1 LS thick and cut a strip 15mm (¾in.) wide to fit round base of clock. Attach with egg white.

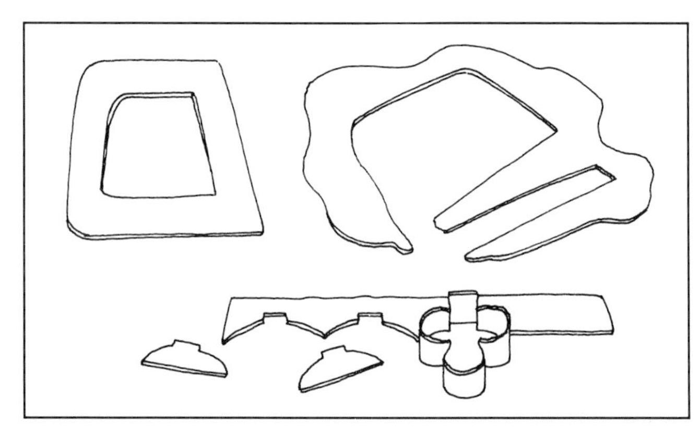

6. With fondant still 1 LS thick, cut a door frame to fit on front of clock. Round off two corners. Cut a fancy strip to go round top of clock – use a cocktail cutter for decorative edging, as shown.

7. Model four conical shapes, position on base ledge at each corner. Secure with egg white. Top each with a silver ball. Model four smaller cones for top of clock. Secure, then add silver balls. Model cones for candles, push candles in while fondant is soft.

8. Break off some white fondant. Roll to 1 LS thick and cut a circle 30mm (1¼in.) diameter. Colour some more white fondant yellow. Cut clock face 60mm (2¼in.) diameter and a pendulum 15mm (⅝in.). Apply white circle to clock face. Position pendulum inside door frame. Colour remaining white fondant pink.

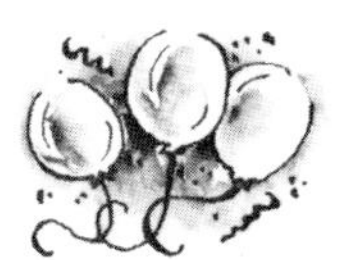

9. Model the mouse (leave enough fondant for the tail which can be attached later). Make body from a fat roll, tapering at one end. Make head from a ball, pinching out the ears. Position on top of clock, head overhanging a little. Secure with egg white.

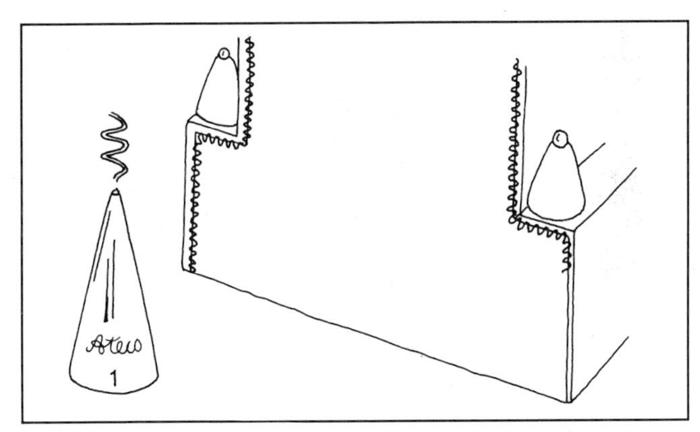

10. Make up the 60g (2oz) of royal icing. With *No. 1 nozzle* and white icing, outline the decorative strip at top of clock. Pipe a narrow zigzag line down side and back seams of fondant. Pipe a line of dots around inside and outside of door frame.

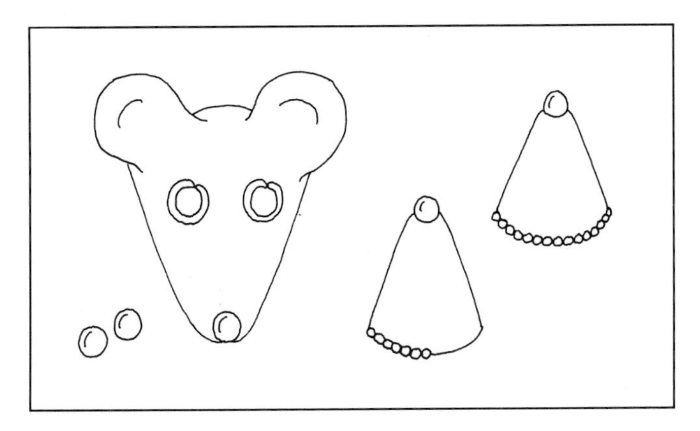

11. Pipe small circles on mouse's head, and gently press in two silver balls. Press a ball in for nose, securing with egg white. Pipe line of dots around cones on base ledge, around base of clock and down front and back seams of base.

12. Pipe the chain holding pendulum and the filigree on door frame. With dark blue icing pipe a line of dots on seam above door. Pipe door hinges as shown and a small circle for handle; press in a silver ball. Pipe numbers and hands on clock face and **Happy Times!** on front of base.

13. Using *No. 15 nozzle* pipe small stars along bottom ledge. Carefully brush back of clock face with egg white and attach to clock.

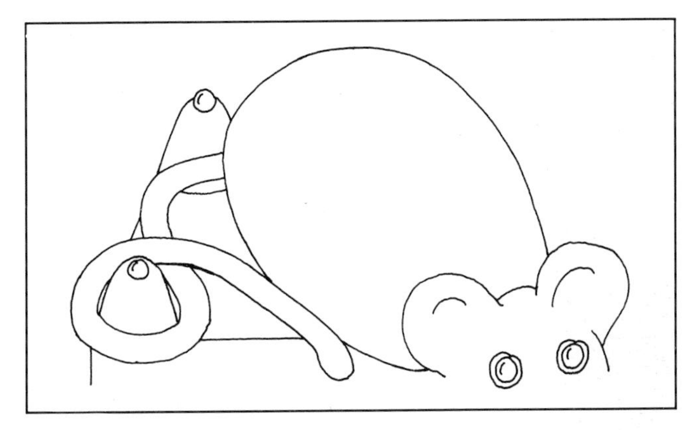

14. Roll a pink tail for mouse. Attach to body and top of clock, curling round one of the cones. Stick candle to silver board using egg white.

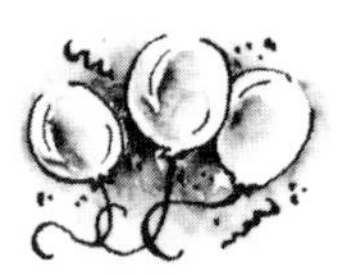

Humpty Dumpty

Humpty Dumpty, famous for his fall from the wall, can be decorated in two days. The piping is very simple, just straight lines (though these may have to be practiced on the kitchen table if you have not piped before). The two pudding basins used for making Humpty are 125mm (5in.) diameter and hold just under 560ml (1pt) of water. Dried fruit can be added to the ingredients as none of the cakes needs to be cut into pieces. Butter cream or jam is used to sandwich the pudding cakes together.

The stone wall can be made to look more realistic by leaving the fondant to dry for about 20 minutes before applying it to the sponge – the surface will develop fine cracks.

Please read the General Notes on pages 6 to 9 before starting to decorate the cake. Also, read through the step-by-step instructions and check the ingredient and equipment lists.

Ingredients for cake

220g (8oz) butter
170g (6oz) caster sugar
280g (10oz) self-raising flour
170g (6oz) ground rice
140ml (3fl oz) milk beaten with 3 large eggs
filling
dried fruit or flavouring (optional)
Make from this recipe: 2 pudding cakes
1 × 900g (2lb) loaf cake

Ingredients for fondant and royal icing

900g (2lb) icing sugar, plus 60g (2oz)
2 egg whites, plus ¼
2 tblsp liquid glucose
flavouring (optional)
Also: warm sieved apricot jam; 50/50 mixture of cornflour and icing sugar in dusting dredger; blue, red, yellow, black and green food colouring.

Equipment

Basins for mixing icings; spoons; sieve; rolling pin; steel rule; sharp-pointed knife; lolly sticks (LS) as spacers; pastry brush; small paint brush; greaseproof paper for icing bag; Ateco (or equivalent) icing nozzle No. 2; 250mm (10in.) square silver board.

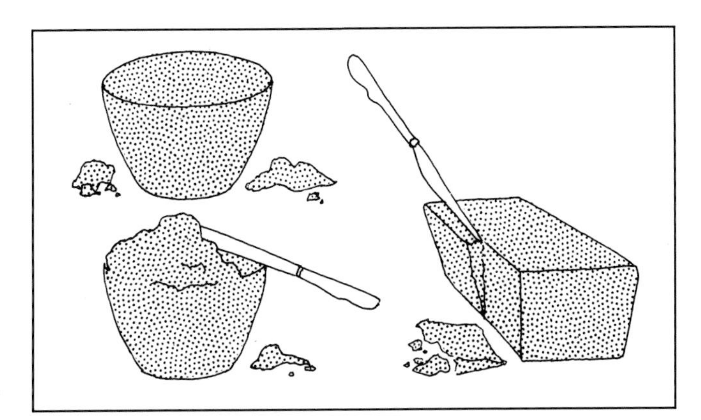

1. Having left the cakes overnight, slice the tops from the two puddings so that the surfaces are flat. Slice the top and one of the long sides from the loaf cake. Stand loaf cake on its side, in the centre of the silver board.

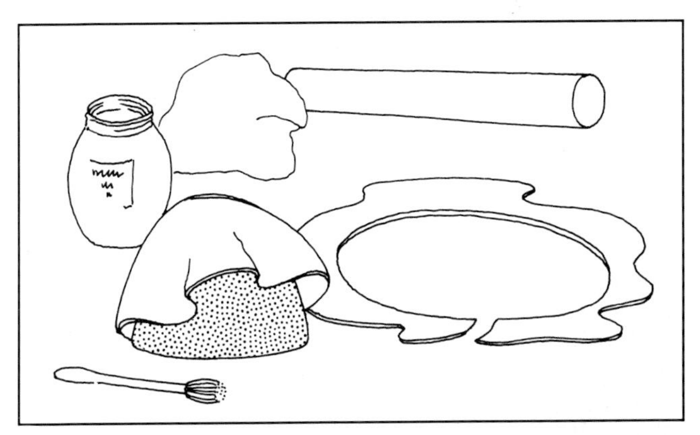

2. Make 450g (1lb) of fondant. Colour half of it cream (drop of blue and red with a little yellow) and the other half pale blue. Measure pudding over round surface. Roll cream fondant to 2 LS thick then cut a circle to fit. Brush sponge with jam and carefully apply fondant, smoothing the surface with your hands.

3. Repeat with the other cake and blue fondant. If edges need trimming, stand cake on upturned basin and carefully slice away excess – keep trimmings for arms and legs.

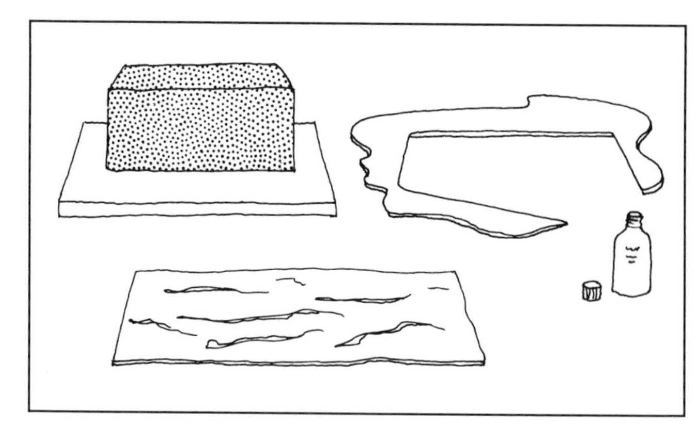

4. Make another 450g (1lb) of fondant. Break off 340g (12oz) and add black colouring – mix only partially to give streaky effect. Roll to 2 LS thick. Measure front and sides of wall, cut one piece of fondant to fit. Leave to dry for 20 minutes.

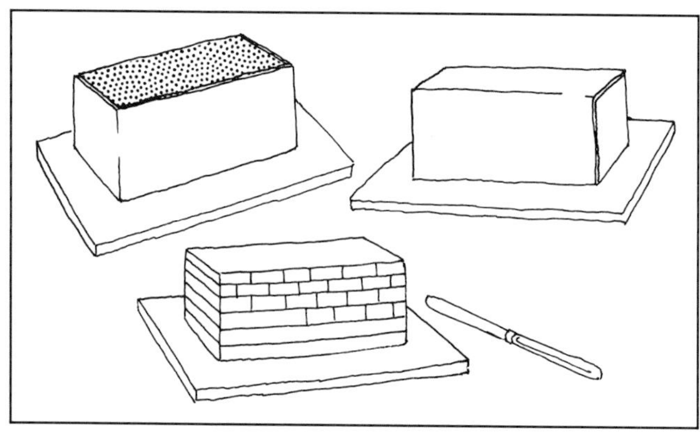

5. Brush cake with jam and apply fondant. Measure back and top. Roll fondant to 2 LS thick and cut fondant to fit. Apply as before. Score horizontal lines all round wall, then vertical lines to form stones. Leave everything to dry overnight.

6. Using a dry paint brush, lightly paint a corner of each stone in the wall. Sandwich the two pudding cakes together with butter cream and/or jam. Stand Humpty on dusted greaseproof paper.

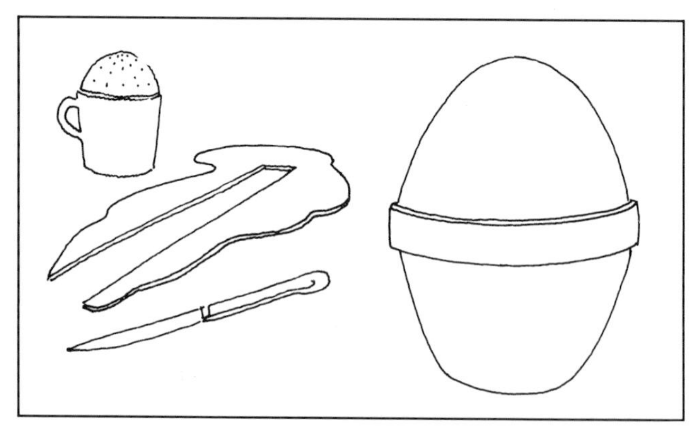

7. Colour remaining white fondant red, roll to 2 LS thick. Measure circumference of Humpty and cut a belt to fit, 20mm (¾in.) wide. Brush back of belt with egg white and carefully attach around his middle.

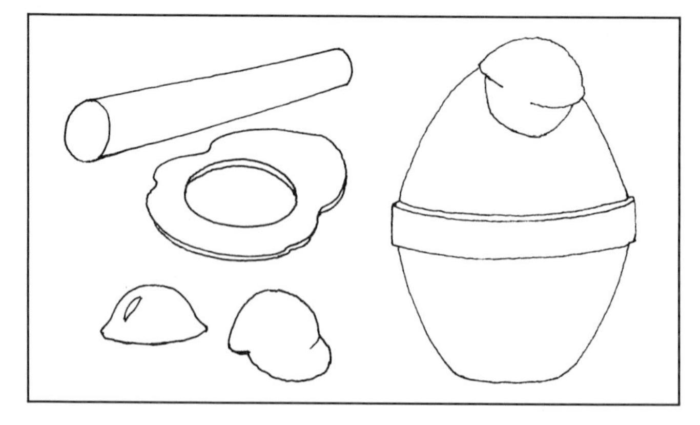

8. Roll fondant to 2 LS thick. Cut a circle and model into shape of a cap. Attach to head with egg white. (If you have one, a tiny dish can be used as a mould for the cap; I use one belonging to a tea-strainer.)

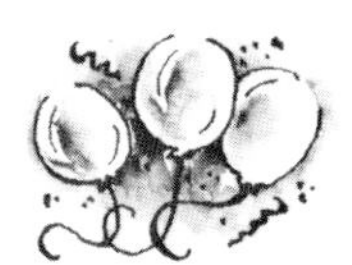

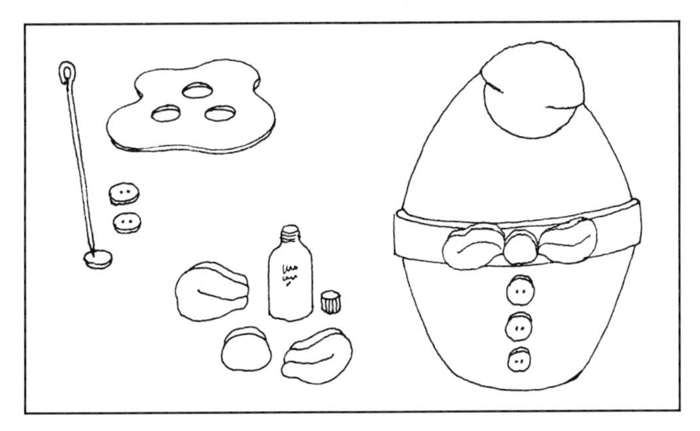

9. Roll fondant to 1 LS thick. Cut three buttons, pierce holes with skewer or similar. Brush backs with egg white and attach below belt. Add more red and a little blue to remaining fondant and model a bow-tie. Attach front of belt with egg white.

10. Break off some of the remaining blue fondant and model a nose. Roll some of cream fondant to 1 LS thick, cut out eyes, then add smaller circles in blue. Roll a strip of cream for mouth. Attach all the pieces to the face using egg white.

11. With blue colouring, paint in eyes and a line along the mouth. Position Humpty on wall, using egg white to secure. Roll cream fondant to form two legs, flatten the feet slightly. Attach them to body and wall with egg white.

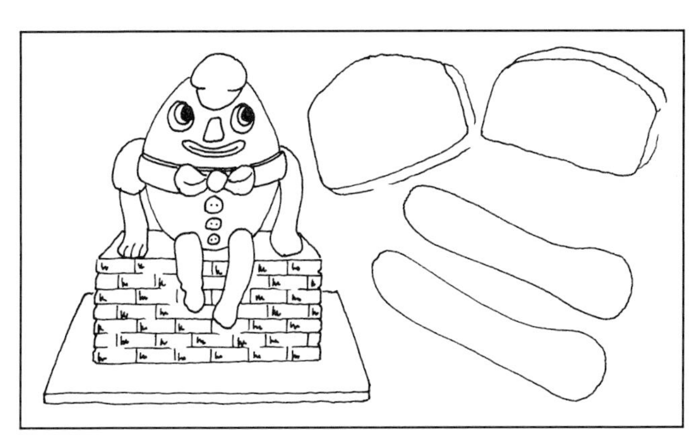

12. Roll blue fondant to form two arms. Attach to body and edge of wall with egg white. Mark fingers with blunt side of knife. Break off some of remaining grey fondant, add red, and mould around top of arms to make sleeves.

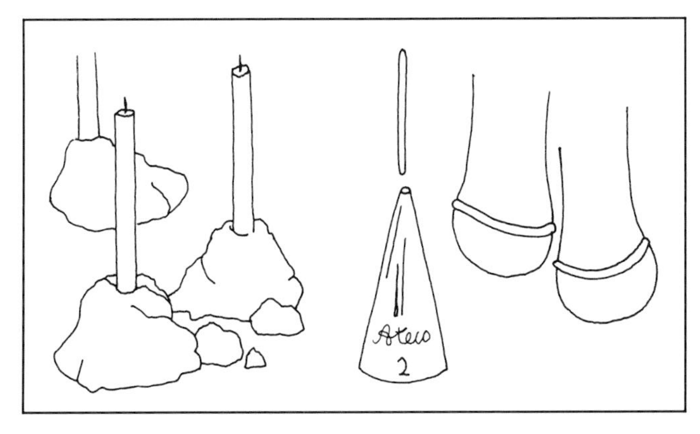

13. Break off more of remaining grey fondant and form into little rocks. Stick them to board with egg white. Poke candles into larger rocks. Make up the 60g (2oz) of royal icing. Pipe pink icing down Humpty's sleeves and a line of pink on each shoe.

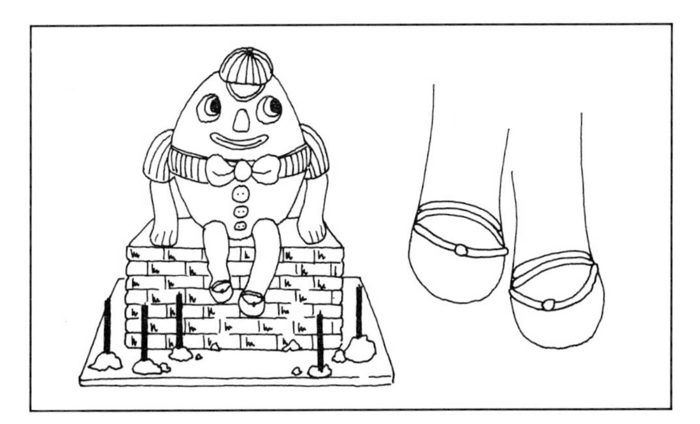

14. Pipe red lines on belt and lines going to centre of hat, ending with a blob in the middle. Pipe a line on each side of buttons. Pipe a double strap on each shoe and a tiny button on the pink icing. Pipe green grass along bottom edge of wall, in crevices and around some of the stones on the board.

Music

Recorder and music

For those children who play the recorder at school, this cake will be a special treat. You could even score their favourite tune on the sheet of music!

The cake itself is easy to decorate, but putting the lining in can be a little awkward – the fondant must be very soft because the folds and gathers will crack if it has been handled or rolled out too much.

The lid has to be left until completely hard – about two days and nights – before attaching to the case.

Please read the General Notes on pages 6 to 9 before starting to decorate the cake. Also read through the step-by-step instructions and check the ingredient and equipment lists.

Ingredients for cake

170g (6oz) butter
110g (4oz) caster sugar
220g (8oz) self-raising flour
110g (4oz) ground rice)
110ml (4 fl oz) milk beaten with 2 large eggs
Make from this recipe: 2 × 450g (1lb) loaf cakes

Ingredients for fondant and royal icing

560g (1¼lb) icing sugar, plus 60g (2oz)
1¼ egg whites, plus ¼
just under 3 tblsp liquid glucose
flavouring (optional)
Also: warm sieved apricot jam; 50/50 mixture of cornflour and icing sugar in a dusting dredger; blue, brown, red, black and silver food colouring.

Equipment

Basins for mixing icings; spoons; sieve; rolling pin; steel rule; sharp-pointed knife; lolly sticks (LS) as spacers; wooden spoon; pastry brush; greaseproof paper for icing bags; Ateco (or equivalent) icing nozzles 1, 2, 3 and 15; 255mm (10in.) square silver cake board.

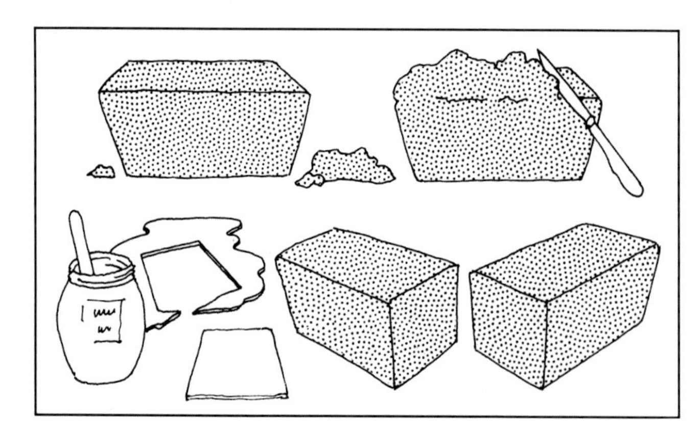

1. Leave the cakes overnight, then slice the tops flat. Trim two of the narrow sides so that the cakes fit flush. Make the 670g (1½lb) of fondant. Take a piece and roll to 1 LS thick. Brush the cut sides of cake with warm jam, then sandwich fondant in middle. Push the two cakes together.

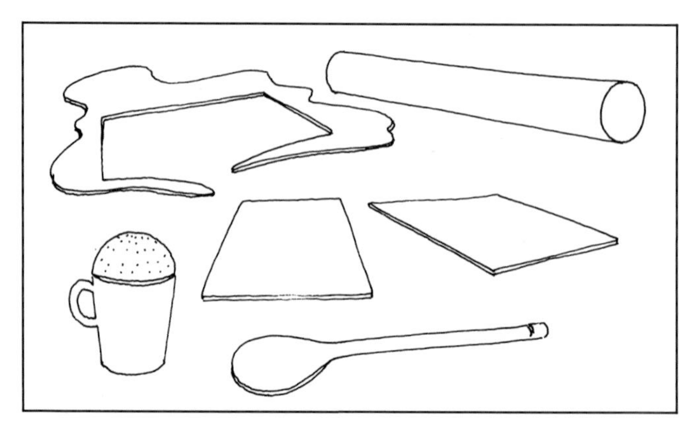

2. Take another piece of fondant. Roll to 1 LS thick and cut two oblongs 120mm (4¾in.) deep, 90mm (3½in.) wide. Dust a working surface and the wooden spoon handle with dusting mixture.

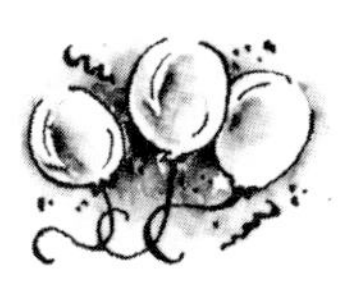

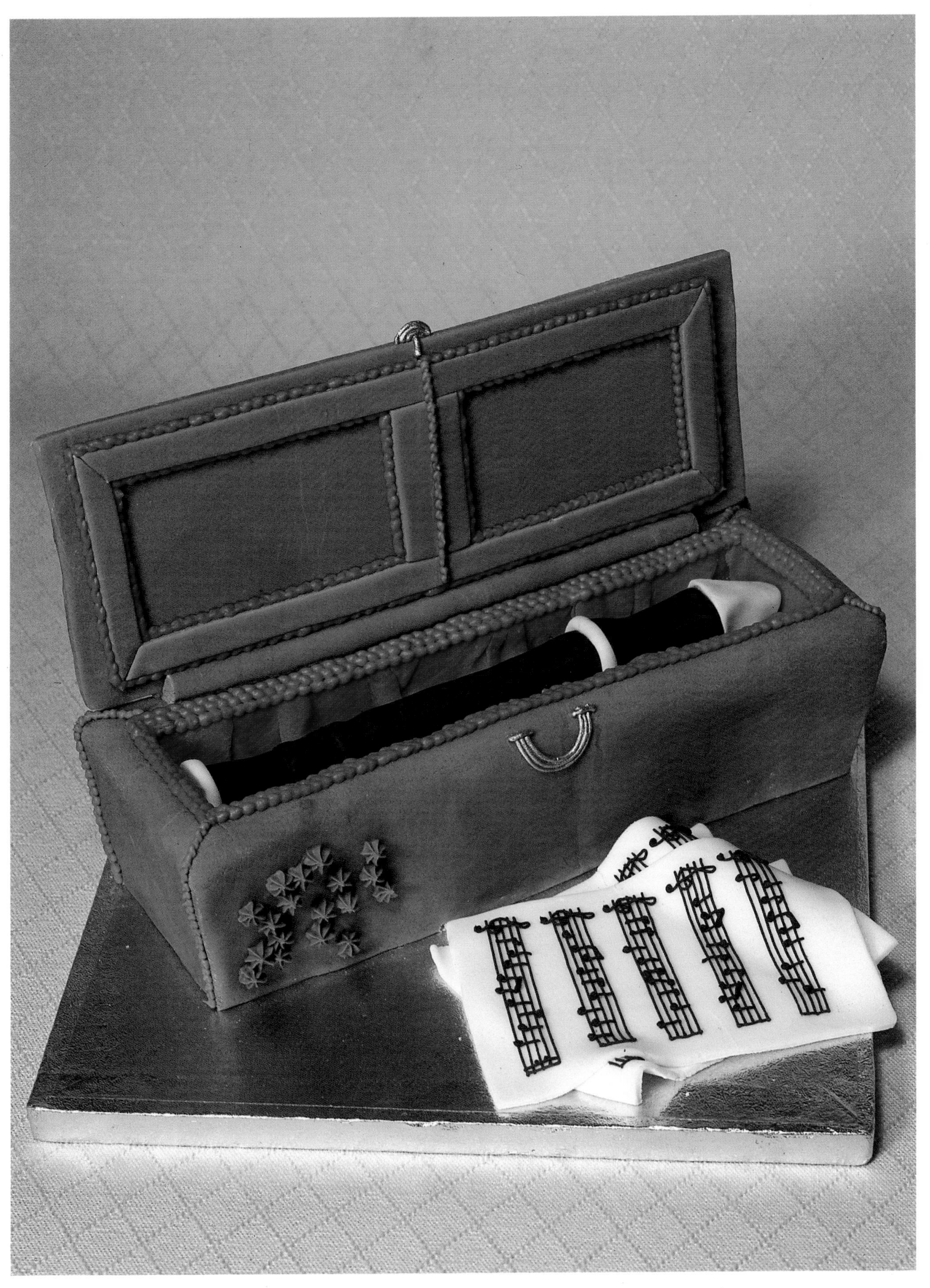

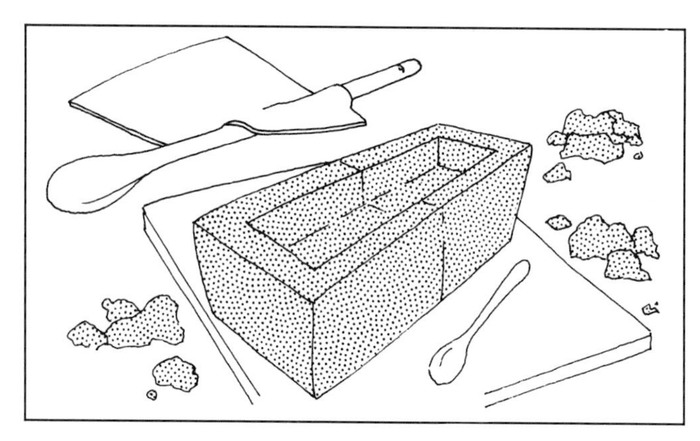

3. Carefully lay one of the fondant oblongs across handle. Lay the other on top at an angle. Leave the two to dry for at least 24 hours.

Cut an oblong in the cake,as shown. Carefully scoop out sponge to 20mm (¾in.) deep. Blow out all crumbs and position cake, on a slant, on silver cake board.

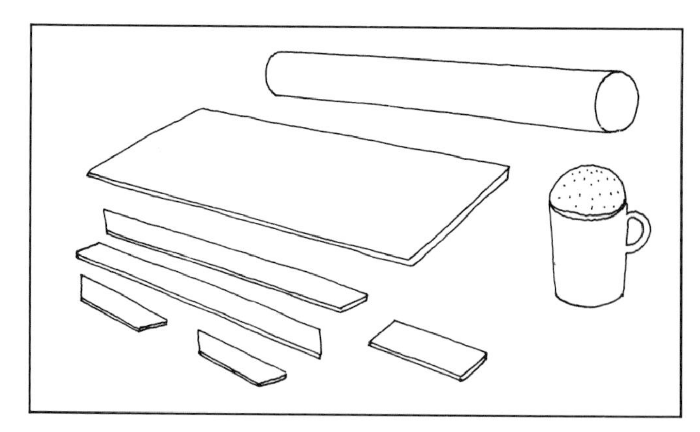

4. Keep back a little white fondant, then colour the remainder blue. Measure length and width of cake. Roll a piece to 2 LS thick, cut a lid for the case and five strips for inside lid. Leave to dry for 1 hour.

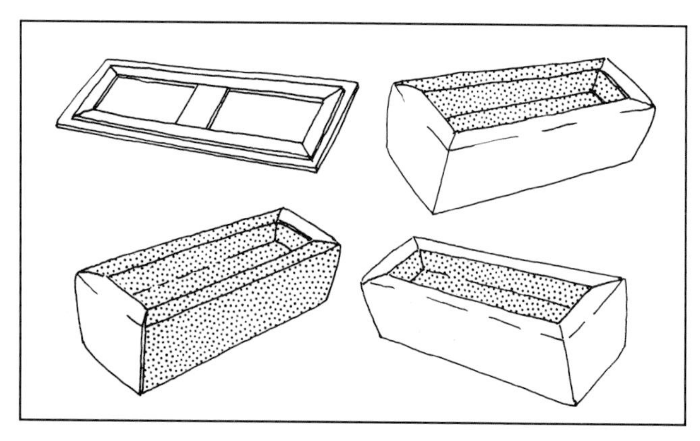

5. Brush backs of strips with egg white and carefully attach to inside lid, as shown. Dust a surface with dusting mixture and leave lid to dry for at least 48 hours.

Measure sides of cake, including top edge. Brush cake with warm jam. Roll fondant to 2 LS thick and cut to fit. Apply sides first, then front and back.

6. Keep a piece of blue fondant for lid support, add brown to remainder. Model the recorder in separate pieces as shown, keeping a check on length.

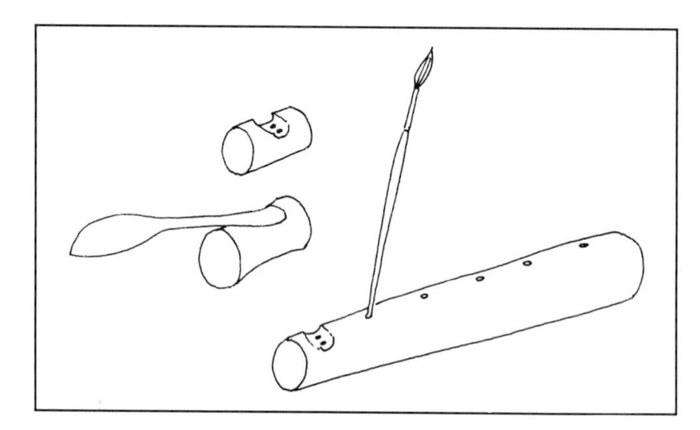

7. Make holes while the fondant is still soft. The top hole beneath mouth-piece is made with a teaspoon handle, other holes are made with a knitting needle or paint brush handle.

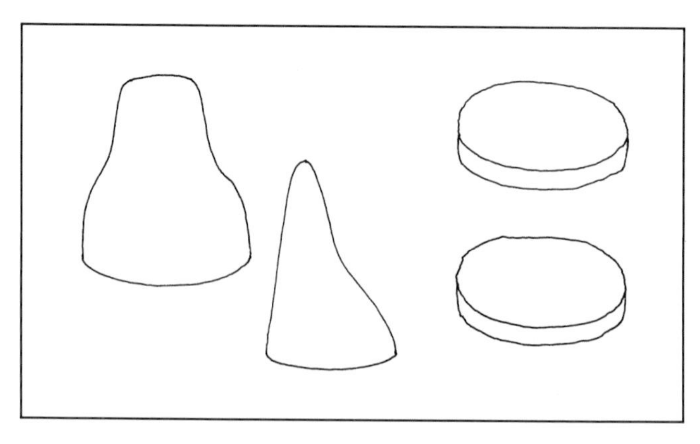

8. Using white fondant, model mouth-piece and centre and end pieces, as shown. Leave all the parts to dry for a few hours before sticking together with egg white.

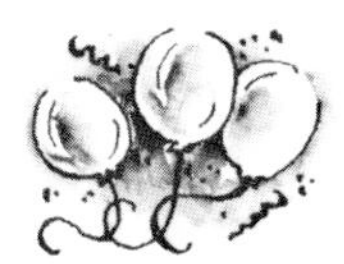

9. Colour the remaining white fondant red. Roll to 1 LS thick and cut pieces to line case (use two pieces for each long side, as shown). Brush top edge of inside case with egg white, then carefully apply pieces, gathering to make folds. Cut a piece to fit base.

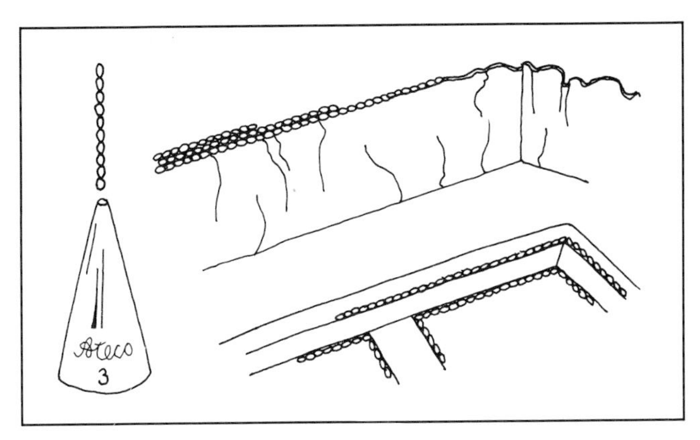

10. When recorder pieces are dry, assemble and lay in case. Make up the 60g (2oz) of royal icing. Colour some red and with *nozzle No. 3* pipe three lines of continuous dots around top edge of lining. Pipe same along edges of strips on lid.

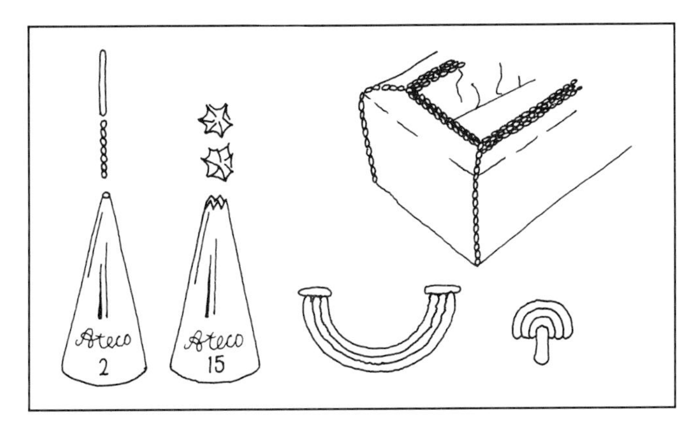

11. Using *No. 2 nozzle* and blue icing pipe lines of continuous dots down the four corner seams of fondant on case. Pipe the handle and catch on top of lid, as shown – when dry paint with silver. With *nozzle No. 15* pipe little flowers on corner of case.

12. When little sheets of white fondant are dry, remove wooden spoon. Using *No. 1* and black icing, carefully pipe staves, treble clefs and notes – start with visible areas of bottom sheet first, then top sheet. Transfer to silver board with a fish slice, first dabbing board with egg white.

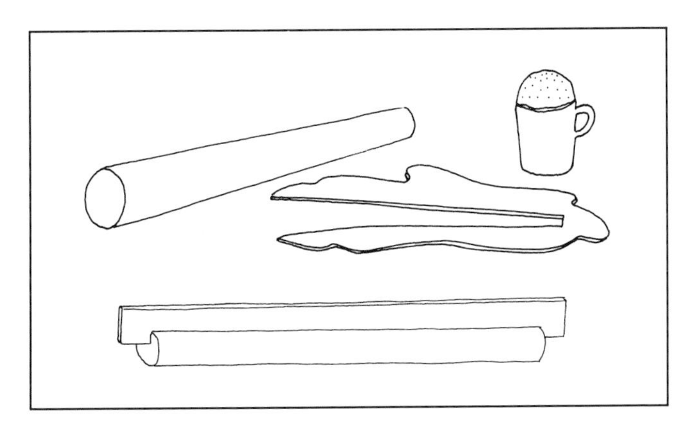

13. When lid is perfectly dry, roll remaining blue fondant to 4 LS thick and cut a strip 15mm (⅝in.) wide. Make a groove down centre (with steel rule or blunt edge of a knife) wide enough to fit edge of lid.

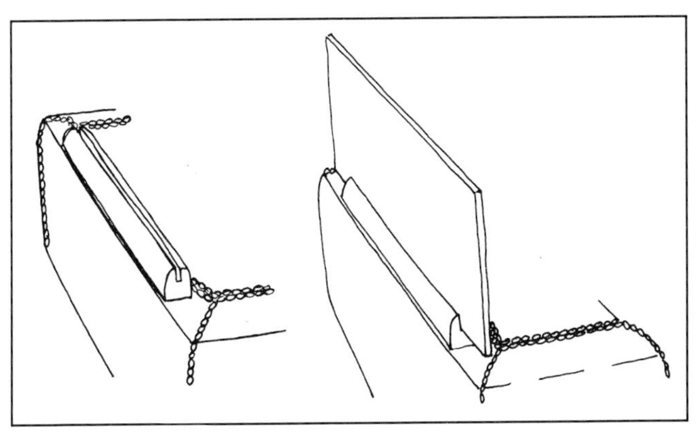

14. Attach strip to back edge of case with egg white. Brush egg white inside groove. Carefully lift lid and place in groove. Hold or support it in position until egg white has dried and the lid can support itself.

Drum

The cake itself can be decorated in a day, but the drum sticks must be left to harden for at least 24 hours. As the sponge does not need to be trimmed to a particular shape, dried fruit or nuts can be added to the mixture (see page 6). Alternatively, each of the two cakes can be split in half and filled with jam and/or butter cream.

Please read the General Notes on pages 6 to 9 before decorating the cake. Also read through the step-by-step instructions and check the ingredient and equipment lists.

Ingredients for cake

220g (8oz) butter
170g (6oz) caster sugar
280g (10oz) self-raising flour
170g (6oz) ground rice
140ml (5fl oz) milk beaten with 3 large eggs
Make from this recipe: 2 × 150mm (6in.) round cakes

Ingredients for fondant and royal icing

790g (1¾lb) icing sugar, plus 110g (4oz)
1¾ egg whites, plus ½
just under 4 tblsp liquid glucose
flavouring (optional)
Also: warm sieved apricot jam; 50/50 mixture of cornflour and icing sugar in a dusting dredger; red, green, yellow and brown food colouring.

Equipment

Basins for mixing icings; sieve; spoons; rolling pin; steel rule; sharp-pointed knife; lolly sticks (LS) as spacers; pastry brush; greaseproof paper for icing bags; Ateco (or equivalent) icing nozzles 1, 2 and 3; 230mm (9in.) round silver cake board.

1. Having left the cakes overnight, slice the tops flat and sandwich together with jam and/or butter cream. Brush with jam. Make the 670g (1¾lb) of fondant. Roll a piece for the top to 2 LS thick (cut around the cake tin). Carefully apply fondant.

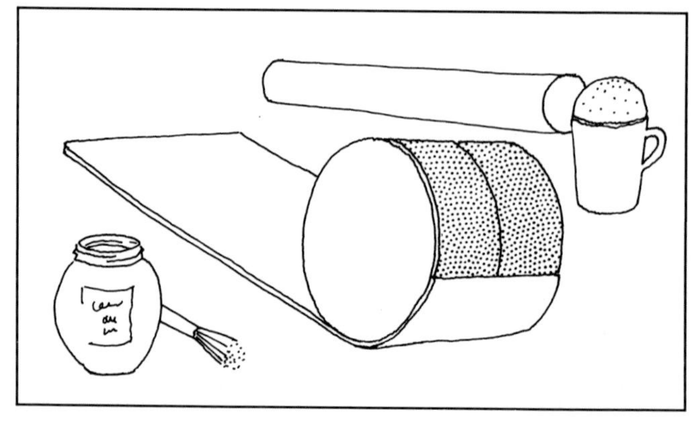

2. Measure circumference and depth of cake. Roll fondant to 2 LS thick and cut a piece to fit. Lay cake on fondant and roll along. Carefully transfer cake to centre of silver board. Measure circumference again. (Keep back 110g (4oz) of the fondant.)

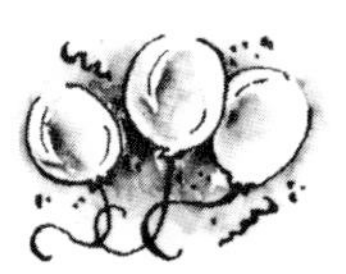

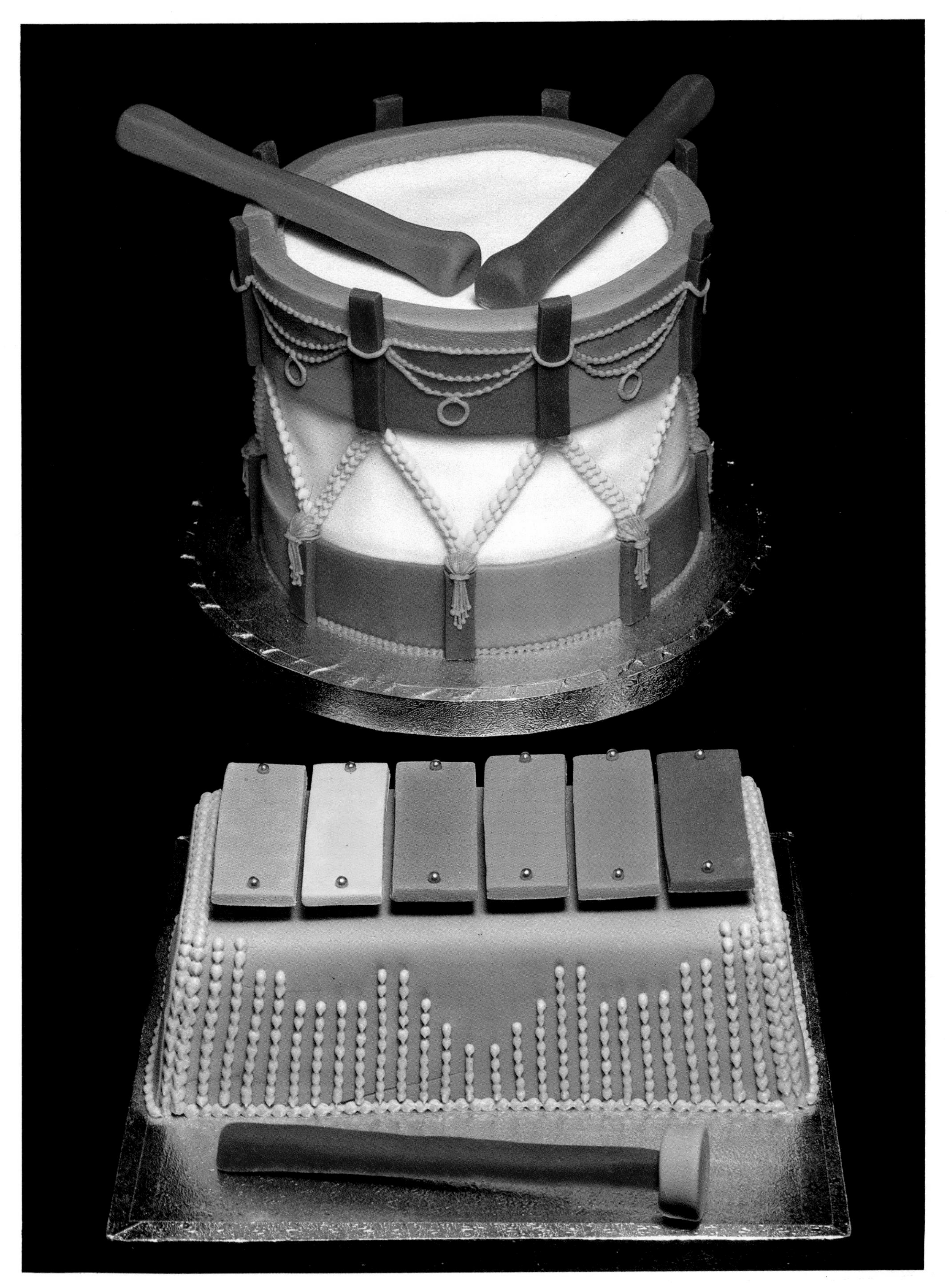

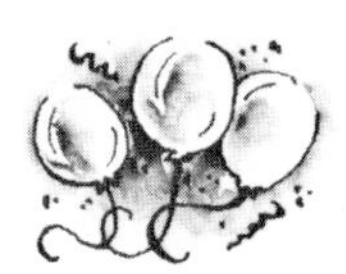

3. Cut remainder in two. Colour half red, half green. Roll to 1 LS thick, cut eight strips in each colour 65mm 2½in.) long, 30mm (1¼in.) deep. (Work four in each colour for base of drum first, then roll out and repeat for top of drum.) Brush backs with egg white and carefully apply.

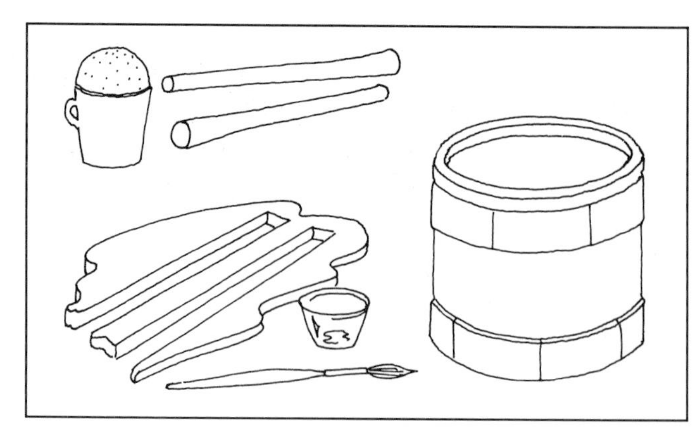

4. Roll two drum sticks, one red, one green, 150mm (6in.) long. Shape as shown. Leave to dry on a dusted surface for 24 hours. Take remaining white fondant, colour it orange (mix red and yellow) and roll to 4 LS thick. Cut a strip 10mm (⅜in.) wide, to go around top of drum. Brush egg white around drum edge, attach strip.

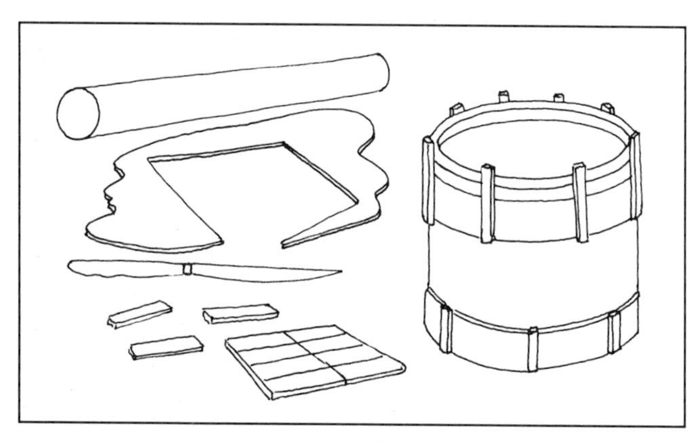

5. Add brown to orange trimmings. Roll to 1 LS thick. Cut sixteen strips 10mm (⅜in.) wide – cut eight pieces 30mm (1¼in.) long and eight pieces 50mm (2in.) long. Brush backs with egg white, position over joins of red and green fondant, shorter strips at bottom, longer strips at top.

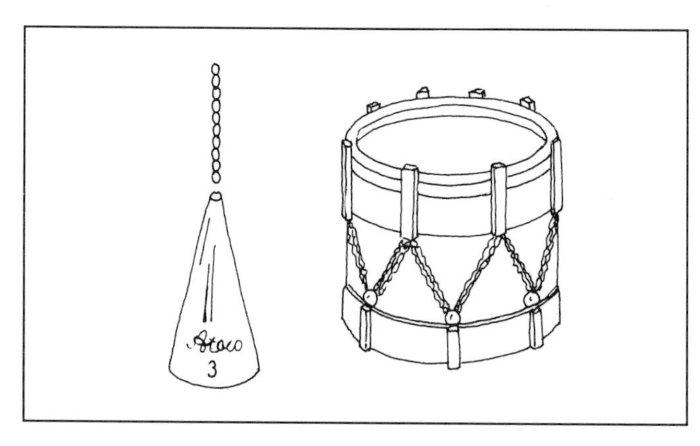

6. Make the 110g (4oz) of royal icing. With *No. 3 nozzle* and yellow icing, pipe a line of continuous dots to and from the brown strips, as shown. Go around the cake, then start again with a second line next to the first. Pipe a large dot at top of each strip, as shown.

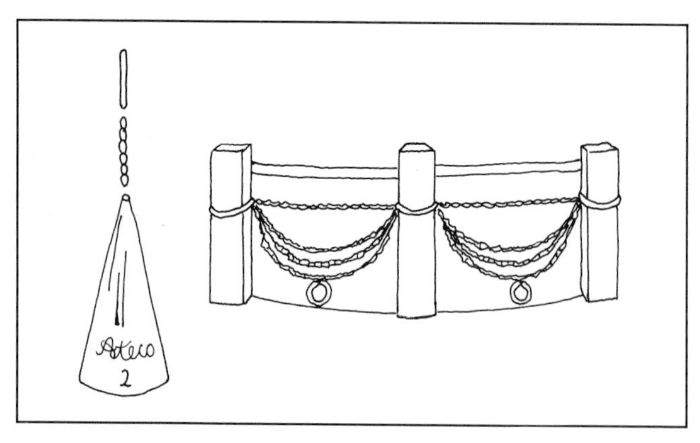

7. With *No. 2 nozzle* and orange icing, pipe a line of continuous dots inside orange strip on top of drum; three lines on red and green panels, as shown, and a line on base of bottom panels. Pipe a line across each brown strip and a circle on panels, as shown.

8. With *No. 1 nozzle* pipe a tassel on each large yellow dot. Pipe top part first, then the strands – each ending with a dot, then the tie, as shown.

Xylophone

This cake can also be decorated in a day, but as with the previous one, the hammer and bars should be left to dry for at least 24 hours. The cake can have added fruit or nuts, or can be sliced lengthways and filled with jam and/or butter cream.

There should really be eight bars on the xylophone (an observant child will no doubt point this out). Unfortunately the loaf cake is not long enough to accommodate eight and thinner ones would, I think, look rather mean. If comments are made, perhaps you can formulate an imaginative retort!

Please read the General Notes on pages 6 to 9 before starting to decorate the cake. It is a good idea also to read through the step-by-step instructions and check the ingredients and equipment lists.

Ingredients for cake

170g (6oz) butter
110g (4oz) caster sugar
220g (8oz) self-raising flour
110g (4oz) ground rice
110ml (4fl oz) milk beaten with 2 large eggs
Make from this recipe: 1 × 900g (2lb) loaf cake

Ingredients for fondant and royal icing

450g (1lb) icing sugar, plus 110g (4oz)
1 egg white, plus ½
2 tblsp liquid glucose
Also: warm sieved apricot jam; 50/50 mixture of cornflour and icing sugar in a dusting dredger; red, blue, yellow, mauve and brown food colouring; twelve edible silver balls.

Equipment

Basins for mixing icings; sieve; spoons; rolling pin; steel rule; sharp-pointed knife; lolly sticks (LS) as spacers; pastry brush; greaseproof paper for icing bag; Ateco (or equivalent) icing nozzle No. 3; 230mm (9in.) square silver cake board.

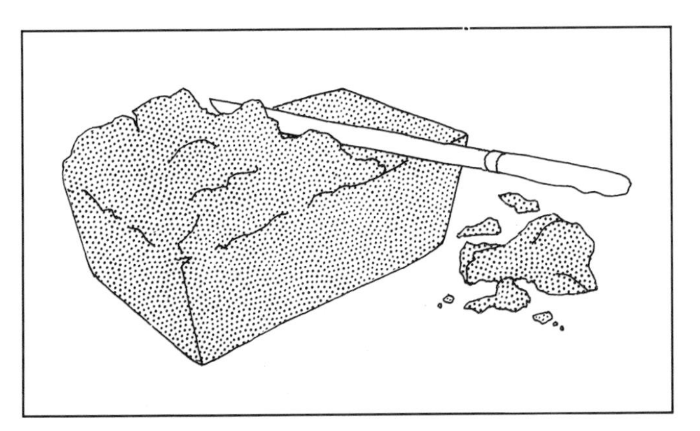

1. Having left the cake overnight, slice the top flat. If desired, slice in half and fill with jam and/or butter cream.

Make the 450g (1lb) of fondant.

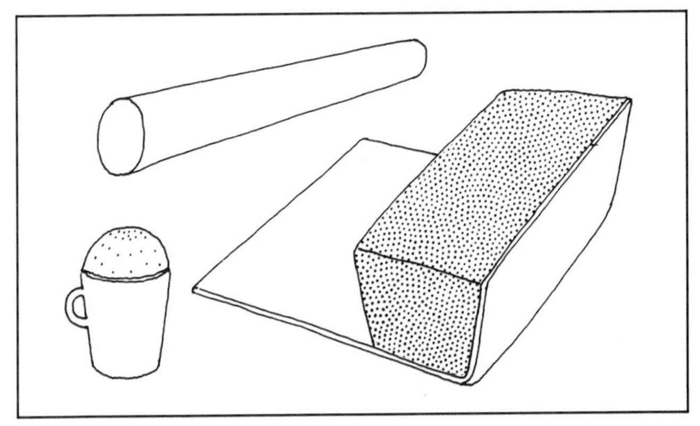

2. Take 340g (12oz) of the fondant and colour it greeny-blue. Measure across cake, then brush it with warm jam. Roll fondant to 2 LS thick and lay one side of cake on top. Carefully roll cake over, covering the three sides. Transfer cake to centre of silver board.

3. Measure short sides of cake. Roll fondant to 2 LS thick and cut to fit. Carefully apply. Trim if necessary. Make a circle 25mm (1in.) diameter and about 10mm (½in.) deep. Push a hole in centre, as shown.

4. Take pieces of remaining white fondant. Colour red, orange, yellow, mauve, pink and green. Roll each piece to 2 LS thick, cut to 75mm (3in.) by 25mm (1in.). Carefully put to one side on a dusted surface.

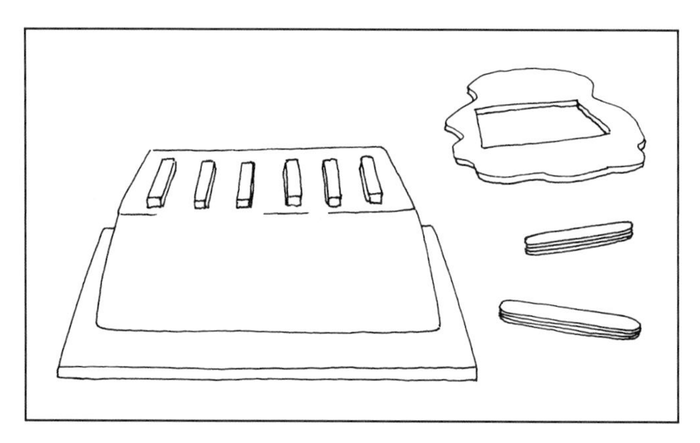

5. Mix all coloured and white trimmings together. Roll fondant to 4 LS thick. Cut into 6 pieces 50mm (6in.) long, 10mm (½in.) wide. Brush backs with egg white and attach to cake as shown.

6. Add brown to remaining fondant. Roll a handle 140mm (5½in.) long, tapering slightly at one end. Leave to dry on a dusted surface for at least 24 hours.

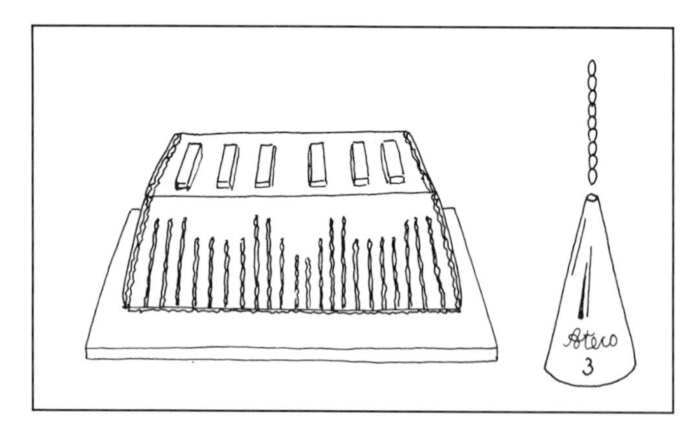

7. Make the 110g (4oz) of royal icing. Colour slightly paler than fondant on cake. Pipe double lines of continuous dots on seams of fondant, then a single line round base and lines down front and back, as shown.

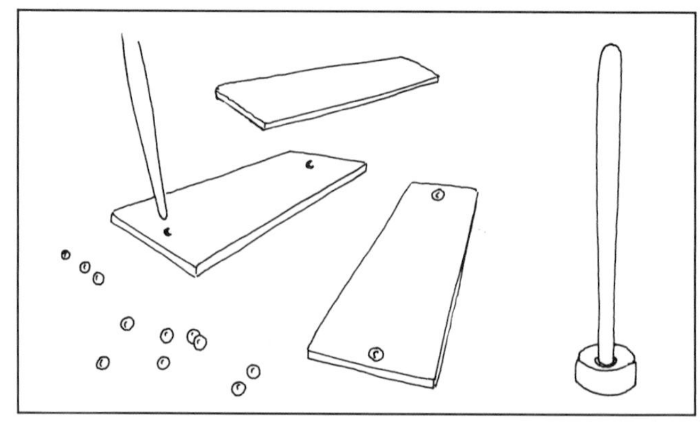

8. Make a slight indent with paint brush handle, at each end of bars. Dab on a little egg white, then drop in a silver ball. Brush tops of bar supports with egg white, then carefully position the bars on top. Attach handle to hammer-head securing with egg white.

Rock group

This cake will take two to three days to decorate. Many of the little pieces have to be completely dry before everything can be assembled. My children (ever critical) complained that the members of the group had rather thick legs! This was done to ensure adequate support for those who were carrying guitars.

The stars on the sides of the cake are cut with a cocktail cutter, but they can easily be made by cutting around a template of card.

As the cake remains whole, dried fruit or nuts can be added to the recipe; or it can be sliced in half and filled with flavoured butter cream.

Please read the General Notes on pages 6 to 9 before starting to decorate the cake. Also read through the step-by-step instructions and check the ingredient and equipment lists.

Ingredients for cake

280g (10oz) butter
220g (8oz) caster sugar
360g (13oz) self-raising flour
200g (7oz) ground rice
220ml (8fl oz) milk beaten with 4 large eggs
dried fruit, nuts or filling (optional)
Make from this recipe:
1 × 200mm (8in.) square cake

Ingredients for fondant and royal icing

900g (2lb) icing sugar, plus 60g (2oz)
2 egg whites, plus ¼
4 tblsp liquid glucose
flavouring (optional)
Also: warm sieved apricot jam; 50/50 mixture of cornflour and icing sugar in a dusting dredger; yellow, red, orange, blue, green, flesh, brown, black, silver and gold food colouring (mix red & yellow for orange; red, blue & yellow for brown; yellow & blue for green).

Equipment

Basins for mixing icings; spoons; sieve; rolling pin; steel rule; sharp-pointed knife; lolly sticks (LS) as spacers; pastry brush; star cocktail cutter; greaseproof paper for icing bags; Ateco (or equivalent) icing nozzles 1 and 2; 255mm (10in.) square silver cake board.

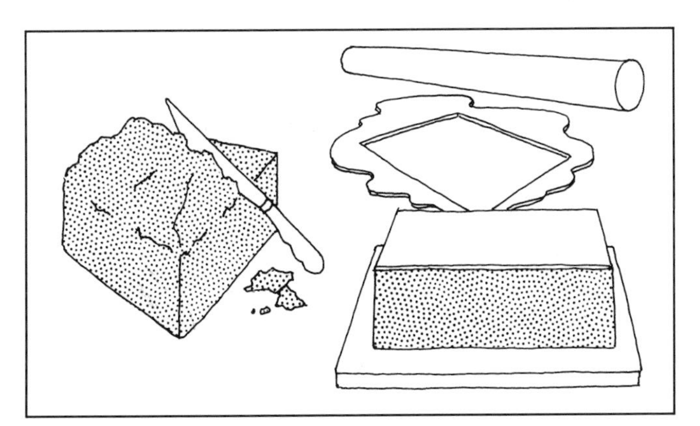

1. Having left the cake overnight, slice the top flat. Turn over and position it in centre of silver board. Make 900g (2lb) of fondant. Colour 560g (1¼lb) with red and yellow – partially mix to give streaky effect. Measure dimensions of cake. Roll fondant to 2 LS thick. Brush cake with warm jam. Cut and apply the top.

2. Apply the four sides. Using fondant trimmings, model spotlights from a roll 20mm (¾in.) diameter, cut five pieces 10mm (⅜in.) wide. Smooth edges and cut a small piece from one side, as shown. Model three drums, one 40mm (2½in.) diameter and two 20mm (¾in.) diamenter – all 13mm (½in.) deep.

THE
Birthday
BUNCH

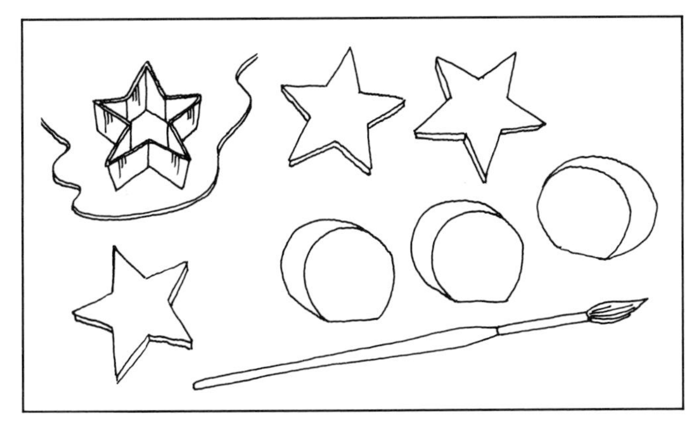

3. Roll fondant to 1 LS thick. Cut twelve stars. Paint backs of floodlights with gold and stars with silver. Leave to dry for an hour, then attach three stars to each side of cake with egg white.

4. Take 220g (8oz) of white fondant, form into an oblong and divide, as shown, into eight sections. Form first four sections into balls and colour red, blue, green and yellow. Model four pairs of legs, as shown – position one pair sitting, the others standing.

5. Divide next section into four, leave one white, colour others orange, green and blue. Model four bodies as shown. Attach to legs with egg white.

6. Colour next section flesh. Divide into four, roll each into a head keeping a tiny piece for nose. Attach noses with egg white. Attach heads to bodies. Colour the next section flesh, wrap and put to one side.

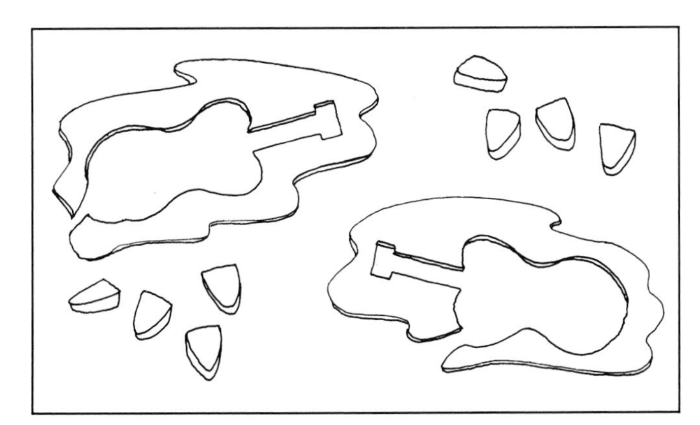

7. Divide last section in two. Colour half brown, half grey. Roll each to 2 LS thick and carefully cut two guitars, as shown. Use trimmings to model two pairs of grey shoes, two pairs brown, as shown.

8. Using white fondant, roll to 1 LS thick and cut circles to fit tops of drums. Apply with egg white. Cut a circle for symbol – paint gold when dry. Colour more fondant blue, make a seat for drummer. Make five small balls in different colour, attach them to front of spotlights with egg white.

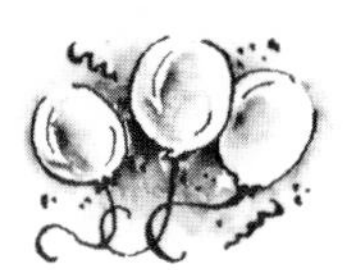

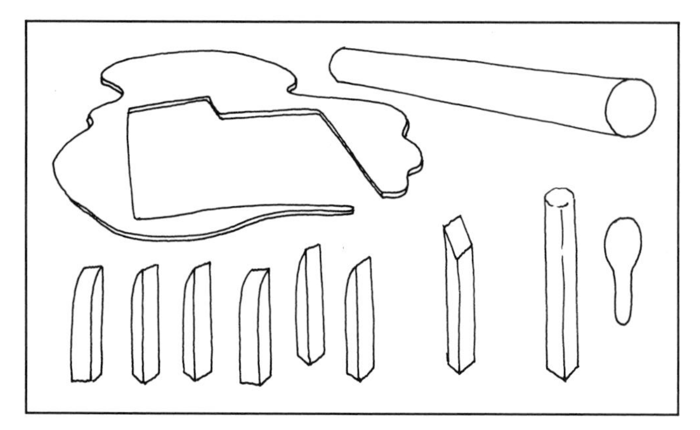

9. Colour more fondant black, roll to 2 LS thick and cut six pieces 30mm (1¼in.) high to support small drums. Cut a support cymbal and microphone. Taper all at one end as shown. Model a microphone.

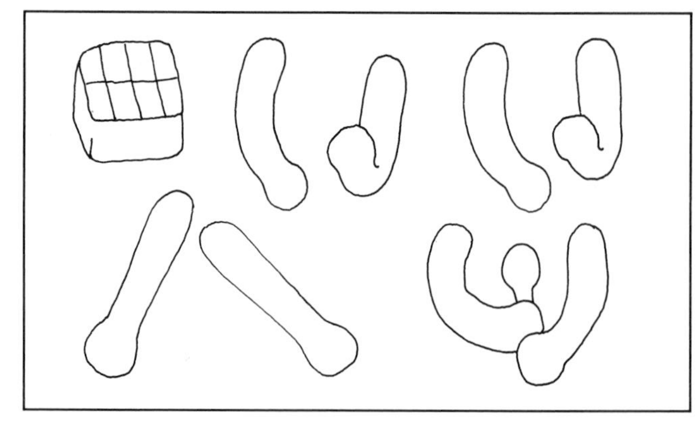

10. Take remaining flesh coloured fondant. Divide into eight and model four pairs of arms. Bend two pairs to support guitars and one pair to go across drums. Attach little microphone to last pair. Do not attach to bodies until dry.

Leave everything to dry overnight.

11. Turn little drums upside down and attach three legs to each with egg white. Turn cymbal upside down, attach support on sloping side, as shown. Cut small hole in cake fondant and push in microphone support. Do same with cymbal, when support is dry and secure.

12. Make up the 60g (2oz) of royal icing. With *No. 2 nozzle* pipe yellow hair on two men. Pipe black hair on other two men, then eyes, as shown. Pipe lines on sides of drums, a dot in centre of cymbal, details on guitars and a little line down front of each shoe. With *No. 1* pipe **THE Birthday BUNCH** on large drum.

13. Position seat next to cymbal. Attach drummer to seat with egg white. Position drums around drummer, secure with egg white or hidden dabs of icing. Attach arms to men. Position men and feet, secure with smear of icing. Secure guitars in arms with hidden dabs of icing.

14. With *No. 2 nozzle* pipe black wire from microphone and guitar to microphone stem. Pipe red lips on men, then narrow zigzag lines along fondant seams of cake and around base. Position spotlights with a smear of icing.

Chess set

This chess set with movable men will take 2–3 days to decorate, depending on how quickly you can get into the swing of modelling the separate pieces. It also takes a little time to get the squares of the board to fit correctly without large gaps between each. Time and patience will be rewarded, though, when your chess enthusiast sees the cake.

As the cake remains whole for this subject, dried fruit and/or nuts can be added to the recipe. The orange and purple fondant can be given separate flavours.

Please read the General Notes on pages 6 to 9 before starting to decorate the cake. Also read through the step-by-step instructions and check the ingredient and equipment lists.

Ingredients for cake

450g (16oz) butter
340g (12oz) caster sugar
560g (20oz) self-raising flour
340g (12oz) ground rice
280ml (10fl oz) milk beaten with 6 large eggs
fruit and/or nuts (optional)
Make from this recipe:
1 × 280mm (11in.) square cake

Ingredients for fondant and royal icing

1.340kg (3lb) icing sugar, plus 220g (8oz)
3 egg whites, plus 1
6 tblsp liquid glucose
flavouring (optional)
Also: warm sieved apricot jam; 50/50 mixture of cornflour and icing sugar in a dusting dredger; orange and purple food colouring.

Equipment

Basins for mixing icings; spoons; sieve; rolling pin; steel rule; sharp-pointed knife; lolly sticks (LS) as spacers; pastry brush; greaseproof paper for icing and bags; Ateco (or equivalent) icing nozzles 2, 15, 22 and 98; 280mm (14in.) square silver board.

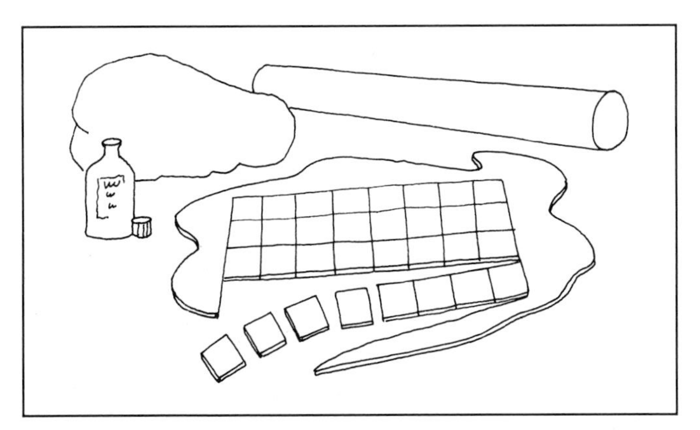

1. Having left the cake overnight, slice the top flat. Turn it over and place in centre of silver board. Make 670g (1½lb) of fondant. Colour 340g (12oz) orange. Roll to 2 LS thick and cut carefully into 32 × 30mm (1¼in.) squares.

2. Take the remaining half of fondant and colour it purple. Cut another 32 squares as before. Roll trimmings from each colour into two balls, cover and put to one side. Make another 670g (1½lb) of fondant.

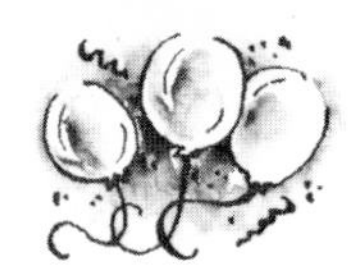

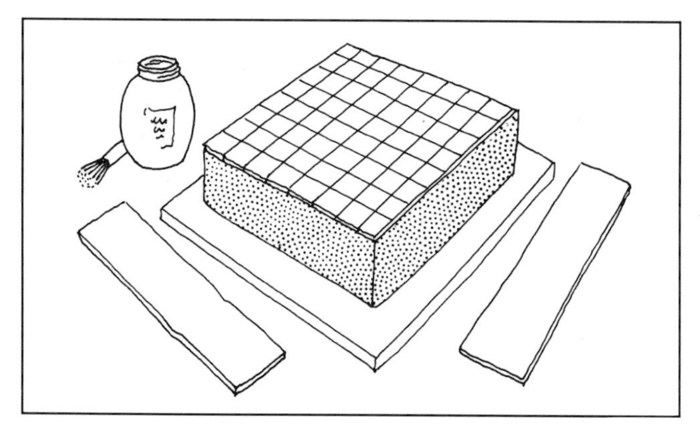

3. Brush top of cake with warm jam. Work about 10mm (⅜in.) from edges of cake and carefully apply squares. Take 450g (1lb) of the fondant. Measure cake sides, including top edge, roll fondant to 2 LS thick and cut to fit. Brush cake with jam and carefully apply fondant.

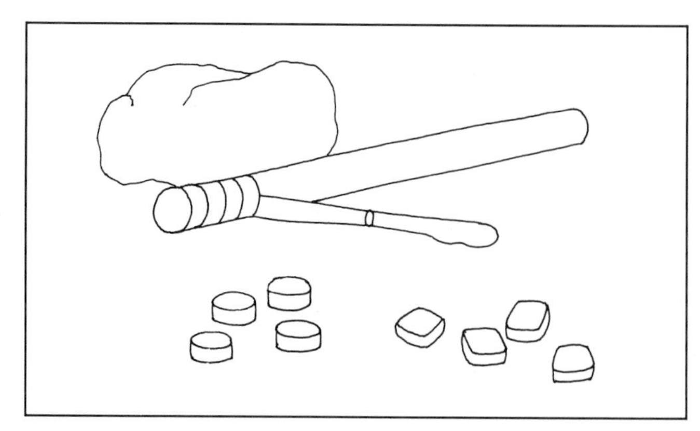

4. Add more white fondant to white trimmings. Cut in half and roll into sausage 22mm (⅞in.) diameter. Cut into slices just less than 10mm (⅜in.) wide and form into round-edged squares – work four at a time. Repeat with second half of fondant. Make 40 in all.

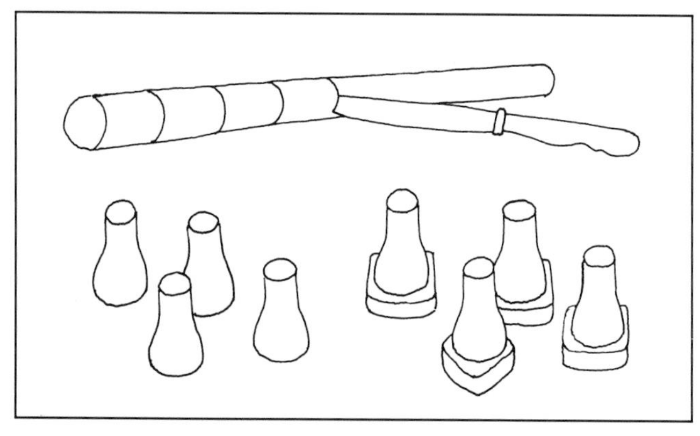

5. Take some of the remaining orange fondant. Roll into sausage 12mm (½in.) diameter and cut into eight pieces, 25mm (1in.) long. Form into pawns, as shown, working four at a time. Repeat with purple fondant. Stick pawns to white bases with egg white.

6. Take more white fondant, roll to 2 LS thick and cut circles 15mm (⅝in.) diameter to fit on top of pawns. Apply with egg white.

7. Roll little orange and purple balls and attach them to top of each pawn. Model the knights (two each colour) from sausages 15mm (⅝in.) diameter. Roll to a slight taper, then bend a little. Make four triple bases with coloured fondant sandwiched in middle, as shown.

8. Stick knights onto bases with egg white. Model ears – take a tiny ball, flatten, then wrap around paint brush handle (or knitting needle). Leave to dry for 10 minutes, then attach to heads with egg white.

9. Cut the remaining chess men from a roll 15mm (⅝in.) diameter. All pieces 30mm (1¼in.) long and tapering slightly, except rooks which are 25mm (1in.) long and do not taper. Roll white fondant to 2 LS thick and cut circles 15mm (⅝in.) diameter. Apply to tops with egg white. Stick men to remaining bases.

10. Make tops for bishops (two each colour) from tapered rolls. Add small white ball to top of each. Make tops for rooks from straight rolls. Attach four tiny white pieces to top, as shown.

11. Make tops for kings and queens, tapering slightly. Add two white balls to queen, slightly flattened. Make white crosses for kings – roll fondant to 1 LS thick, cut four pieces and stick together as shown. Leave to dry, then make small cut in tops of kings, drop in a dab of egg white, then stick in crosses.

12. With *No. 2 nozzle* and white icing pipe wavy lines down back of each knight's head, then eyes. Pipe crowns and mitres on kings, queens and bishops, as shown. Pipe circle around tops of rooks.

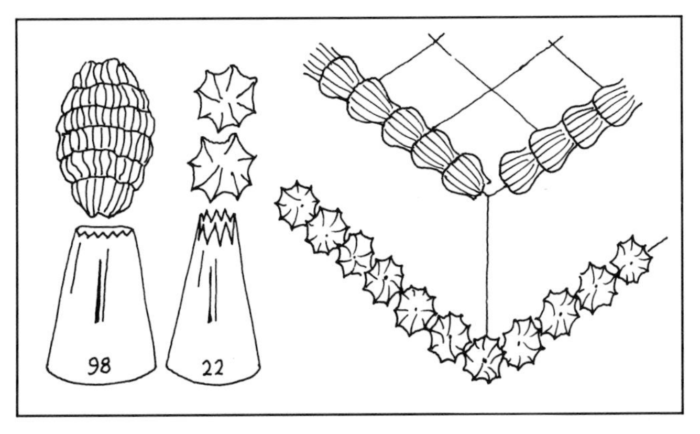

13. With *No. 98* pipe shell line in pale orange on two top edges of cake. Pipe other two edges in pale purple. With *No. 22* pipe line of dark orange flowers around bottom edge. Pipe dark purple flowers around other two bottom edges.

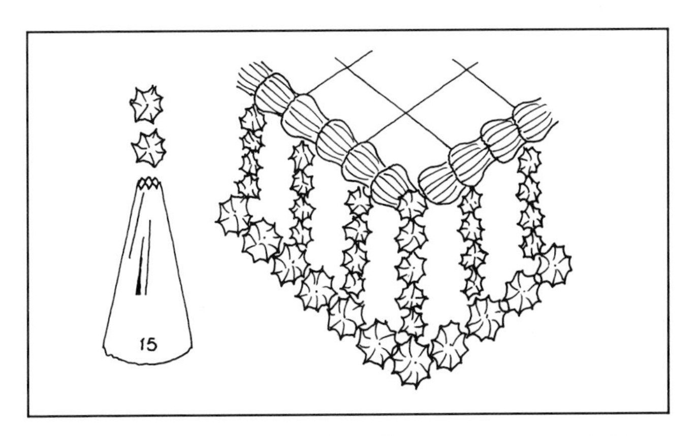

14. With *No. 15* pipe white flowers in vertical lines down each side of cake.

Position chess men on board (leave loose, or secure with a smear of icing).

Building bricks

This edible construction will take two to three days to decorate and build. It would suit a young toddler; or perhaps make an unconventional christening cake by omitting the brithday message and replacing it with the baby's name (the small bricks could each hold a candle for any older brother or sister to blow out).

Please read the General Notes on pages 6 to 9 before starting to decorate the cake. It is also useful to read through the step-by-step instructions and check the ingredient and equipment lists.

Ingredients for cake

280g (10oz) butter
220g (8oz) caster sugar
360g (13oz) self-raising flour
200g (7oz) ground rice
220ml (8fl oz) milk beaten with 4 large eggs
Make with this recipe: 1 × 200mm (8in.) square cake

Ingredients for fondant and royal icing

1,800kg (4lb) icing sugar, plus 280g (10oz)
4 egg whites, plus 1¼
8 tblsp liquid glucose
flavouring (optional)
Also: warm sieved apricot jam; 50/50 mixture of cornflour and icing sugar in a dusting dredger; yellow, pink, blue, green, purple and orange food colouring.

Equipment

Basins for mixing icings; spoons; sieve; rolling pin; steel rule; sharp-pointed knife; lolly sticks (LS) as spacers; pastry brush; greaseproof paper for icing bags; Ateco (or equivalent) icing nozzles 3, 4, 13 and 15;) 350mm (14in.) round silver cake board; small cocktail cutter.

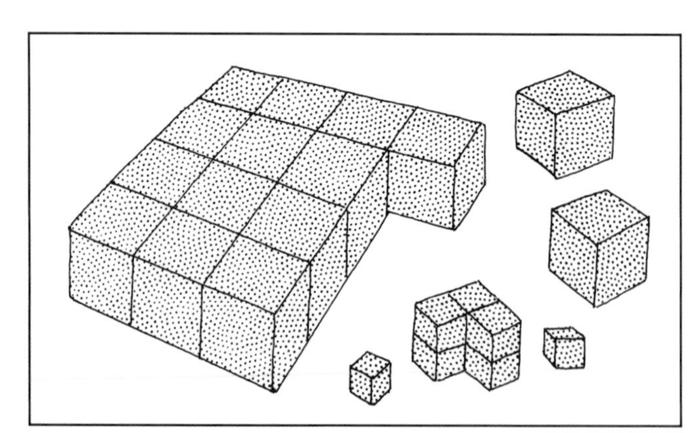

1. Having left the cake overnight, slice the top perfectly flat. Carefully cut into 16 × 50mm (2in.) squares. Cut one of these into eight small squares, as shown.

2. Make the 1,800kg (4lb) of fondant (in two lots). Measure three sides of a large brick, then brush the sides with jam. Roll fondant to 2 LS thick and cut to fit. Place brick on fondant and roll carefully, covering the three sides as shown.

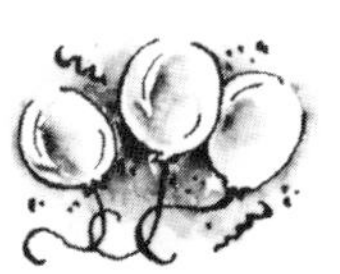

HAPPY
BIRTHDAY
EMMA JANE

3. Repeat with all bricks (including little ones) then repeat again, covering remaining three sides. Trim if necessary, so that all edges are perfectly smooth. Leave to dry on a dusted surface overnight.

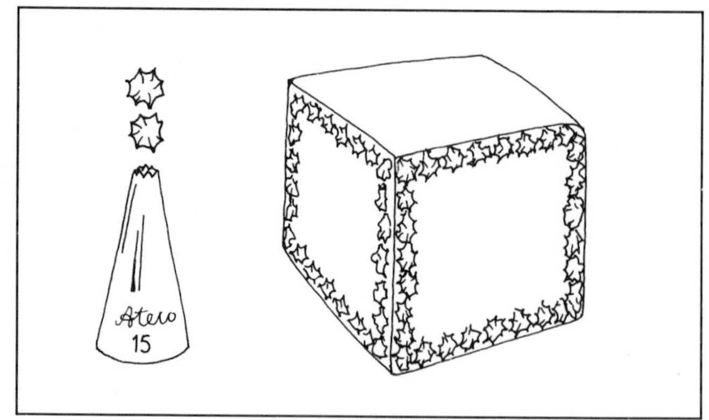

4. Make the 280g (10oz) of royal icing. With *No. 15 nozzle* pipe stars along seams and down corners of each large brick, as shown. Pipe three bricks with pink, three with pale blue, three yellow, three pale green and three pale purple. Push required number of candle holders into a pink brick.

5. With *nozzle No. 13* and pale orange icing, pipe stars along seams and down corners of small bricks. Using same colour and *nozzle No. 3* pipe name of child (if there are enough bricks) or an appropriate message.

6. With *nozzle No. 4* and following the colour scheme, pipe **HAPPY BIRTHDAY** on large bricks.

7. Using fondant trimmings, colour small pieces, roll to 1 LS thick and cut small flower shapes – four yellow, three pink, three pale green, two pale blue and two pale purple. Brush backs with egg white and apply to appropriate bricks. Leave to dry overnight.

8. Assemble bricks on silver board, as shown. Secure them (including ones actually on board) with smears of royal icing.

Snakes & ladders

This is a fairly straight-forward cake which can be decorated in a day and evening, but some patience is required with the ladders. As the cake is large it might taste better with a filling of flavoured butter cream or jam – either slice the whole cake in half; or cut it into nine cubes, smear the filling on each of the cut sides then press them together again.

Gum Tragacanth is added to the fondant which forms the sides of the cake, and acts as a hardener. The powder can be bought from most chemists but it is rather expensive and unless you intend to do more fondant decorating you may feel it too costly – the cake will survive without it.

Please read pages 6 to 9 before starting to decorate the cake. Also read through the step-by-step instructions and check the ingredient and equipment lists.

Ingredients for cake

450g (16oz) butter
360g (13oz) caster sugar
560g (20oz) self-raising flour
340g (12oz) ground rice
280ml (10fl oz) milk beaten with 6 large eggs
filling, flavouring or dried fruit
Make from this recipe:
1 / 280mm (11in.) square cake

Ingredients for fondant and royal icing

900g (2lb) icing sugar, plus 220g (8oz)
2 egg white, plus 1
1 teasp gum tragacanth (optional)
4 tblsp liquid glucose
flavouring (optional)
Also: 450g (1lb) marzipan or almond paste; warm sieved apricot jam; 50/50 mixture of cornflour and icing sugar in a dusting dredger; yellow, red, blue, green and brown colouring; silver balls for decoration.

Equipment

Basins for mixing icings; sieve; spoons; rolling pin; steel rule; sharp pointed knife; lolly sticks (LS) as spacers; pastry brush; greaseproof paper for icing bags; fine paint brush; Ateco (or equivalent) icing nozzles 1 and 15; 350mm (14in.) square silver board.

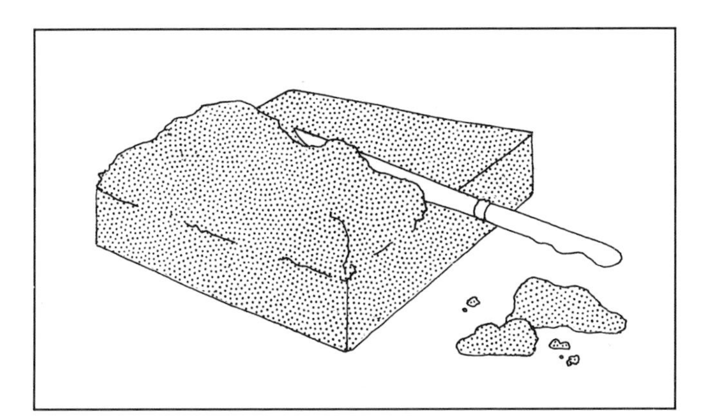

1. Having left the cake overnight, slice the top so that the surface is completely flat. Turn the cake over and position it in centre of the silver board.

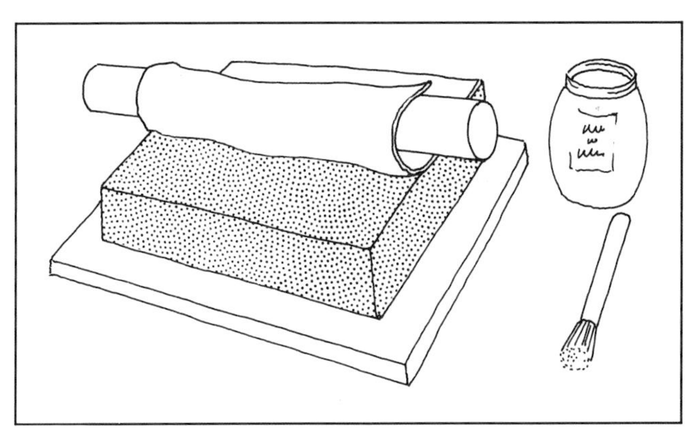

2. Brush top of cake with the warm sieved jam. Knead marzipan (almond paste), knock into a square then roll out on a dusted surface to 2 LS thick. Cut round baking tin. Carefully place (with the help of the rolling pin) on top of cake.

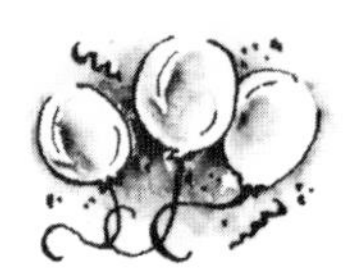

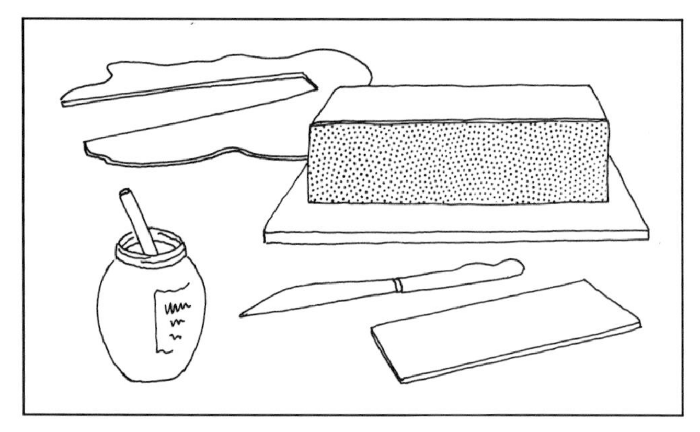

3. Make 900g (2lb) fondant. Take just over 670g (1½lb), add gum tragacanth and flavour if desired, then colour pale greeny-blue. Brush sides of cake with jam. Roll fondant to 2 LS thick, cut to size then apply to cake sides.

4. Roll fondant again to 2 LS thick, cut four strips to fit around top edges of cake, 25mm (1in.) wide. Brush outer area of marzipan with jam then position fondant strips.

5. Mix left-over trimmings with remaining fondant and divide into three equal portions. Colour them red, blue and yellow (because some of the original fondant was coloured, you will have subtle shades of red, blue and green).

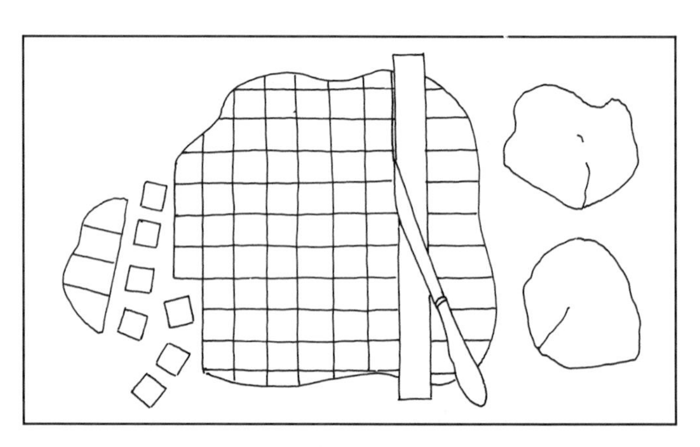

6. Dust the working surface. Roll fondant to 1 LS thick and cut into neat 25mm (1in.) squares. You will need 27 squares of each colour.

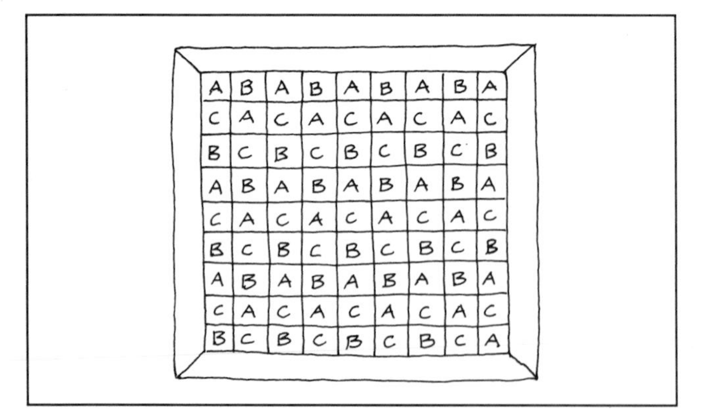

7. Brush a thin film of jam over the marzipan. Carefully position each square as indicated on diagram.

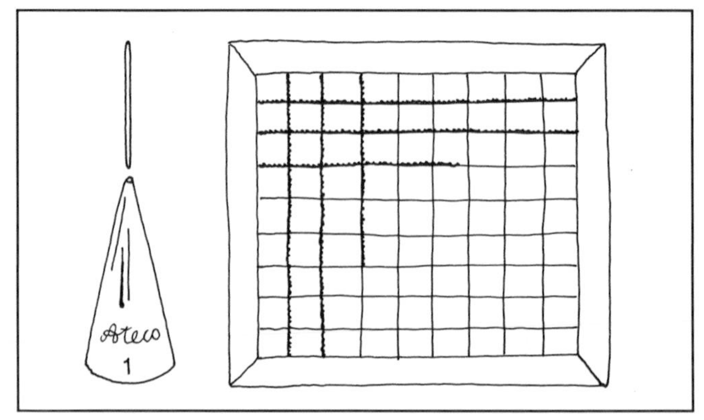

8. Make up the 220g (8oz) of royal icing and keep in an airtight container. Using *No. 1 nozzle* pipe very small white dots along seams of squares.

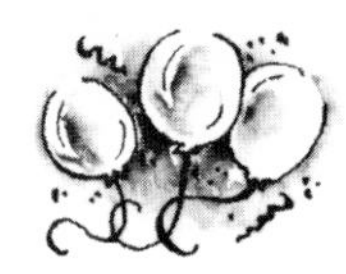

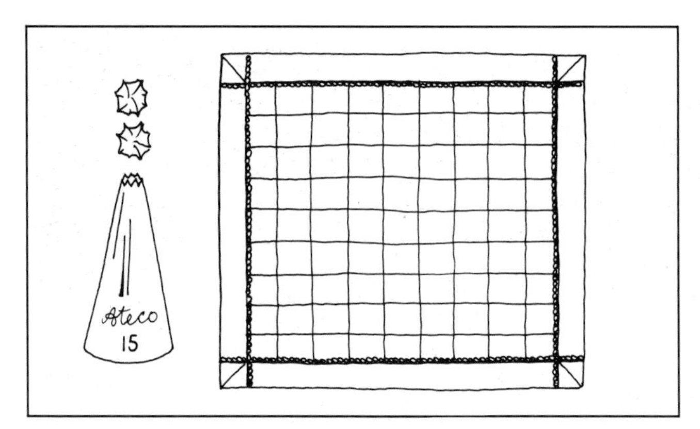

9. Mix yellow into royal icing. Using *No. 15* pipe small stars around outer edge of coloured squares, making a small square at each corner as shown.

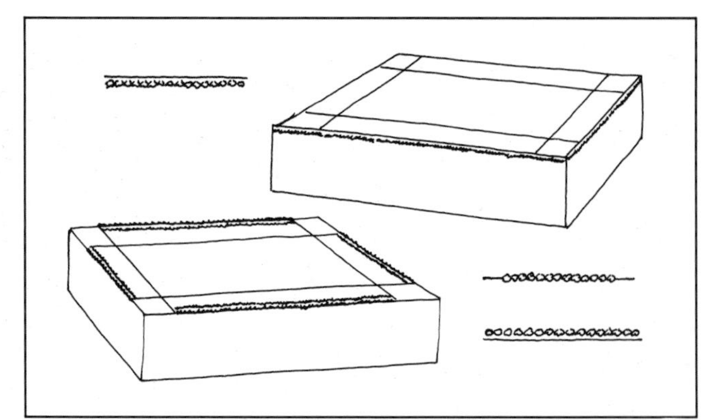

10. Pipe one line of stars along top edge of each side. Then, stopping at the square in each corner, pipe one line of stars on join of fondant and one line at edge of each strip, as shown.

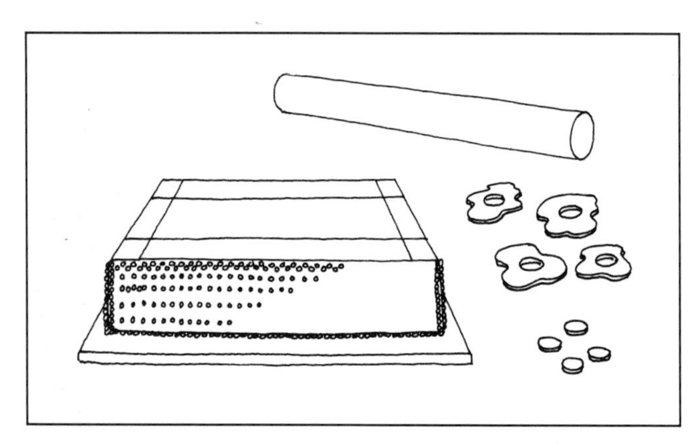

11. Pipe gradating stars on sides of cake as shown, then pipe stars round base of cake.

Add more colour to small pieces of fondant. Roll to 1 LS thick and cut round counters. Place in one corner of cake.

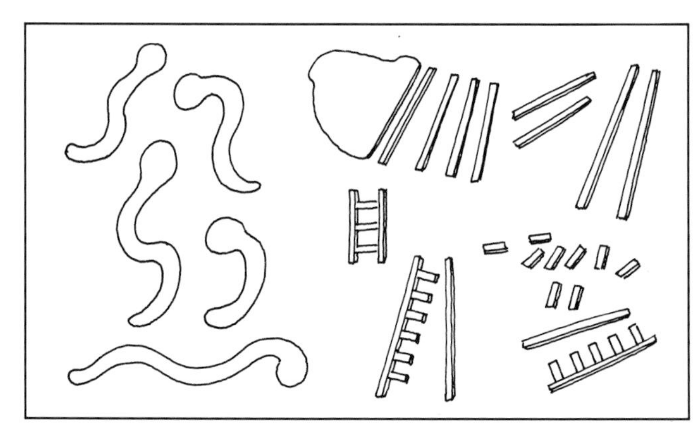

12. Add more green to green fondant. Roll five snakes of varying sizes. Flatten heads slightly and bend bodies. Add brown to red fondant. Roll to 1 LS thick and cut into narrow strips. Attach ladder rungs as shown, with a dab of egg white. Leave snakes and ladders to dry.

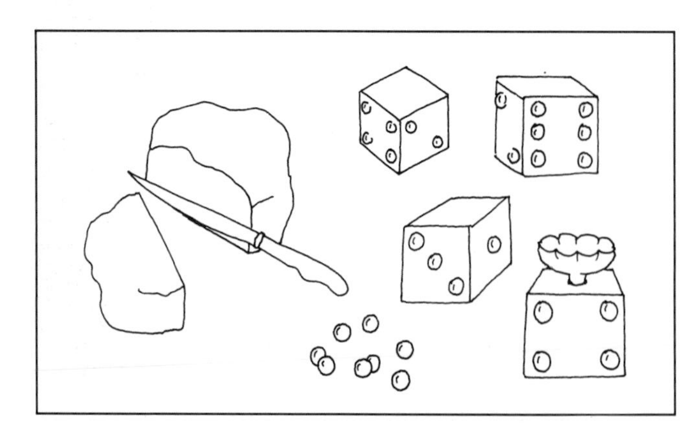

13. Add more blue to remaining blue fondant. Knead, then cut into four cubes. Press in silver balls secured with tiny dabs of egg white. Place a dice at each corner of cake, securing with a dab of royal icing. Push candle holders carefully into dice.

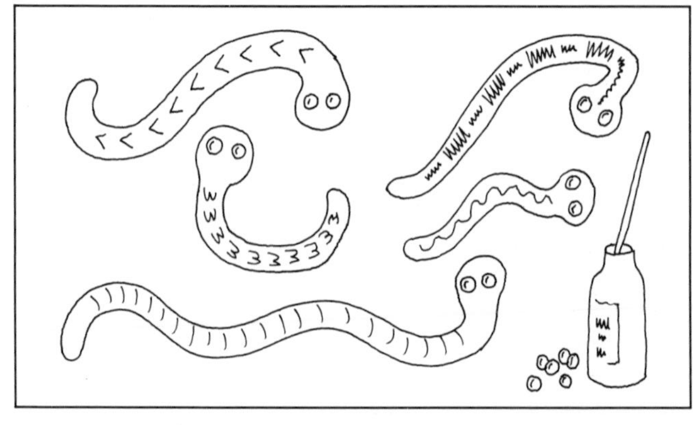

14. Paint patterns with red and blue colour on backs of snakes. Pipe 2 dots of icing on each head and attach silver balls (eyes). Secure ladders and snakes to cake with hidden dabs of icing. Place candles in holders.

Bobsleighs

This was originally intended as a ski slope, but after various minor traumas trying to balance the skiers, my son suggested bobsleighs. The fact that the sleighs are likely to go flying over the edge (as one already has) must be overlooked!

The trickiest part of decorating is in applying the white fondant. Fortunately, in order to look realistic, it does not have to be perfectly smooth. I made this cake during the half-term holidays and, because of interruptions by 'The young Pinder Cake-decorating Advisory Service' it took almost a week to complete. However, it should be done in two or three days.

Please read the General Notes on pages 6 to 9 before starting to decorate the cake. Also read through the step-by-step instructions and check the ingredient and equipment lists.

Ingredients for cake

450g (16oz) butter
340g (12oz) caster sugar
560g (20oz) self-raising flour
340g (12oz) ground rice
280ml (10fl oz) milk beaten with 6 large eggs
filling
Make from this recipe: 1 × 280mm (11in.) square cake

Ingredients for fondant and royal icing

1.570kg (3½lb) icing sugar, plus 220g (8oz)
3½ egg whites, plus 1
7 tblsp liquid glucose
flavouring (optional)
Also: warm sieved apricot jam; 50/50 mixture of cornflour and icing sugar in a dusting dredger; red, blue, yellow, green and brown food colouring.

Equipment

Basins for mixing icings; spoons; sieve; rolling pin; sharp-pointed knife; steel rule; lolly sticks (LS) as spacers; pastry brush; greaseproof paper for icing bags; Ateco (or equivalent) icing nozzles 1, 2, 3 and 41; 280mm (11in.) square silver cake board.

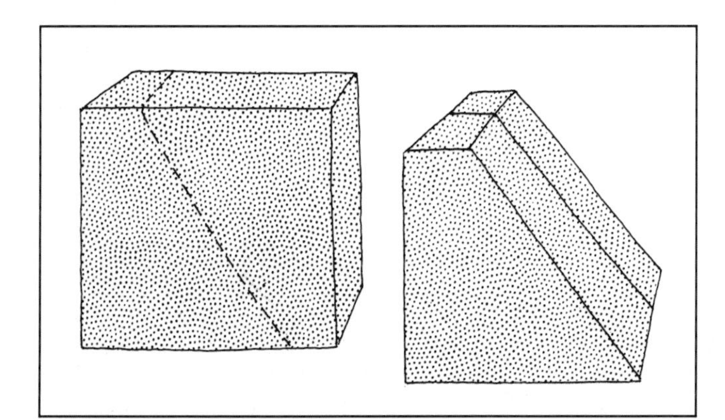

1. Having left the cake overnight, slice the top flat. Measure 40mm (1½in.) from top and bottom opposite sides and cut the cake across, as shown. Join the two pieces together with filling (jam and butter cream). Trim if necessary, to make a smooth slope.

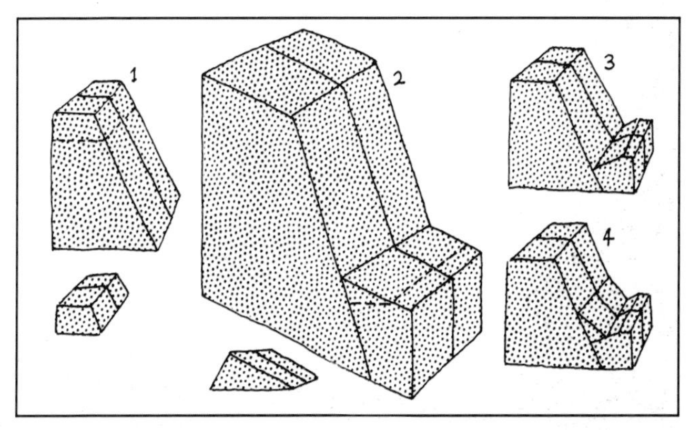

2. Cut 75mm (3in.) off the top. Turn this piece upside down and position at bottom of slope (with filling). Cut a piece out, as shown and position against main slope, using filling to secure.

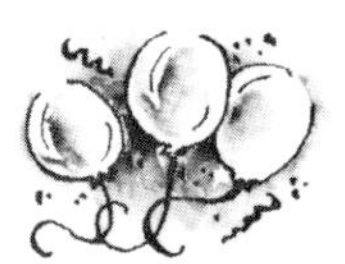

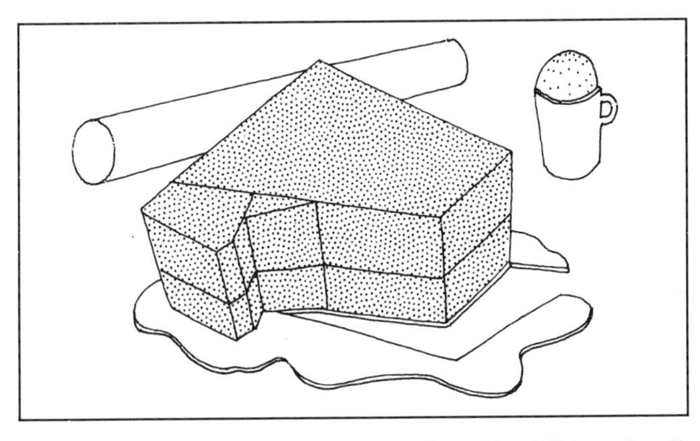

3. Make 900g (2lb) of fondant. Take 450g (1lb) and roll to 2 LS thick roughly the shape of one side of cake. Brush side with jam. Slide cake along table to bottom edge of fondant and lay cake on. Cut around fondant and carefully lift cake.

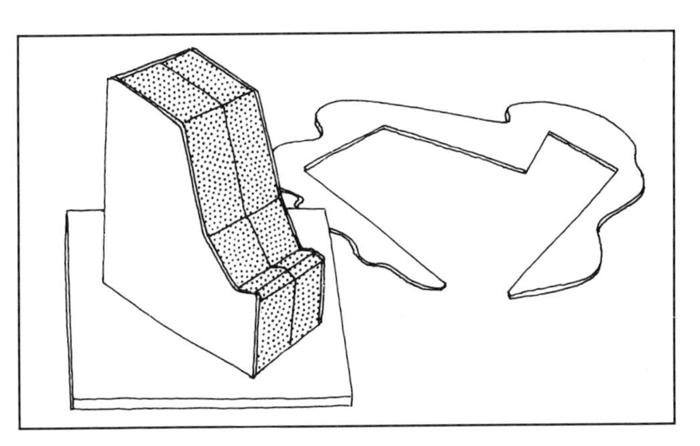

4. Slide cake to another part of table. Brush other side with jam. Roll out fondant and apply as before. Carefully lift cake up, slide to edge of table and on to silver board. Position diagonally.

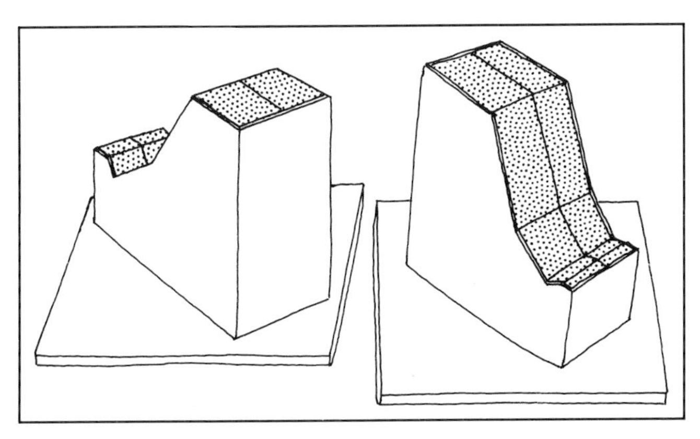

5. Add more fondant to trimmings. Measure back of slope then brush with jam. Roll fondant to 2 LS thick and cut to fit. Apply carefully, smoothing with hands. Measure facing front of slope, cut and apply fondant as before.

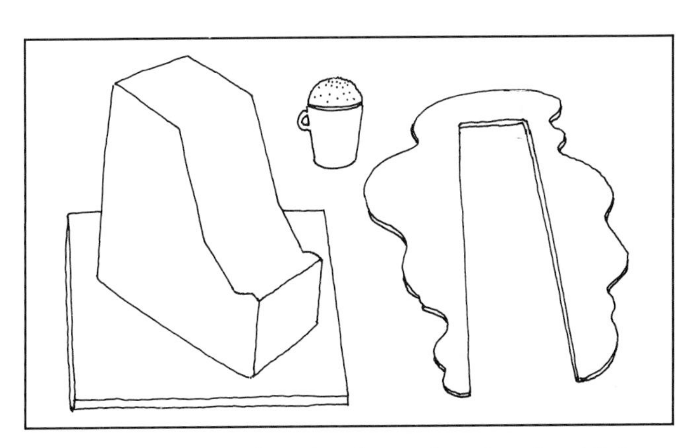

6. Measure top and entire slope, then brush with jam. Roll fondant to 2 LS thick and cut to fit, in one piece if possible. Carefully apply, then smooth with hands. Mark three pairs of grooves in snow (one pair going off edge) using wooden skewer or knitting needle.

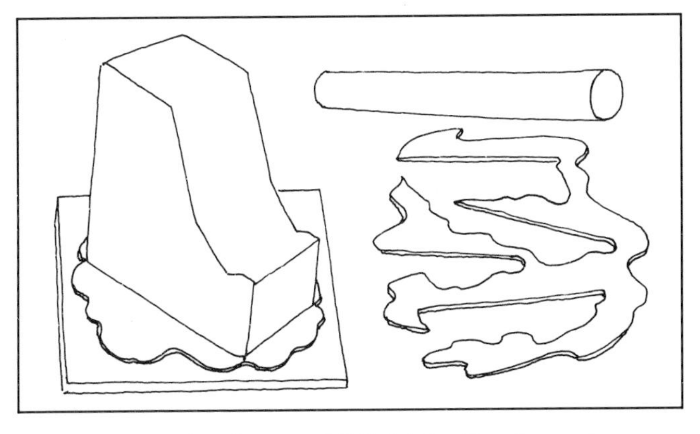

7. Roll more fondant to 2 LS thick. Cut four pieces as shown, to fit around base of cake. Brush bottom edge of cake and part of silver board with egg white. Lay pieces down.

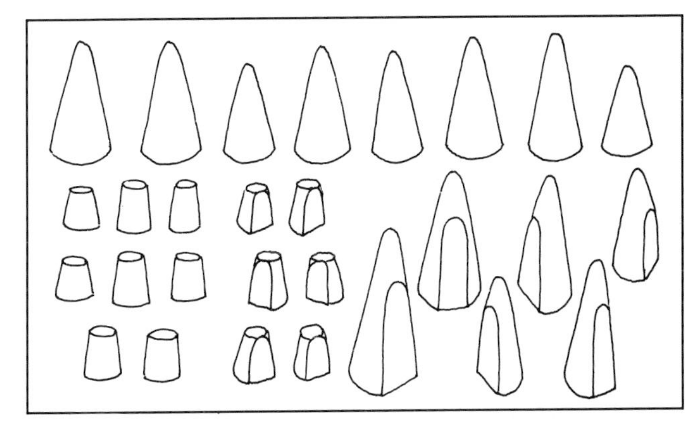

8. Make up the remaining fondant 675g (1½lb) – but use some to complete snow around cake base. Make fourteen green trees and fourteen brown trunks, as shown. Slice the backs off six trees and flatten one side of six trunks, as shown – so they can be attached to sides of slope.

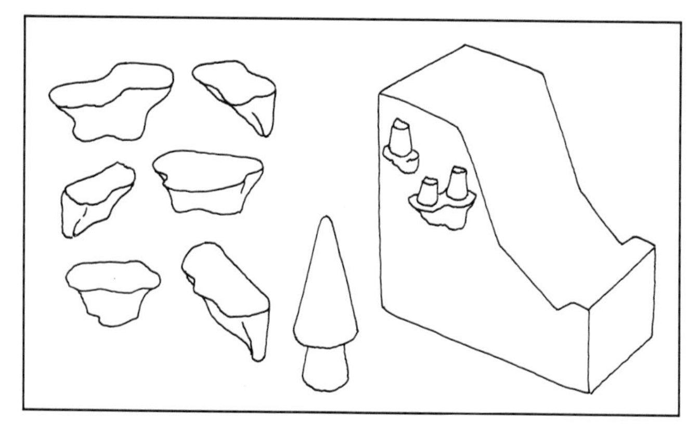

9. Make six shelves to support trees. Model the shapes, brush backs with egg white and attach to cake, two on each side, one at back. Attach trunks to free-standing trees. Position flat-sided trunks on shelves, brushing egg white on base and flat side.

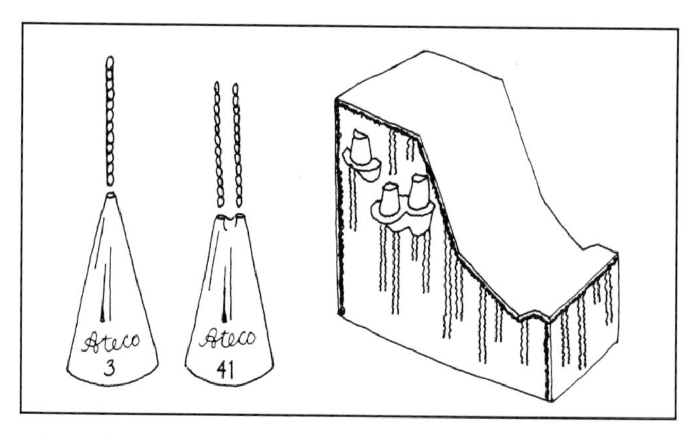

10. Make the 220g (8oz) of royal icing. Using *nozzle No. 3* pipe continuous dots on all cake seams. With *nozzle No. 41* pipe lines down walls to give impression of falling snow.

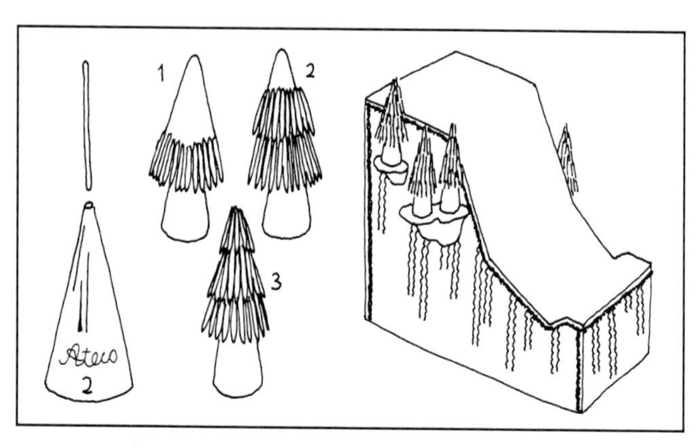

11. Attach flat-sided trees to trunks and wall of cake. With *nozzle No. 2* pipe green branches on all trees, starting at bottom and working up. Leave free-standing trees to dry, then carefully position on flat snow using egg white to secure.

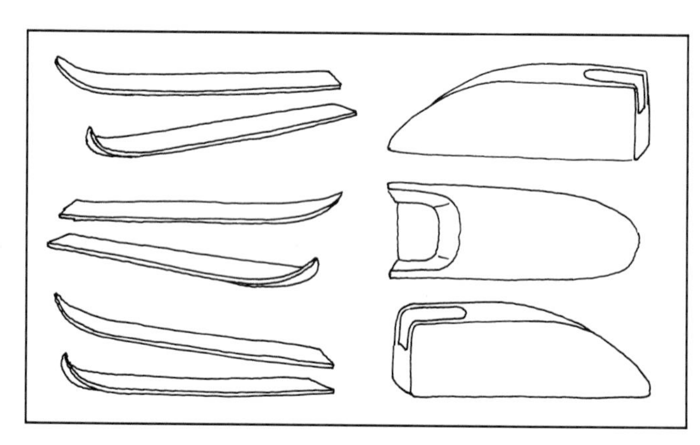

12. Roll brown fondant to 2 LS thick. Cut three pairs of skis 6mm (¼in.) wide, 75mm (3in.) long, pointed at one end. Leave to dry on dusted surface, support at one end to give a slight curve. Model sleighs in red, blue and yellow from a sausage, as shown. Cut pieces out where man is to sit.

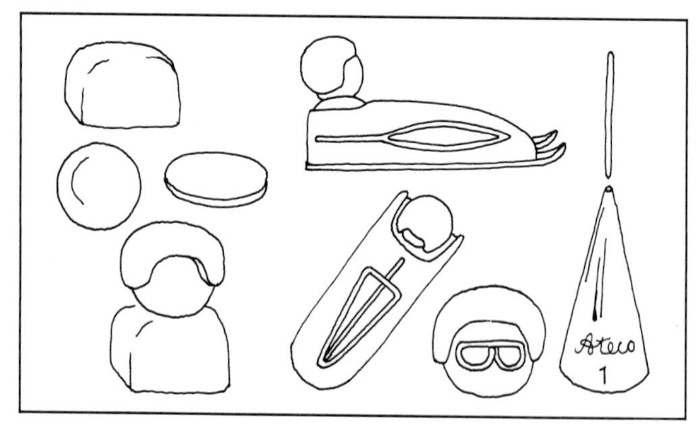

13. Model bodies, heads and helmets, as shown, in different colours. Place in sleighs securing with egg white. Position sleighs on skis, secure with egg white. Using *No. 2 nozzle* pipe coloured markings on sleighs. With *No. 1* and brown icing, pipe goggles on men. Leave to dry.

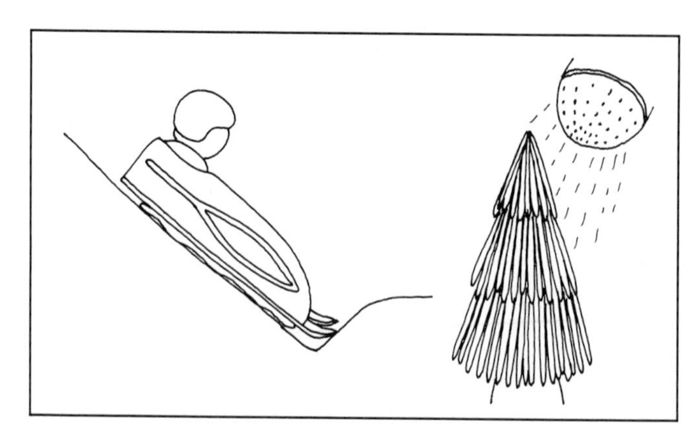

14. Place a lump of white fondant at base of cake, position yellow sleigh as if fallen (safely) from slope – secure with egg white. Position other sleighs as shown, securing lower one with piece of soft white fondant underneath. Gently shake dredger over all the trees.

American football

This subject is made from two cakes. Although both are baked in 280mm (11in.) square tins, the upright cake needs to be deeper than the flat one, so the ingredient quantities are increased. Working with such a large mass of ingredients can be tricky – I first combined the butter and sugar in my blender, then added the remaining ingredients in a washing-up bowl. I then blended everything in two separate batches.

My players appear to be slightly inebriated. This was not intended – although I did leave a glass of wine by the cake one night! One of my teams is the New England Patriots, the other is made up. I suggest you use the colours of your child's two favourite teams.

The cake will take three to four days to decorate.

Please read the General Notes on pages 6 to 9 before starting to decorate. Also read through the instructions and check the ingredients and equipment lists.

Ingredients for cake

450g (1lb) butter
340g (12oz) caster sugar
560g (20oz) self-raising flour
340g (12oz) ground rice
280ml (10fl oz) milk beaten with 6 large eggs
Make from this recipe: 1 x 280mm (11in.) square cake

670g (1½lb) butter
450g (1lb) caster sugar
840g (30oz) self-raising flour
510g (18oz) ground rice
420ml (15fl oz) milk beaten with 9 large eggs
Make from this recipe: 1 x 280mm (11in.) square cake

Ingredients for fondant and royal icing

2.470kg (5½lb) icing sugar, plus 220g (8oz)
5½ egg whites, plus 1
11 tblsp liquid glucose
flavouring (optional)
Also: warm sieved apricot jam; 50/50 mixture of cornflour and icing sugar in a dusting dredger; green, brown, flesh, yellow, red, blue and silver food colouring.

Equipment

Basins for mixing icings; sieve; spoons; rolling pin; sharp-pointed knife; steel rule; lolly sticks (LS) as spacers; pastry brush; small paint brush; greaseproof paper for icing bags; Ateco (or equivalent) icing nozzles 1, 2 and 3; 400mm (16in.) square silver cake board.

1. Having left the cakes overnight, slice the top of the shallower one flat, then turn it over. Stand the deeper cake upright, against the other and draw a line, as shown (the pencil mark will be cut away). Lay cake flat and cut out a piece, as shown, cutting just above pencil line.

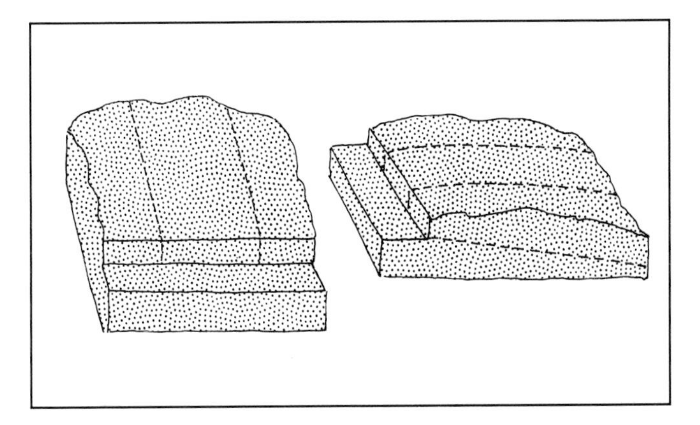

2. Measure 90mm (3½in.) in from each side (mark with pencil again) and cut the two side pieces out, sloping towards the top, as shown.

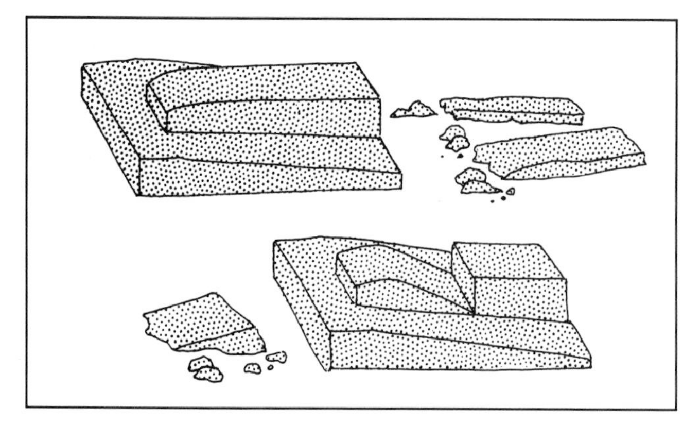

3. Cut the centre piece flat, sloping in a little (following natural curve of cake) at the bottom, as shown. Then cut the piece in half and cut a slope upwards to the top of the bottom slope, as shown.

Make 900g (2lb) of fondant and colour green.

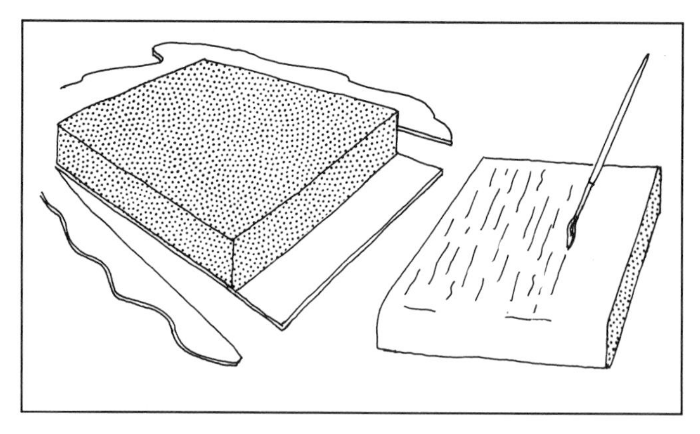

4. Brush top and front of 'pitch' with warm jam. Roll fondant (on well dusted surface) to 2 LS thick. Lay jammed surface of cake on to fondant and cut around three sides. Lift cake onto fourth side to cover, then trim. Carefully position cake towards front of silver board. Paint strokes of green colour on top surface.

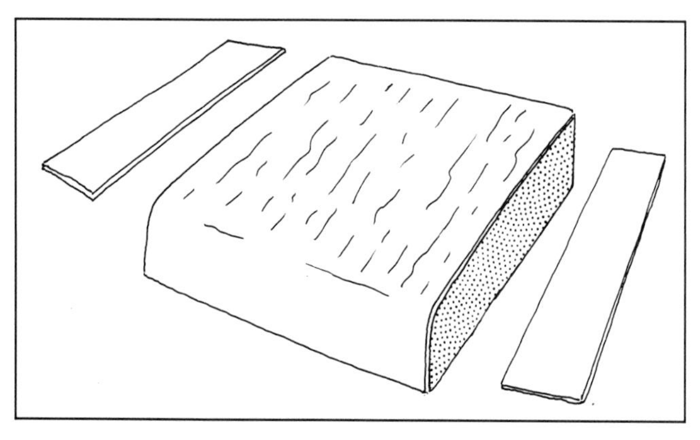

5. Brush right and left sides of pitch with jam. Roll fondant to 2 LS thick. Measure each side, cut fondant to fit and carefully apply.

Make 1.570kg (3½lb) of fondant – in two batches for ease. Keep well wrapped.

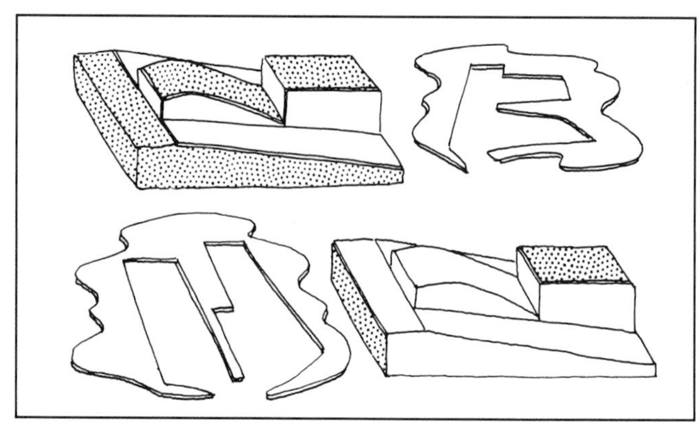

6. Take 670g (1½lb) of fondant, add it to green trimmings and mix in brown colour. Brush top surfaces of carved cake with jam. Measure each surface in turn (apart from top middle surface), roll fondant to 2 LS thick, cut to fit and carefully apply. Brush sides and top of cake with jam and apply fondant as before.

7. Take 450g (1lb) of fondant. Roll a piece to 2 LS thick, cut to fit remaining top middle surface (score board). Brush surface with jam and apply piece of fondant.

Take more white fondant, colour some flesh, some darker flesh and some dark brown.

8. Roll about 46 balls (slightly varying in size) and cut each in half. Make the 220g (8oz) of royal icing. Using *No. 1 nozzle* with black, yellow and red icing, pipe different expressions on faces and different hairstyles, as shown. Leave on a dusted surface to dry.

GREAT
SCORE
12
TODAY
65
72

9. Trace the above letters (with child's age) on to greaseproof paper. Attach paper, with two dabs of white icing, to score board. Stick a pin through pencil lines, then remove. Fill in area made by pin marks with regular dots, as shown.

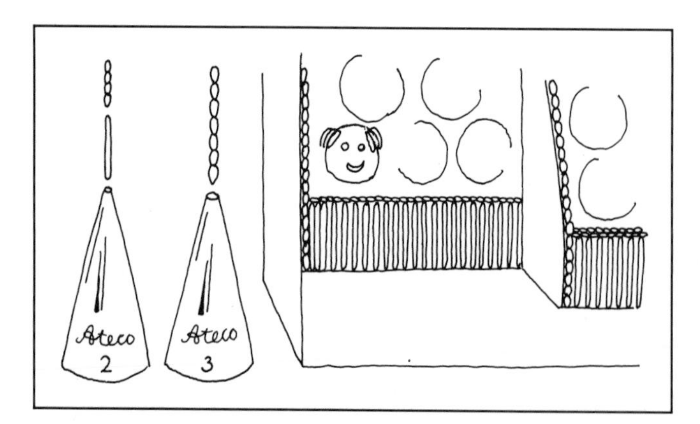

10. With *No. 3 nozzle* and brown icing, pipe continuous dots on all top surface seams of fondant. With *No. 2 nozzle* pipe fencing, as shown. Pipe double row of dots on middle fence, single row on other two fences. Pipe circles of icing on back of each head and attach to cake.

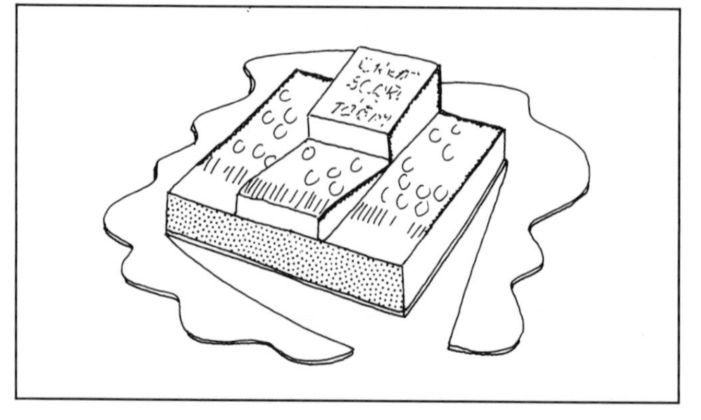

11. Take remaining brown fondant, add about 110g (4oz) of white. Roll to 1 LS thick. Carefully stand brown cake upright. Brush back with jam then gently lower onto fondant. Trim around edge then carefully lift upright again.

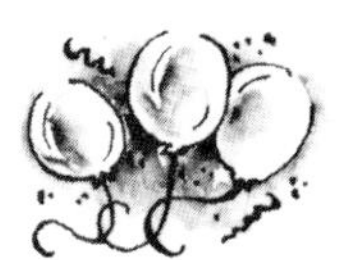

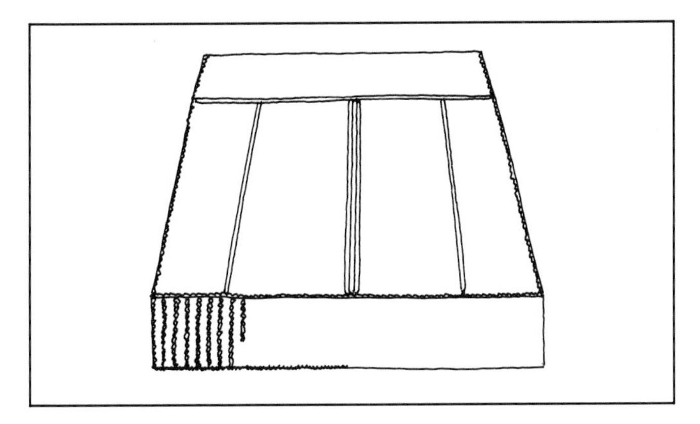

12. With *No. 2 nozzle* and white icing, pipe the pitch lines, as shown. Pipe team colours on each side of centre line. With same nozzle and green icing, pipe continuous dots on fondant seams, along front, around base and down front panel.

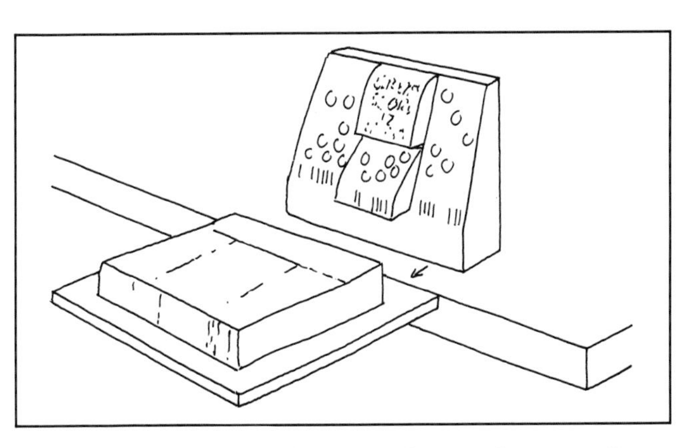

13. Smear back edge of pitch with jam, then pipe lines of icing over jam. Pipe lines underneath protruding centre piece of brown cake. Ask someone to hold silver board level with table top and carefully slide brown cake to join back of pitch.

14. With brown icing and *No. 3 nozzle* fill in any gaps at join of the two cakes, then pipe continuous dots over join, on all remaining fondant seams and around base of brown cake.

15. Take about 110g (4oz) of white fondant and colour flesh. Make eight heads. Add more brown colour to some of brown trimmings, make two more heads. Model the football from brown trimmings. Leave all to dry on a dusted surface.

16. Choose your own colours for the following: take some fondant and model eight helmets – roll a ball slightly smaller than heads, flatten and mould around heads. Model eight bodies for the players, as shown. Model two cheer-leader bodies, arms, legs and boots, as shown.

17. Model remaining pieces for players, apart from arms and hands. After four hours, stick cheer-leaders together using egg white – the arms will have to be supported for a few minutes until secure. Stick boots, legs and trunks of players together, then stick heads to bodies.

18. Model arms and hands and stick to bodies while still fairly soft; they will have to be supported (use a stack of coins) until secure. Leave overnight.

19. Attach all legs to bodies, using icing to secure. With your own colour choice and *No. 2 nozzle*, pipe guards on helmets, numbers on back and front of players, stripes down sides of legs, on helmets and boots. Pipe pleats on cheer-leaders' dresses and little loops on hems.

20. With *No. 1 nozzle* pipe all eyes. Pipe crinkly hair on one cheer-leader, straight hair on the other. With same nozzle build up white pompoms on each hand of cheer-leaders. Pipe red lips and bows in hair. Pipe a yellow band around the ball. Leave to dry for a while, standing players against supports if necessary.

21. Carefully paint the face guards and cheer-leader's pompoms with silver. Position the ball on the pitch, securing with egg white.

22. Pipe icing on to soles of feet and position cheer-leaders at edge of pitch. Repeat with each player, allowing them to support each other if they look as if they might fall! Lay one player on the pitch. Push candle holders into top of scoreboard.

Cricket

I have been told by a very keen cricketer (my husband) that 'rain stop(s) play' (not enough spaces for good grammar!) is never put up on the scoreboard; but this theme makes a change from the usual cake-cricket pitch – and is probably more true to life, in England anyway!

As you can see, the players and pavilion are not in proportion; one could make the men smaller, but then detail would be lost. A slight improvement might be to make the windows wider and deeper.

The cake will take two to three days to decorate. The players are very easy; because they are supported by the steps you will not have to wait for each piece to dry before assembling.

Please read the General Notes on pages 6 to 9 before you start to decorate the cake. Also read through the step-by-step instructions and check the equipment and ingredient lists.

Ingredients for cake

450g (16oz) butter
340g (12oz) caster sugar
560g (20oz) self-raising flour
340g (12oz) ground rice
280ml (10fl oz) milk beaten with 6 large eggs
Make from this recipe 1 × 280mm (11in.) square cake

280g (10oz) butter
220g (8oz) caster sugar
360g (13oz) self-raising flour
200g (7oz) ground rice
220ml (8fl oz) milk beaten with 4 large eggs
buttercream for filling
Make from this recipe: 1 × 200mm (8in.) square cake

Ingredients for fondant and royal icing

2.040kg (4½lb) icing sugar, plus 110g (4oz)
3¾ egg whites, plus ½
7½ tblsp liquid glucose
flavouring (optional)
Also: warm sieved apricot jam; 50/50 mixture of cornflour and icing sugar in a dusting dredger; green, red, brown, black, flesh, blue and silver food colouring.

Equipment

Basins for mixing icings; sieve; spoons; rolling pin; steel rule; sharp-pointed knife; lolly sticks (LS) as spacers; pastry brush; small paint brush; greaseproof paper for icing bags; Ateco (or equivalent) icing nozzles 1, 2 and 3; 350mm (14in.) square silver cake board.

1. Having left the cakes overnight, slice the tops flat. Slice 20mm (¾in.) from one side of smaller cake. Lay this piece flat and cut off a third. Cut a 50mm (2in.) piece from the cake. These pieces will form the steps, as shown – the main cake standing a little back on the top step.

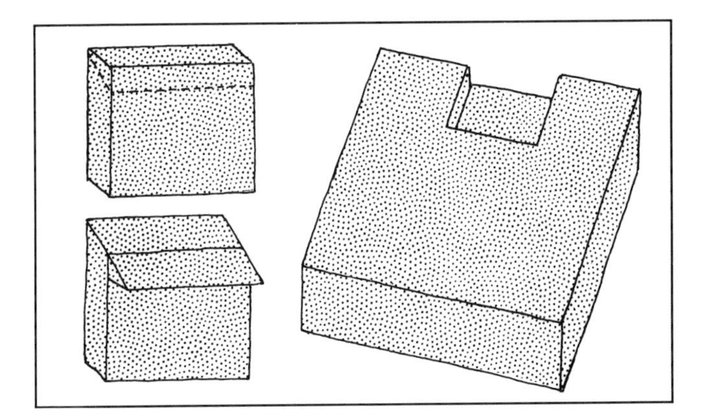

2. Slice a sloping piece from top of cake, as shown. This piece will be turned over and attached to continue the sloping roof. Take the larger cake, with smooth base facing up, cut a piece from edge 90mm (3½in.) long, 75mm (3in.) wide, 20mm (¾in.) deep, as shown. Position the cake in centre of silver board.

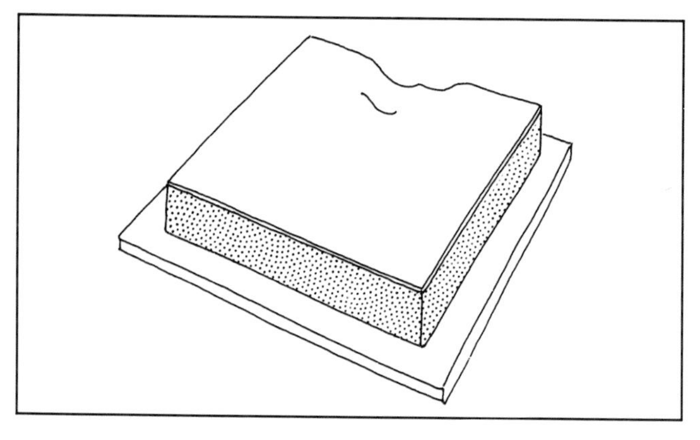

3. Make 670g (1½lb) of fondant and colour green. Measure top of large cake, then brush with warm jam. Roll fondant to 2 LS thick, cut to fit and, with help of rolling pin, carefully apply – allow fondant to fall loosely into cut-out square.

4. Measure front and sides, then cover with fondant 2 LS thick, as before. Make 1kg (2¼lb) of fondant. Add green trimmings and more green colour. Lay largest piece of pavilion on its back. Stick sloping roof on with buttercream.

5. Measure dimensions of roof, front and underneath roof. Brush with jam. Roll fondant to 2 LS thick and cut to fit (front and underneath roof in one piece). Mark planks on roof after application. Leave to dry.

6. Colour a small piece of fondant brown. Roll to 1 LS thick, cut door and shutters to fit inside, as shown. Before attaching mark grooves with knife. Paint inside surrounds black, as shown. Roll white fondant to 1 LS thick cut door and shutters to fit inside, as shown – before attaching mark grooves with knife.

7. Roll green fondant to 1 LS thick. Brush scoreboard (piece taken out of large cake) with jam. Cover back, top and bottom with one piece; cover sides and front with one piece. Leave to dry on dusted surface.

Sandwich steps and pavilion together with buttercream, as shown. Brush steps with jam.

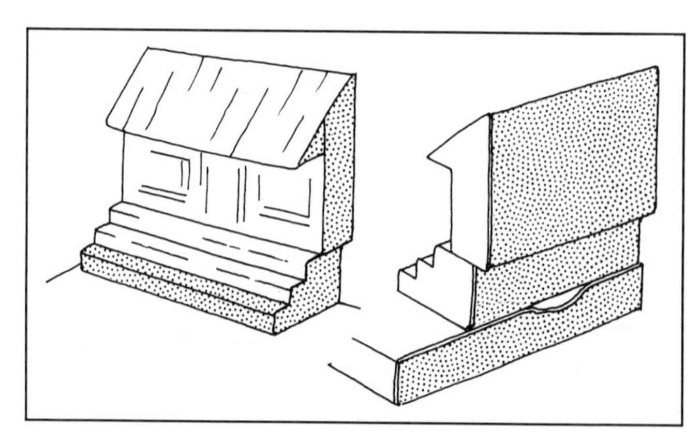

8. Roll fondant to 2 LS thick, measure the three steps in turn, cut fondant to fit then apply. Brush sides of pavilion with jam. Cut fondant roughly to shape, carefully apply, then trim. Add about 110g (4oz) fondant to green trimmings. Roll to 1 LS thick. Brush back of cakes with jam. Cut fondant to fit, then apply.

RAIN
STOP
PLAY

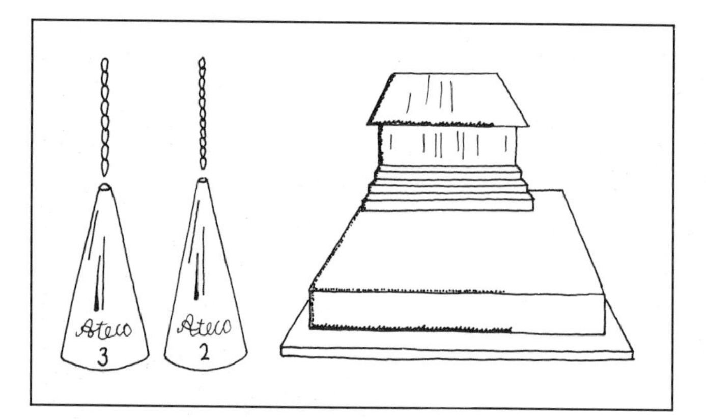

9. Make the 110g (4oz) of royal icing. With dark brown icing and *No. 3 nozzle*, pipe continuous dots down edges of roof, along front edge, down sides of front wall and around base of cake. With *No. 2*, pipe continuous dots down sides of steps, around base of bottom step and on all fondant seams.

10. Roll white fondant to 1 LS thick, cut 26 posts 45mm (1¾in.) high, with point at one end. Attach around steps with egg white. Cut horizontal pieces for fence and attach. Cut a step for door and attach.

Make a fourth green step and position between opening of fence.

11. Colour some fondant trimmings black. Make supports for score-board. Attach to cake with egg white. Roll black fondant to 1 LS thick, cut oblongs to fit on score-board, attach with egg white. With *No. 2 nozzle*, pipe **RAIN STOP PLAY** on black pieces. Pipe markings on pitch, as shown.

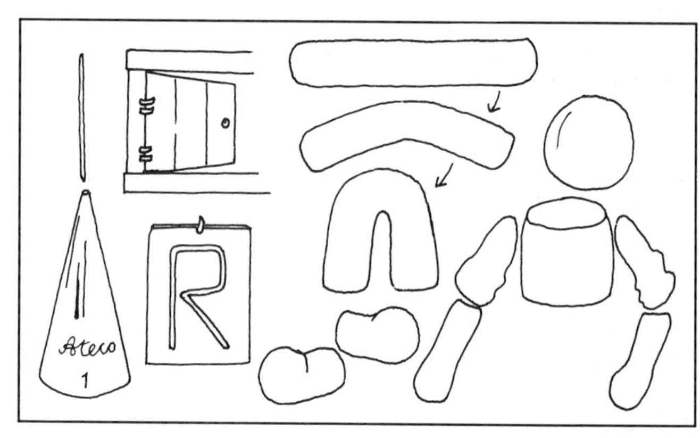

12. With *No. 1 nozzle* and light brown icing, pipe hinges and knobs on door and shutters, then a hook on each scoreboard letter.

With white fondant model boots, legs (from a roll bent in half), bodies and sleeves. Attach to steps with egg white. Model flesh and brown heads and arms.

13. Attach little noses to faces. Make blue and red caps from flat circles, as shown. Attach to heads. Attach heads to bodies. Paint edging of sweaters, in little dots, as shown and eyes and lips on faces.

Attach scoreboard to supports with dabs of icing.

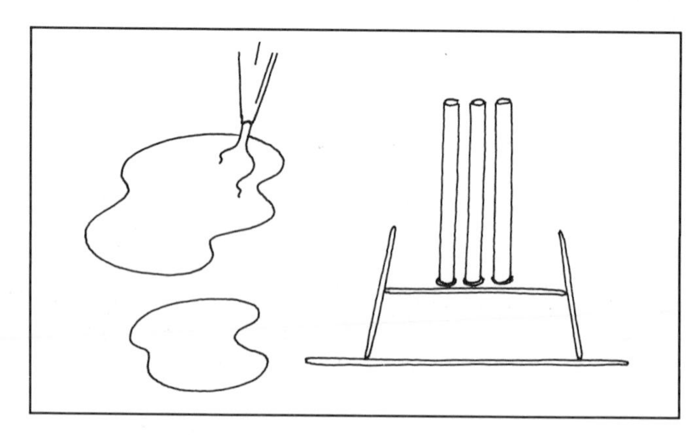

14. With *No. 2 nozzle* and 'runny' white icing, pipe puddles on pitch, lines down roof and drops on roof edge. After an hour, paint silver. Add a drop of brown to white fondant. Roll to make wickets 30mm (1¼in.) high. Carefully poke three holes just behind white line. When dry, stick in wickets with egg white.

Alice in Wonderland

'There was a table set out under a tree in front of the house, and the March Hare and the Hatter were having tea at it: a Dormouse was sitting between them, fast asleep . . .'

Of all the charming incidents which occur in the book, this scene is probably the most suitable for cake decorating. The crockery is great fun to make – you may have had practice with your children, using plasticine. It is important to leave the toadstools as long as possible before positioning the figures on them – they will crack and possibly collapse if they have not had enough time to dry. I have not given the March Hare any legs because with them he would not fit close to the table; he is at the back anyway – but if you prefer to make them, add a little more fondant to the amount given below.

The cake will take two to three days to decorate. Please read the General Notes on pages 6 to 9 before starting. Also read through the step-by-step instructions and check the ingredient and equipment lists.

Ingredients for cake

450g (16oz) butter
340g (12oz) caster sugar
560g (20oz) self-raising flour
340g (12oz) ground rice
280ml (10fl.oz) milk beaten with 6 large eggs
butter cream for filling
Make from this recipe: 1 × 280mm (11in.) square cake

Ingredients for fondant and royal icing

1.340kg (3lb) icing sugar, plus 110g (4oz)
3 egg whites, plus ½
6 tblsp liquid glucose
Also: warm sieved apricot jam; 50/50 mixture of cornflour and icing sugar in a dusting dredger; red, green, yellow, blue, brown, black, silver and flesh food colouring.

Equipment

Basins for mixing icings; sieve; spoons; rolling pin; steel rule; sharp-pointed knife; lolly sticks (LS) as spacers; pastry brush; small paint brush; knitting needle or wooden skewer; greaseproof paper for icing bags; Ateco (or equivalent) icing nozzles 1, 2 and 13; 280mm (11in.) square silver cake board.

1. Having left the cake overnight, slice the top flat and turn it over. Cut a 180mm (7in.) piece off for the base. Cut the remaining piece in half (this will be the table), then carefully slice one of the halves, as shown.

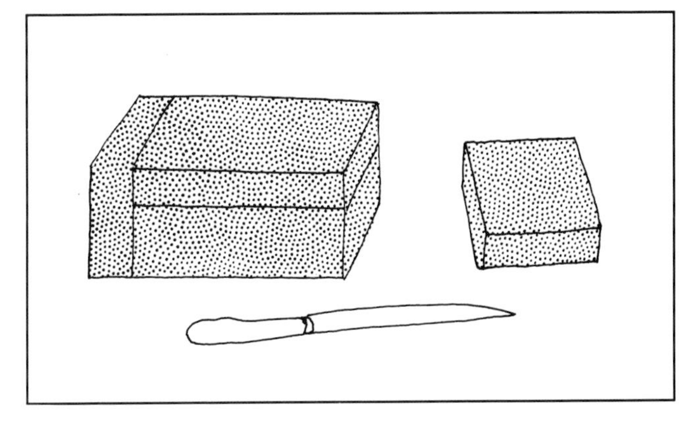

2. Put one of the sliced halves on top of the table to give more depth. Cut the remaining piece in half – put one half at side of table to give more length (the rest of that half is spare).

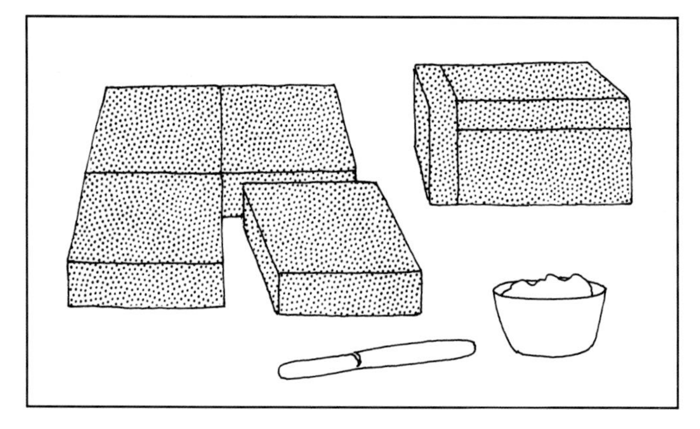

3. Cut the base into four pieces, apply filling, then re-assemble. Stick pieces of sponge to table with filling. Make 670g (1½lb) of fondant and colour pale green.

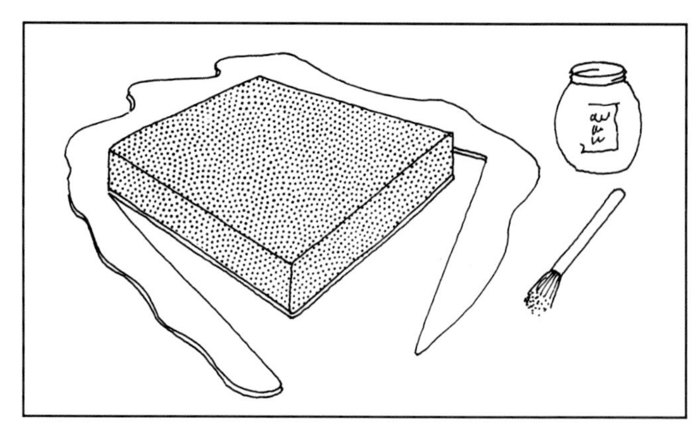

4. Brush top of base with warm jam. Dust working surface liberally and roll fondant to 2 LS thick. Lay jammed surface on fondant, then trim away excess. Carefully lift cake and position in centre of silver board. Brush away excess powder from surface.

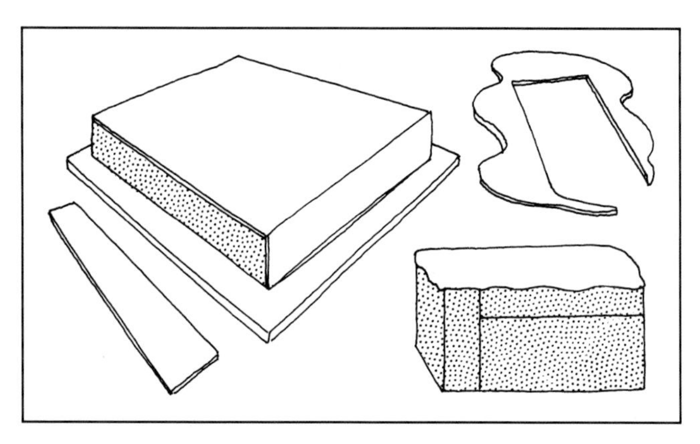

5. Brush sides of base with jam. Measure each in turn, roll fondant to 2 LS thick, cut to fit, then carefully apply. Brush top of table with jam. Roll fondant trimmings to 1 LS thick. Cut to fit and apply, smoothing with hands to make edges round.

Make another 670g (1½lb) of fondant.

6. Brush underside of table with jam, and position it in centre of base. Measure length and width of table, including sides. Colour 220g (½lb) of fondant pale yellow. Roll to 1 LS thick and cut to size. Brush table top with egg white. With help of rolling pin, apply fondant. Allow folds to fall naturally. Trim.

7. Colour 110g (4oz) of fondant red. Divide into four, and model toadstool heads, as shown. Take another 110g (4oz) white fondant, make tiny white flat circles and apply to toadstools with egg white. Make four fat stems with remaining fondant, about 45mm (1¾in.) high and tapering, as shown. Leave to dry.

8. Add more fondant to white trimmings and mix in blue colour. Roll fondant to 1 LS thick for plates and saucers. Plates are roughly 35mm (1½in.) diameter, saucers 25mm (1in.). I used cocktail cutters, but use anything of similar size. Cups are solid, and 20mm (¾in.) high. Make grooves in top with wider end of *No. 1 nozzle*.

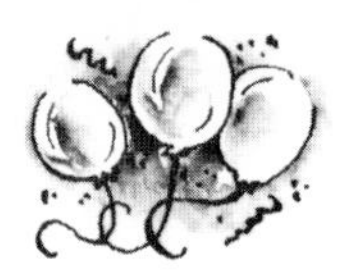

9. Handles are made from small circles (*No. 12 nozzle* if you have it), 1 LS thick, cut in half and attached to cups and jug with egg white. Make a shallow cavity at top of jug and sugar bowl, then put in white fondant – make rough surface for sugar. Make teapot as shown and assemble, using egg white to secure.

10. Spoons are made from thin strips of fondant 1 LS thick, 20mm (¾in.) long and pressed at one end. Make a small hole in sugar, stick a handle in , securing with egg white. Leave overnight to dry.

Paint blue markings on crockery, as shown. Paint tea in cups. Paint spoons and lid handle with silver.

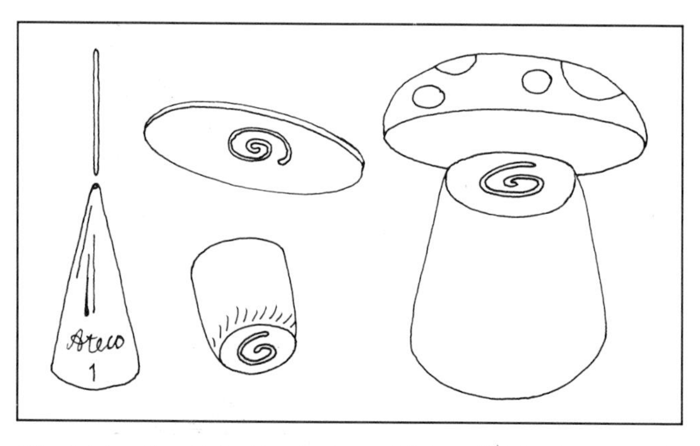

11. Make the 110g (4oz) of royal icing. With *No. 1 nozzle* pipe underneath each piece of crockery and position on table. Position spoons, using egg white to secure. Again used piped icing, secure toadstool heads to stems.

12. With *No. 2 nozzle* and pale yellow icing, pipe a line of continuous dots around hem of tablecloth. Position two toadstools at back and as near to table as possible. Secure to base with icing. Position other two at each side, almost at edge of base.

13. Colour some fondant flesh and model heads and necks for Alice and the Hatter, as shown. Leave to dry on a dusted surface. With dark brown fondant model pieces for Hare, as shown – curl ears around knitting needle to give deep groove. Attach ears to head after 30 minutes, using egg white. Hold until secure.

14. Flatten two little white balls and attach to head. Colour some fondant with drops of black, to make grey mouse. Model head and body in one piece, as shown. Brush base and attach to toadstool while still fairly soft, laying head on plate.

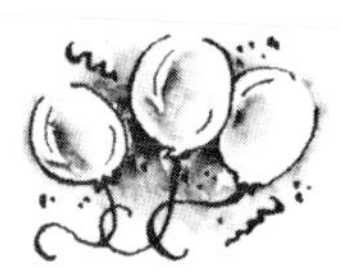

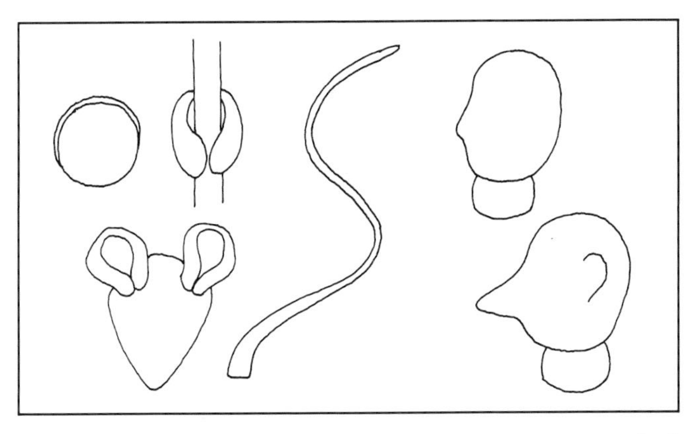

15. Model ears from round circles, bend around end of knitting needle, as shown, and attach to head with egg white. Roll a very thin tail and attach.

Attach Alice's and Hatter's heads to necks, using egg white.

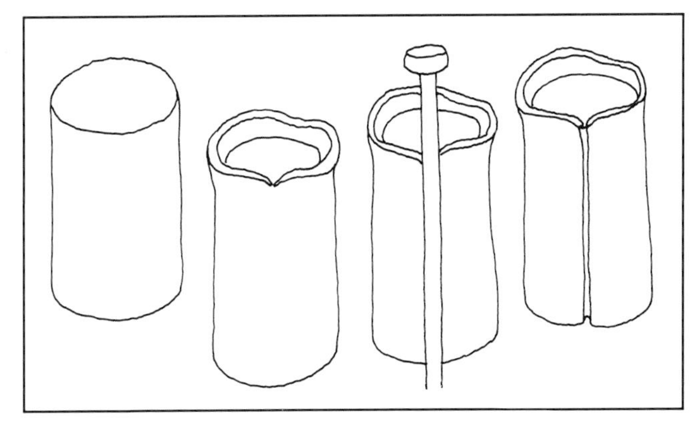

16. Colour some fondant green. Form a roll, then pinch out a collar at top. Make a groove down centre with knitting needle, then press together. Leave on one side on a dusted surface.

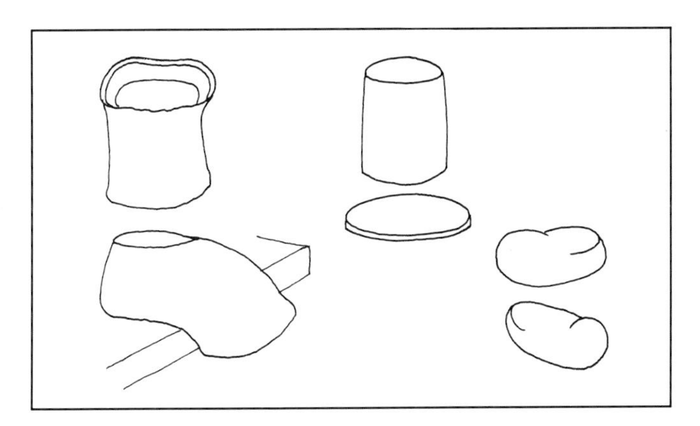

17. Using orange fondant (mix red and yellow colouring) model Alice's body, pinch out a little collar as before. Model skirt as shown and position on (dusted) edge of working surface. Keep a small piece for sleeves. With dark grey fondant cut a circle 1 LS thick for hat brim, roll a piece for main part. Model shoes, as shown.

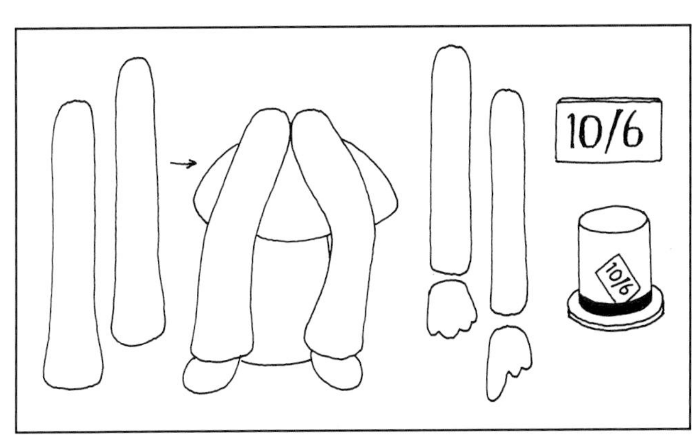

18. Using brown fondant, roll Hatter's legs and attach, with shoes, to toadstool. Position body on legs, attach head to body and hat to head. Model arms and position while still fairly soft. Cut a thin oblong of white fondant, attach to hat. Paint black band around hat and over ticket, then paint 10/6 on ticket.

19. Position Alice's skirt on toadstool, using egg white to secure. Attach body to skirt and head to body. Using flesh fondant, model arms, legs and Hatter's hands. Attach while soft. Model sleeves from oblongs, as shown, and attach. Paint details on faces, as shown, and shoes on Alice.

20. With *No. 1 nozzle* and white icing, pipe lacy apron on Alice. With *No. 2 nozzle* pipe her yellow hair, in two stages as shown.

With *No. 13* and green icing, pipe stars on all fondant seams on base cake.

Winnie-the-Pooh

Winnie-the-Pooh is one of the best loved characters in children's literature. Here he is indulging once more in his favourite pastime, eating honey.

The cake can be completed in two days. To give a more realistic appearance the Chintz design on the chair and tablecloth is painted rather than piped. Pooh himself is modelled from fondant but almond paste (marzipan) may be used instead – deduct 220g (8oz) of icing sugar and half an egg white from the fondant ingredients and replace with 220g (8oz) of almond paste.

As it is difficult to make a really smooth cut when dried fruit is added to a cake, I suggest you only use a filling for this one.

Please read the General Notes on pages 6 to 9 before starting to decorate the cake. Also read through the step-by-step instructions and check the ingredient and equipment lists.

Ingredients for cake

170g (6oz) butter
110g (4oz) caster sugar
220g (8oz) self-raising flour
110g (4oz) ground rice
110ml (4fl oz) milk beaten with 2 large eggs
filling (butter cream)
Make from this recipe: 2 × 130mm (5 in.) square cakes

Ingredients for fondant and royal icing

900g (2lb) icing sugar, plus 60g (2oz)
2 egg whites, plus 1/4
4 tblsp liquid glucose
flavouring (optional)
Also: warm sieved apricot jam; 50/50 mixture of cornflour and icing sugar in a dusting dredger; yellow, brown, pink, green, blue and black food colouring; two silver balls for Pooh's eyes.

Equipment

Basins for mixing icings; spoons; sieve; rolling pin; steel rule; sharp-pointed knife; lolly sticks (LS) or spacers; pastry brush; small paint brush; greaseproof paper for icing bag; Ateco (or equivalent) icing nozzle No. 2; 250mm (10in.) square silver board.

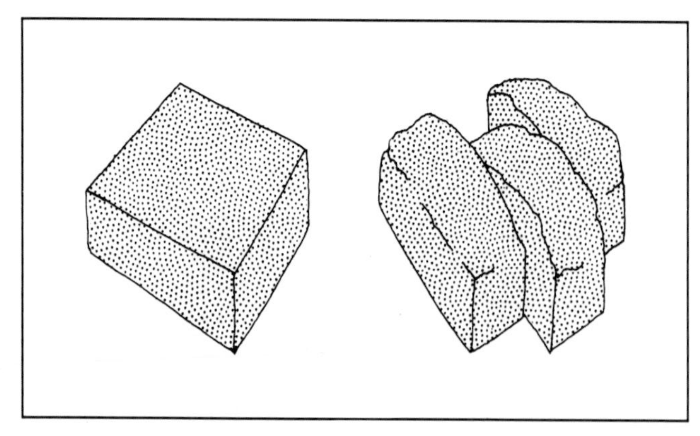

1. Having left the cakes overnight, trim one to form a neat square. Cut middle section out of other cake (leaving a slightly rounded top, which forms back support of chair).

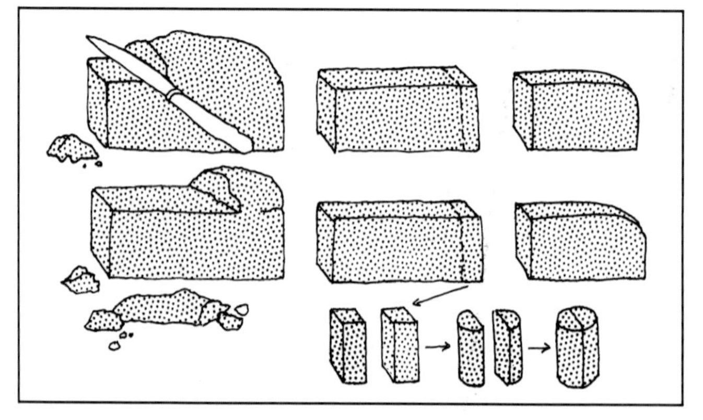

2. The two remaining pieces will form arm rests. Cut a piece from the end of each. Trim these ends into half-circles and join with butter cream to form the little round table.

3. Make 220g (8oz) of fondant (or use equivalent in marzipan). Keep back a small ball for honey, and colour the remainder brown. Make Pooh's body from a roll, rounding off edges at top and bottom. Form top surface to slope forward slightly. Stand body on a piece of dusted greaseproof paper.

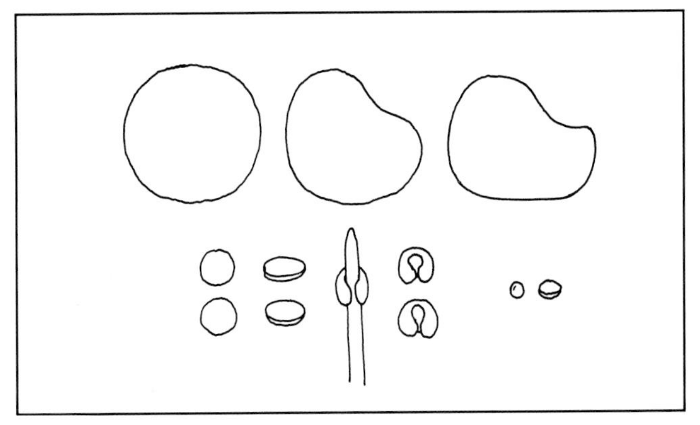

4. Model the head, as shown, from a round ball. Model ears from two small balls – flatten them slightly, then curve around a knitting needle. Make a small ball for the nose and flatten slightly.

5. Make holes for eyes, then press in two silver balls, securing with egg white. Attach ears and nose, secure with egg white. Score mouth as shown, with blunt edge of a knife. Attach head to body using egg white to secure.

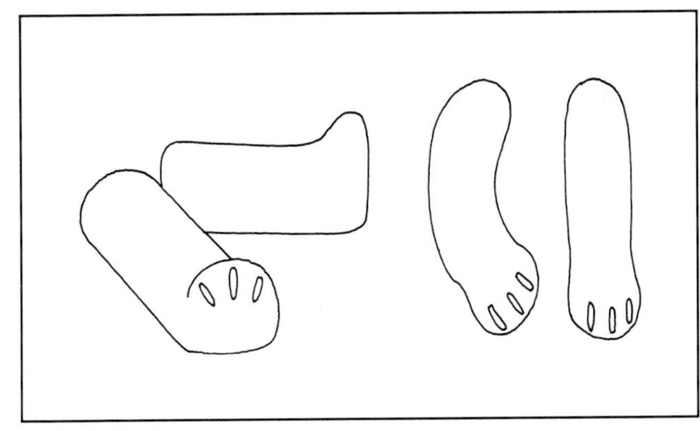

6. Model legs and arms from a roll 15mm (⅝in.) diameter and 160mm (6¼in.) long. Flatten the paws slightly then form the feet. Score paw marks using blunt edge of a knife. Bend one arm round slightly.

Leave everything to dry overnight.

7. Add a little black and some pink to remaining brown frondant. Model the honey jar. With black colouring paint Pooh's eyes, nose, dots round his mouth, rims round top and bottom of jar, then write **honey** on jar. Mix brown – pink with a drop of black and paint inside ears, mouth and paw marks.

8. Colour white ball of fondant with yellow and a little brown – for honey. Put some on top of jar, running down sides. Attach legs to body using egg white. Position jar on legs. Attach arms. Smear blobs of honey to paws and on chest.

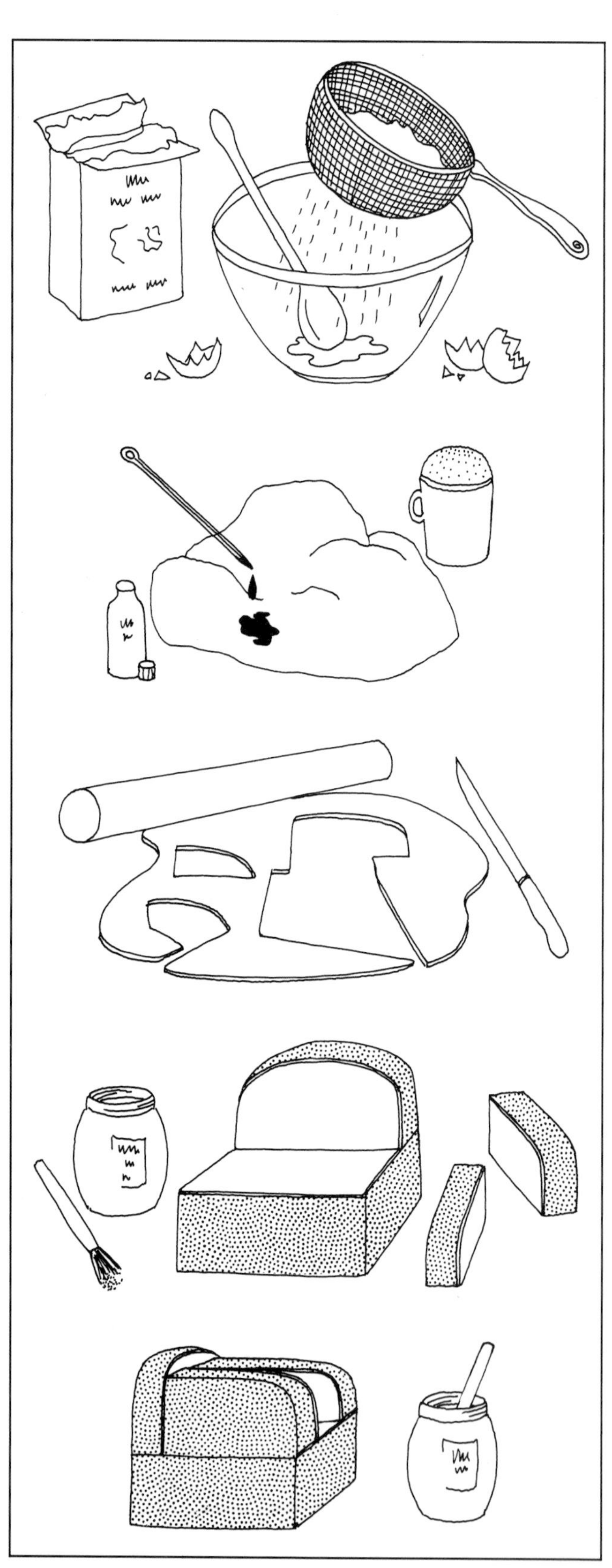

9. Make 670g (1½lb) of fondant. Colour pale yellow. Put chair base on silver board. Roll fondant to 1 LS thick and cut pieces to fit inside arms, inside back and seat of chair. Brush sponge with jam and apply pieces. Attach arms to chair with a film of jam.

Honey

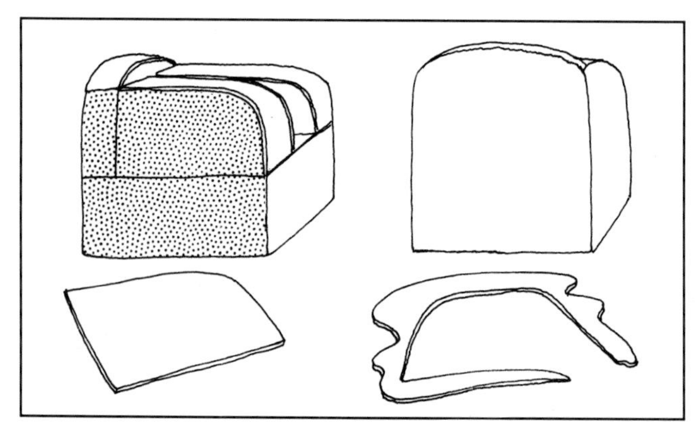

10. Roll fondant to 2 LS thick. First cut and apply front of chair, then arm and back tops, then the sides, finally the back.

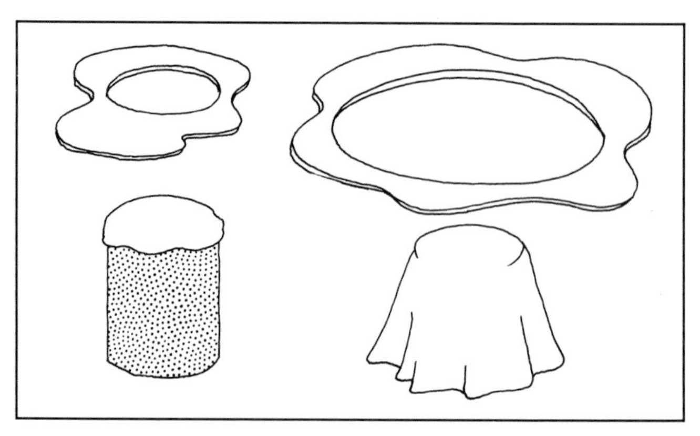

11. Roll fondant to 2 LS thick, cut a circle slightly larger than the table top. Brush sponge with jam and apply fondant, curving over edges of sponge. Roll fondant to 1 LS thick, cut circle about 150mm (6in.) diameter. Place over table, pressing gently in to form folds. Neatly trim edge if necessary.

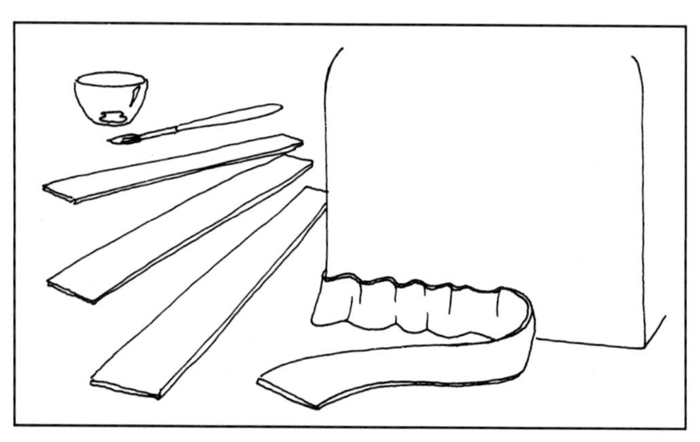

12. Add pink to remaining yellow fondant. Roll to 1 LS thick and cut four strips 200mm (8in.) long and 25mm 1in.) wide. Gather each strip carefully to each side of chair. Attach with egg white. Trim top of frill straight, then press gently into chair side.

13. Paint Chintz design on chair and tablecloth using green, blue and pink colouring. (Follow a reference from a magazine, or copy the simple interpretation above.)

14. Make a square brown cake with fondant trimmings. Apply honey-coloured fondant to top, some down the sides. Paint black currants on cake. Attach cake to top of table using egg white.

15. Push candle into cake. Make up the 60g (2oz) or royal icing. Colour pink. With *No. 2 nozzle* pipe dots along all chair seams, along top edge of frill and round bottom edge of tablecloth. Placve table beside chair on silver board. Carefully position Pooh in the chair.

Tom Sawyer/ Huckleberry Finn

I have to confess that, not having read *Tom Sawyer* or *Huckleberry Finn* since childhood, I cannot remember which character sat by a stream with a fishing line tied to his toe. The scene may even be a figment of my imagination – but it feels indicative of the kind of thing both boys would do.

The cake can be decorated in one or two days. Please, before starting, read the General Notes on pages 6 to 9. It is also a good idea to read through the step-by-step instructions and check the ingredient and equipment lists.

Ingredients for cake

340g (12oz) butter
250g (9oz) caster sugar
420g (15oz) self-raising flour
250g (9oz) ground rice
250g (9fl oz) milk beaten with 5 large eggs
buttercream for filling
Make from this recipe:

1 × 150mm (6in.) round cake
1 × 200mm (8in.) round cake

Ingredients for fondant and royal icing

790g (1¾lb) icing sugar, plus 220g (8oz)
1¾ egg whites, plus 1
3½ tblsp liquid glucose
flavouring (optional)
Also: warm sieved apricot jam; 50/50 mixture of cornflour and icing sugar in a dusting dredger; green, red, black, brown, blue, yellow and silver food colouring.

Equipment

Basins for mixing icings; sieve; spoons; rolling pin; sharp-pointed knife; lolly stiocks (LS) as spacers; pastry brush; paint brush; greaseproof paper for icing bags; Ateco (or equivalent) icing nozzles 1, 2, 13, 66 and 85; 250mm (10in.) round silver cake board.

1. Having left the cakes overnight, slice the tops flat. Cut a piece from smaller cake, as shown, and round off corners – this will be a tree trunk. Sandwich the cakes together with buttercream, small cake towards back of large one. Brush warm jam over both cakes.

2. Make 790g (1¾lb) of fondant. Colour 450g (1lb) green. Roll to 2 LS thick and roughly apply to areas shown above – allow fondant to crinkle and crease. Take 110g (4oz) of white fondant, add a line of black colour and partially mix to give streaky effect. Make creases in waterfall with knitting needle.

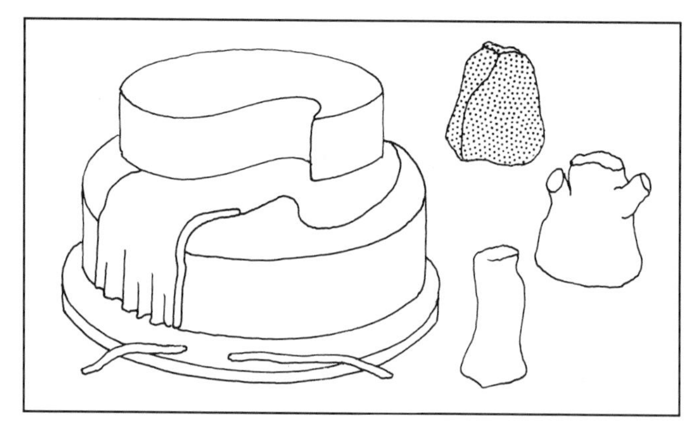

3. Make rough rolls from green trimmings and build up banks of stream, as shown. Add grey trimmings to green and mix in brown colour. Brush tree trunk with jam, cover with fondant, modelling gnarled effect and broken branches. Model a narrower trunk with remaining brown fondant. Position trunks as indicated.

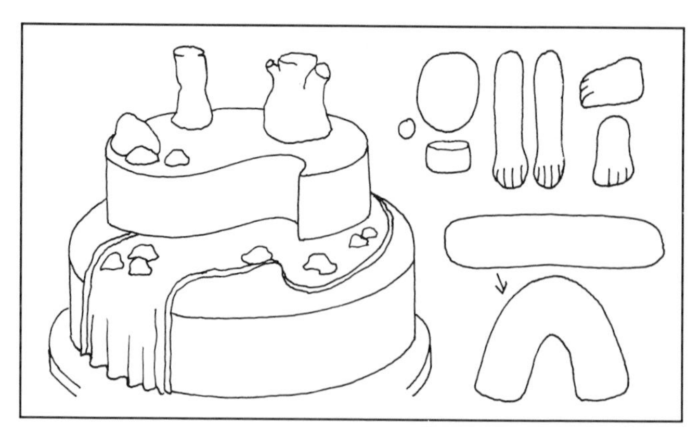

4. Add black to remaining trimmings and model rocks, position with egg white as indicated. Colour some fondant flesh. Model head and nose, neck, feet and arms – mark fingers and toes with knife. Model red trousers from a roll bent in half, as shown. Attach to cake with feet, using egg white.

5. Model blue body and sleeves, as shown. Position, then fit neck inside body. Add drops of yellow and flesh to a piece of white fondant. Model a hat, marking straw with knife. Attach to head. Roll twigs from brown fondant and build fire, securing with egg white.

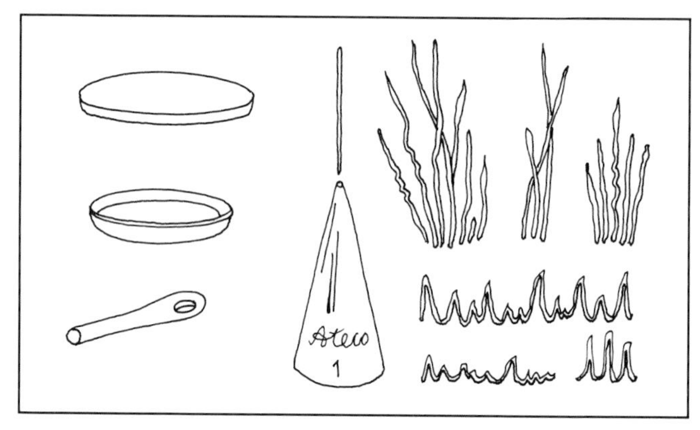

6. Make the frying pan – cut small white circle, curve edges up, attach white handle with hole in end, as shown. Paint when dry, handle brown, pan silver, then position with egg white near fire.

Make the 220g (8oz) of royal icing. With *No. 1 nozzle* and green icing, pipe grass, as shown.

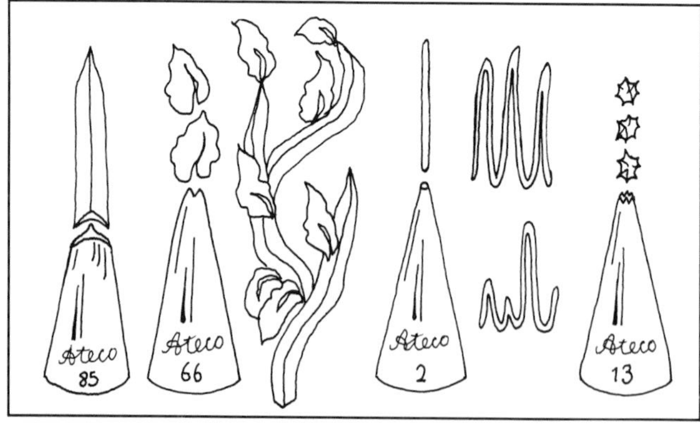

7. With brown icing and *No. 85*, pipe tree trunks up sides of cakes. With dark green and *No. 66*, pipe leaves on trunks. With *No. 2* and paler green, pipe more grasses. Pipe little yellow flowers on grass with *No. 13*. Add a little brown and yellow to remaining white fondant. Roll to 1 LS thick.

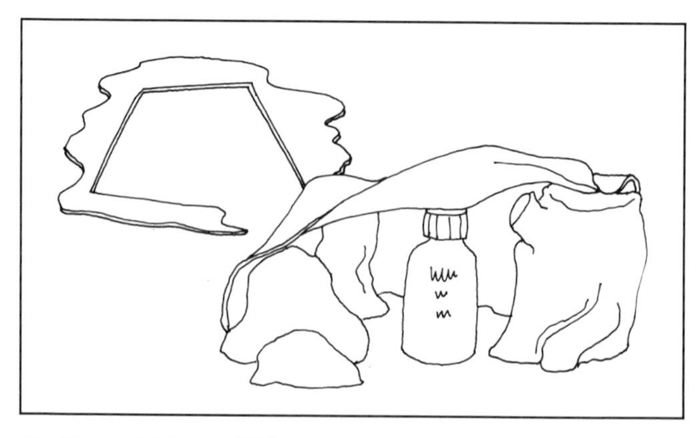

8. Cut a 120mm (4½in.) square. Brush tops of trunks and rock with egg white, carefully lay on fondant turning a corner over on large trunk (support opening until dry). Make a float, position in stream and paint red. With *No. 2 nozzle* and dark icing, pipe a line from toe to float.

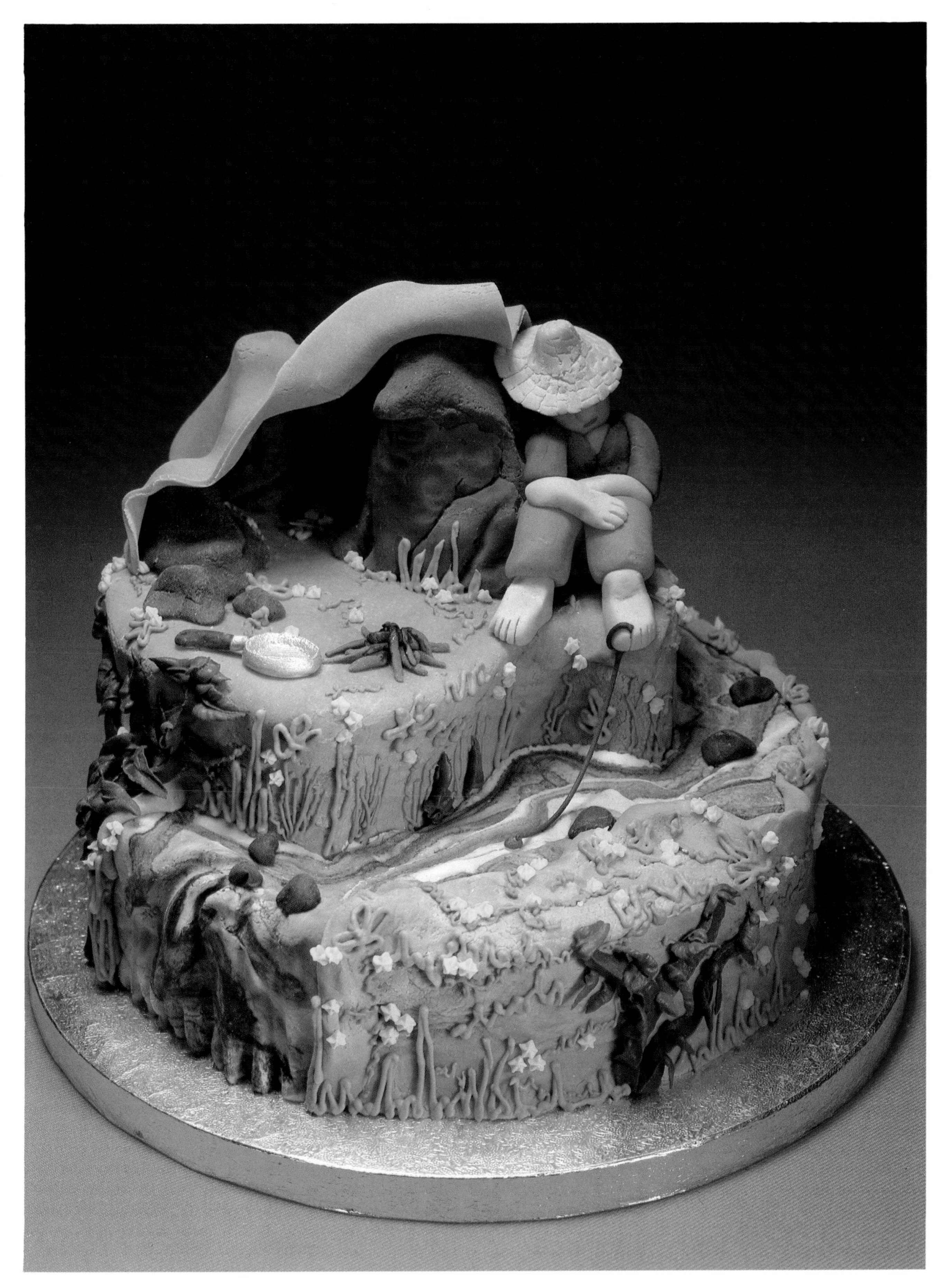

Sleeping Beauty's Castle

This cake will take about four days to decorate, so patience is required – but the result is well worthwhile. I recommend it for a very, very special occasion.

The marbling effect on the tiles is obtained by only partially mixing the colour (or colours) into the fondant.

If any fondant remains after each session, cover it with greaseproof paper, keep in an airtight container, then add it to the next batch or use for making small items (a little egg white may need to be added if it has become hard). The conical shapes on which the roof tiles are stuck are not visible, so these can be made from leftovers.

To vary the greens in the piped foliage add a little more yellow or blue, or even a spot of red, to an existing green.

Please read the General Notes on pages 6 to 9 before starting to decorate the cake. Read also through the step-by-step instructions and check the ingredients and equipment lists.

Ingredients for cake

450g (16oz) butter
340g (12oz) caster sugar
560g (20oz) self-raising flour
340g (12oz) ground rice
280ml (10fl oz) milk beaten with 6 large eggs
flavouring, filling or dried fruit
Make from this recipe:
1 / 200mm (8in.) round cake
1 / 115mm (4½in.) round cake
1 / 400g (14oz) food-can cake
4 / 140g (5oz) food-can cakes

Ingredients for fondant and royal icing

1.570kg (3½lb) icing sugar, plus 110g (4oz)
3½ egg whites, plus ½
7 tblsp liquid glucose
flavouring (optional)
Also: warm sieved apricot jam; 50/50 mixture of cornflour and icing sugar in a dusting dredger; red, blue, yellow, green, brown and black food colouring.

Equipment

Basins for mixing icings; sieve; spoons; rolling pin; steel rule; sharp pointed knife; lolly sticks (LS); pastry brush; greaseproof paper for icing bags; fine paint brush; Ateco (or equivalent) icing nozzles 1 and 15; 350mm (14in.) square silver board.

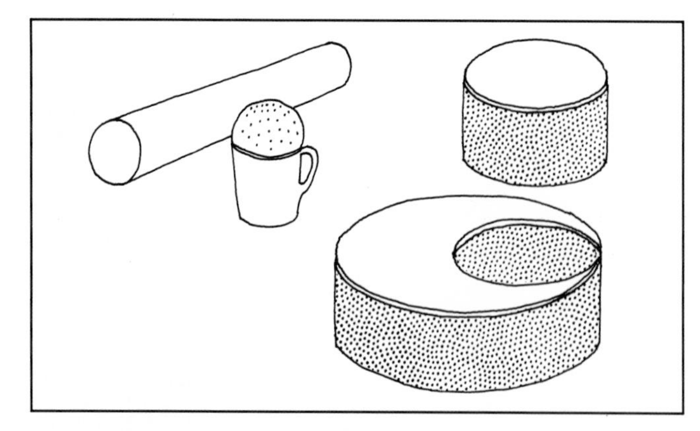

1. Having left the cakes overnight, slice the tops until they are perfectly flat. Make 670g (1½lb) fondant. Colour with drops of red and blue. Roll to 2 LS thick and cut a circle for large cake – then cut from this a circle for the small cake. Coat tops with jam, then cover.

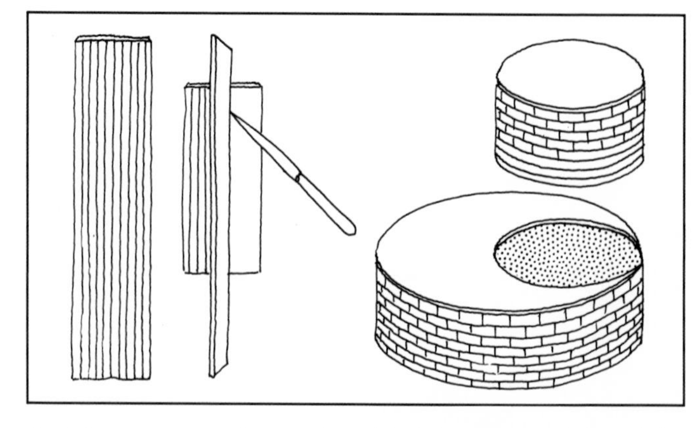

2. Measure round the cakes. Roll fondant to 2 LS thick, then cut to fit. Score horizontal lines using steel rule. Coat cake sides with jam, then cover. Score vertical lines to form bricks.

Make 670g (1½lb) fondant, colour as before.

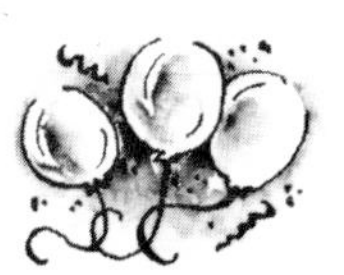

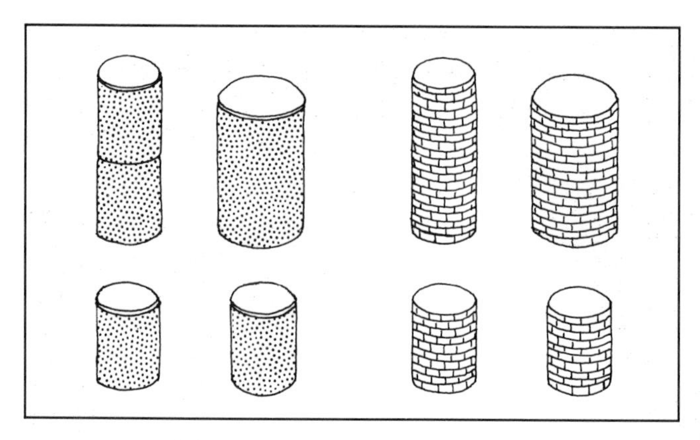

3. Put one of the small cakes on top of another, securing with jam. Cut four circles to fit tops of cakes (2 LS thick), then cover as before. Measure circumference and depth of cakes, cut fondant to fit, and score horizontal lines. Apply fondant and score vertical lines as before. Leave overnight.

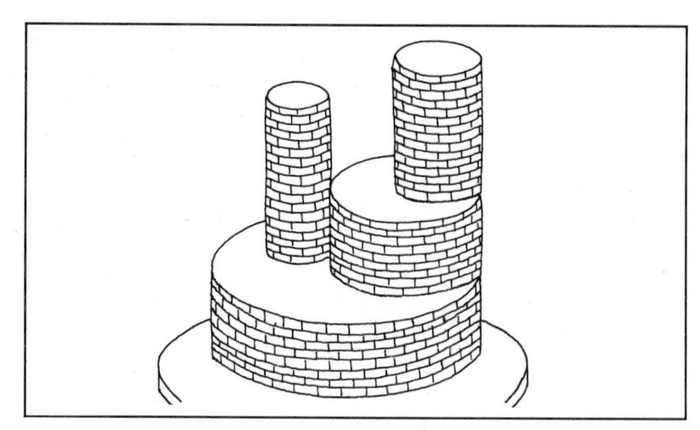

4. Position large cake towards the back of the silver board. Position other three cakes as indicted.

Make up the royal icing and store in airtight container.

Add a little egg white (if necessary) and red colour to remaining fondant. Knead.

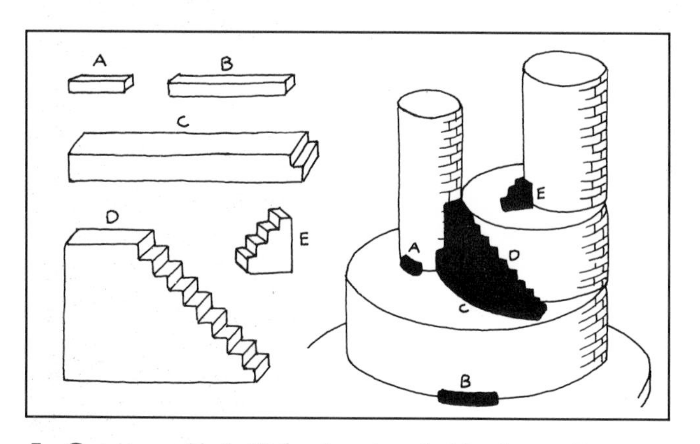

5. Cut steps (A & B) for front and side doors. Position with dabs of royal icing. Cut main steps (D) then cut a double step (C) a little wider. Position as shown. Cut four steps (E) and position.

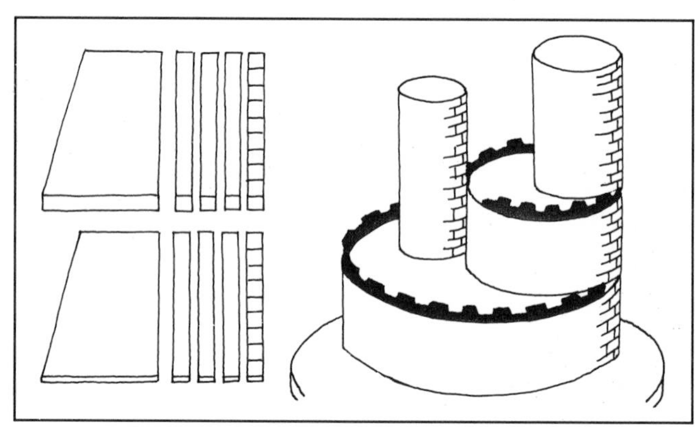

6. Add a little blue to fondant. Roll to 4 LS thick then cut about forty squares. Roll fondant again to 2 LS thick and cut another 40 squares. Position round tops of two main cakes using dabs of icing to secure. Press required number of candles into fondant while still soft, then remove.

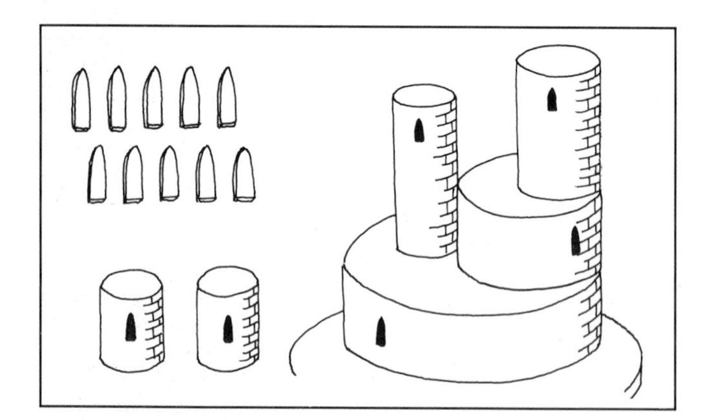

7. Add drops of black to remaining fondant. Roll to 1 LS thick. Cut ten little windows as shown. Brush the backs with egg white and attach where indicated – four go to the back.

8. Add brown to rest of fondant. Roll to 2 LS thick. Cut four doors and score as shown. Brush backs with egg white and attach where indicated.

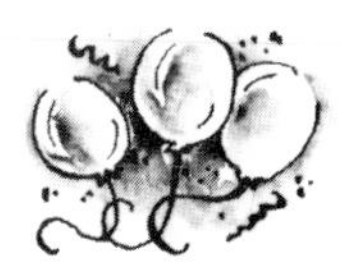

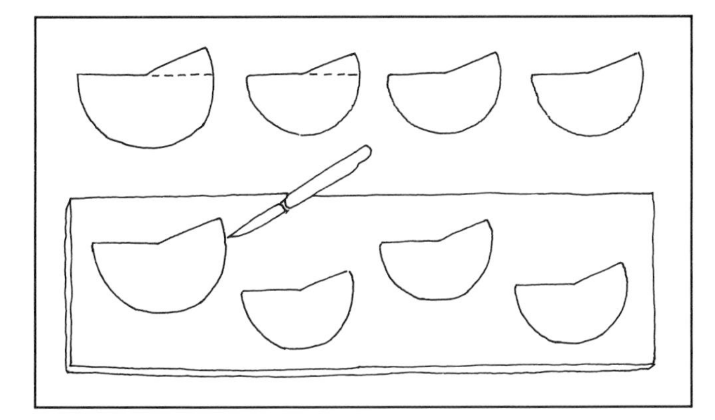

9. Cut from a piece of thin card one circle 190mm (7½in.) diameter and three circles 145mm (5¾in.) diameter. Cut out wedges as shown. Fold cones around and check that they fit the cakes; they should overhang a little. Using cards as templates, cut one large and three small roofs.

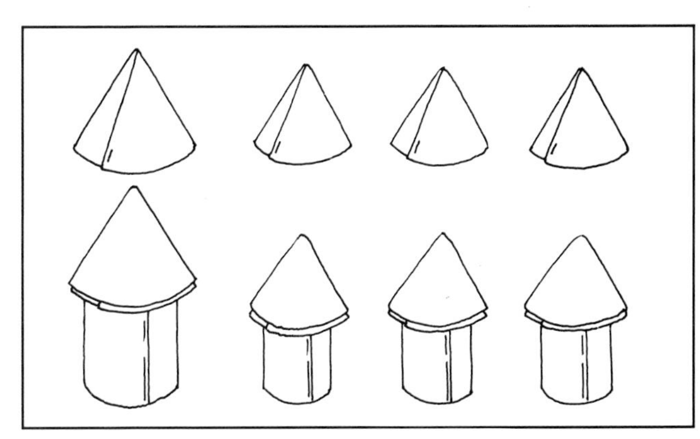

10. Fold templates into cones, secure with staples. Dust outside of cones liberally with cornflour. Place fondant carefully around each cone. Secure edges with egg white. Stand each cone on a can. Leave overnight. Position the two small cakes 20mm (¾in.) from front of castle, secure with icing.

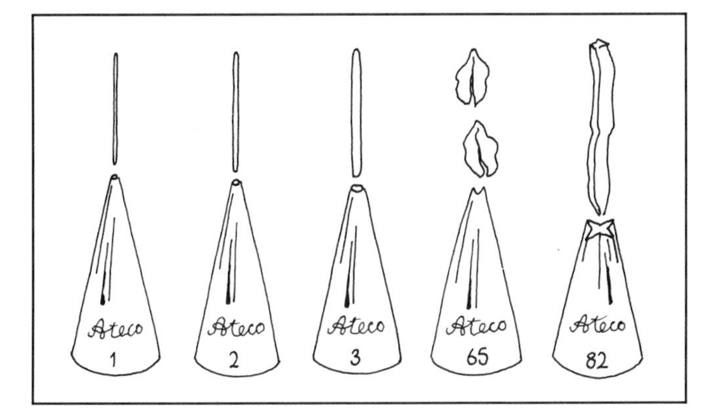

11. Make eight icing bags. With *No. 1 nozzle*, two shades of green, pipe grass at intervals around base and top of cakes, on steps, in crevices. *No. 2*, pipe grey down centre and around each window. *No. 82*, pipe five brown tree trunks, at back, at each side, by steps, on small castle – continue branches with *No. 3*.

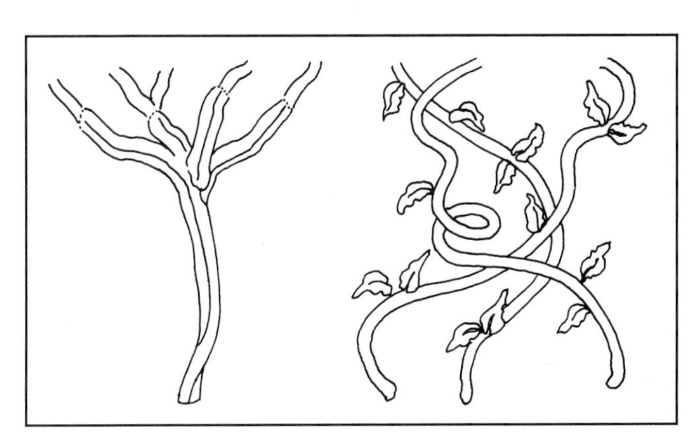

12. With *No. 3* nozzle put two greens in an icing bag and pipe four vine stems – at back, at side, at front and on small castle. *No. 65*, pipe dark green leaves on trees, light green on vines. *No. 1* pipe white flowers (four dots) on trees. *No. 1*, pipe black handles and hinges on doors. Leave to dry overnight.

13. Make 220g (½lb) marbled fondant. Roll to 1 LS thick and cut roof tiles. Start at bottom edge, stick tiles to fondant cones using egg white. Made four blue balls, flatten slightly, score round edges then secure to top of roofs with icing. Leave to dry on cans overnight.

14. Smear icing round top edges of each of the four castle parts. Carefully press the roofs into position. Smear a little icing on the under-sides of the two small towers and position as indicated. Finally, secure the candles in their holes with a little dab of icing.

Superman

The idea for this cake was given me by Joseph, my eldest son. I had intended skyscrapers with Superman heroically diving down to save some helpless victim. An ingenious way of suspending him in mid-flight was eluding me, so Joseph's idea was very welcome.

As I have related in the Introduction, Superman's arm fell off because I did not allow him enough time to dry. Twenty-four hours should be sufficient, but he must be handled with great care.

Please read the General Notes on pages 6 to 9 before starting to decorate the cake. It is also a good idea to read through the step-by-step instructions and check the ingredient and equipment lists.

Ingredients for cake

280g (10oz) butter
220g (8oz) caster sugar
360g (13oz) self-raising flour
200g (7oz) ground rice
220ml (8fl oz) milk beaten with 4 large eggs

Make with this recipe:
1 × 200mm (8in.) square cake

Ingredients for fondant and royal icing

790g (1¾lb) icing sugar, plus 110g (4oz)
1¾ egg whites, plus ½
just under 4 tblsp liquid glucose
flavouring (optional)
Also: warm sieved apricot jam; 50/50 mixture of cornflour and icing sugar in a dusting dredger; red, blue, yellow, flesh and black food colouring.

Equipment

Basins for mixing icings; sieve; spoons; rolling pin; steel rule; sharp-pointed knife; lolly sticks (LS) as spacers; pastry brush; greaseproof paper for icing bags and tracing; card; pencil; sewing needle; Ateco (or equivalent) icing nozzles 1, 2 and 3; 250mm (10in.) square silver cake board.

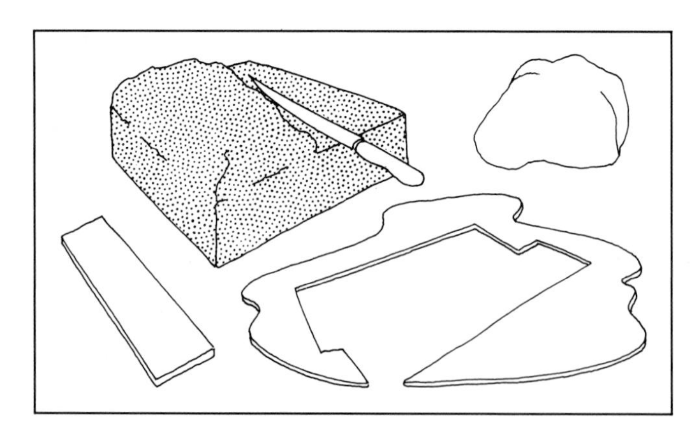

1. Having left the cake overnight, slice the top flat. Make the 790g (1¾lb) of fondant. Colour 340g (12oz) blue and 110g (4oz) red, put the red to one side, wrapped. Measure sides of cake then brush with jam. Roll fondant to 2 LS thick and cut to size.

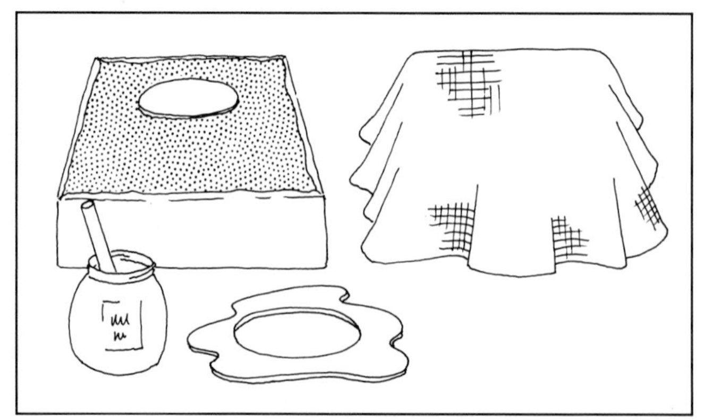

2. Carefully apply each side, rounding off top edge with hands. Roll trimmings to 1 LS thick and cut a circle roughly 90mm (3½in.) diameter. Brush area of top of cake with a thin film of jam and apply fondant in centre towards back, as shown. Cover the cake with a clean tea towel.

HAPPY
BIRTHDAY

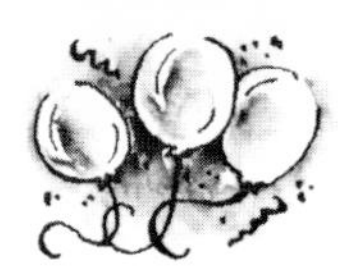

3. Make a card template from the shape given above, then trace the symbol on to greaseproof paper. Colour 45g (1½oz) of fondant yellow, roll to 1 LS thick and cut around template six times. Place tracing over each shape and prick through pencil lines with needle.

4. Make the 110g (4oz) of royal icing. Colour about 4 teasp red. With *No. 2 nozzle* pipe lines over needle marks. When all six are complete, add more egg white to icing to make it runny. With *No. 1 nozzle* fill in areas inside lines. Leave symbols to dry for 24 hours on a dusted surface.

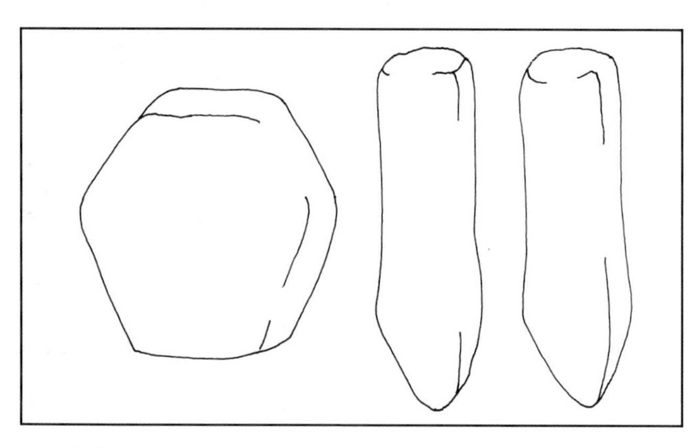

5. Take the remaining blue fondant and model Superman's body and arms, as shown – the body is about 65mm (2½in.) high, the arms 80mm (3¼in.) long. Lay them flat on a dusted surface and attach the arms with egg white.

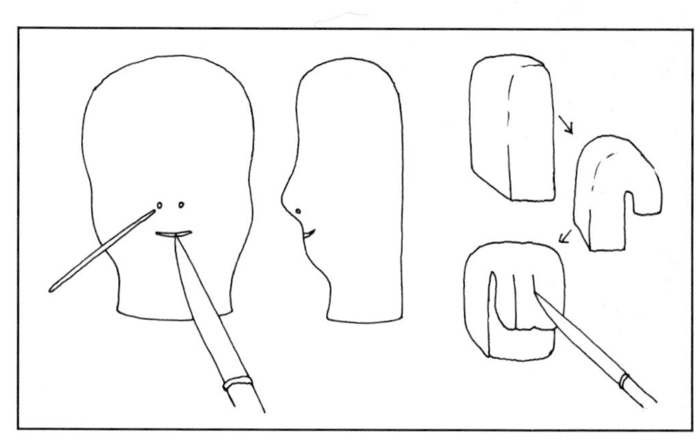

6. Colour a piece of fondant flesh and model a head and neck, in one piece, and hands. Mark nostrils and mouth. Model hands from fat oblongs, bent over to form fists. Mark fingers with blunt edge of knife.

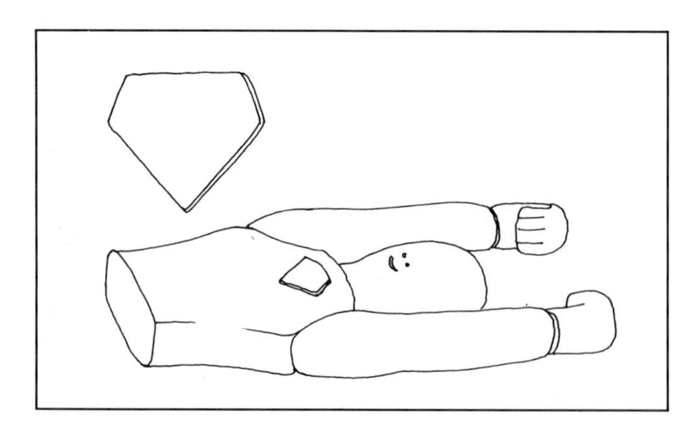

7. Attach head to body and hands to arms. Flatten a small piece of yellow fondant and cut a symbol. Brush back with egg white and attach to chest.

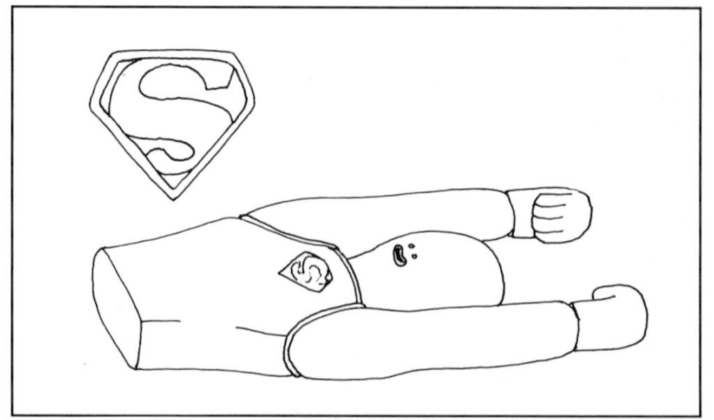

8. With *nozzle No. 2* and red icing, pipe a line around symbol and **S** inside (this is rather too small to fill in, so use the nozzle like a pencil and fill the letter in as you pipe). Pipe around the mouth. Mix a little blue icing and pipe a line around arm and neck joints. Leave to dry on a dusted surface.

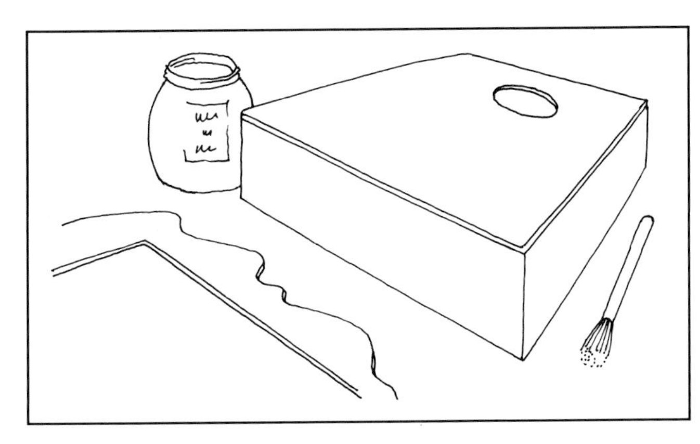

9. Colour the remaining fondant yellow. Roll to 2 LS thick. Measure top of cake then brush with jam, apart from blue circle. Apply fondant. Carefully cut a hole for Superman.

10. Smear inside hole with royal icing. Slide Superman on to a fish slice and carefully position him in hole. Roll yellow fondant to 2 LS thick and cut wedge shapes. Brush around hole with egg white and attach wedges – Superman has just burst through the cake. Mark cracks on cake with blunt edge of knife.

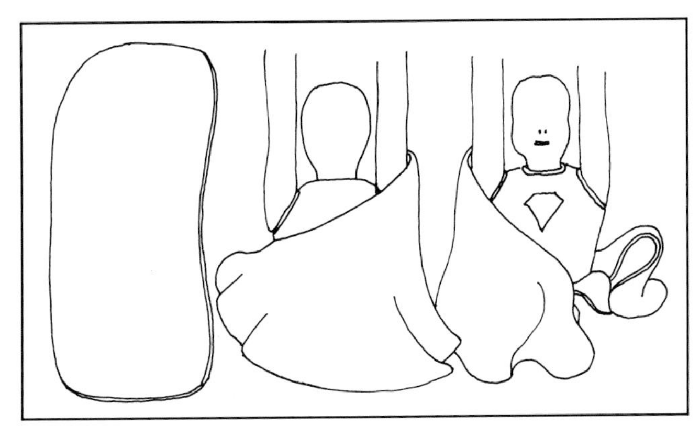

11. Roll red fondant to 1 LS thick and roughly to shape as shown. Quickly brush back of Superman with egg white and carefully attach cape, with a flourish.

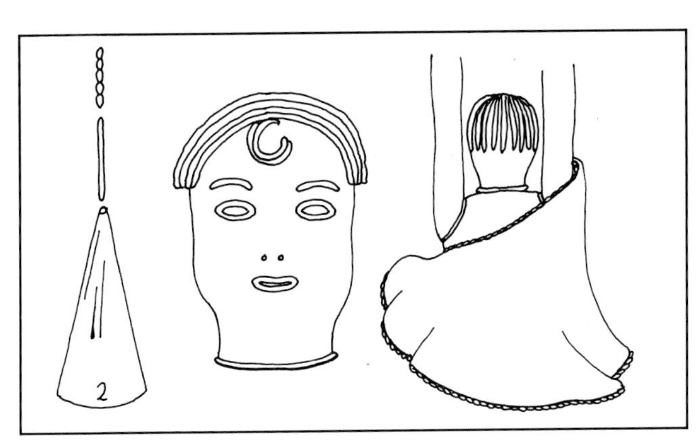

12. With *No. 2 nozzle* and black icing, pipe hair and curl on forehead, the eyes and brows. With same nozzle pipe red dots on edge of cape.

13. Roll the remaining red fondant to 1 LS thick. Cut a strip about 150mm (6in.) long and 12mm (½in.) wide. With nozzle No. 2 and yellow icing, pipe **HAPPY BIRTHDAY** (or appropriate message). Cut strip and centre the two pieces on cake, using icing to secure.

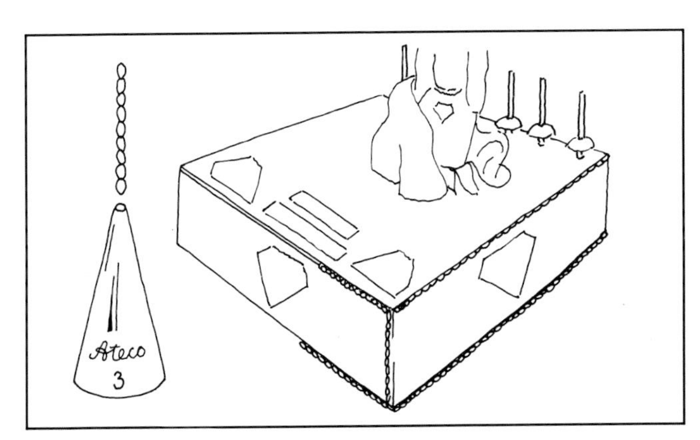

14. Attach symbols, again using icing to secure – one on each side of cake and two at side of writing. Using *No. 3 nozzle* and red icing, pipe continuous dots along seams of fondant on cake. Push required number of candle holders into back of cake.

Rocket on the moon

Decorating this cake will take two to three days. Because of the weight of the rocket it is as well to add a little gum tragacanth (see introductory paragraph on page 49) to the fondant covering the main cake for it will act as a hardener. (If you do not use it, then make the cake as near as possible to the party day so that the rocket will not sink into the cake and spoil the shape.)

The candles used in the photograph are 'Magic Candles' which re-light themselves after being blown out. They are great fun but if used it is best to remove them with the holders (bottom ones first) and douse them under the tap – otherwise you may have to throw a bucket of water over the cake!

Please read the General Notes on pages 6 to 9 before starting to decorate the cake. Also read through the step-by-step instructions and check the ingredient and equipment lists.

Ingredients for cake

280g (10oz) butter
220g (8oz) caster sugar
360g (13oz) self-raising flour
200g (7oz) ground rice
220ml (8fl oz) milk beaten with 4 large eggs
flavouring, filling or dried fruit
Make from this recipe:
1 × 200mm (8 in.) round cake
1 × 420g (15oz) food-can cake

Ingredients for fondant and royal icing

900g (2lb) icing sugar, plus 110g (4oz)
2 egg whites, plus ½
4 tblsp liquid glucose
gum tragacanth (if desired)
flavouring (optional)
Also: warm sieved apricot jam; 50/50 mixture of corn flour and icing sugar in a dusting dredger; blue and green colouring; silver balls for decoration.

Equipment

Basins for mixing icings; sieve; spoons; rolling pin; steel rule; sharp-pointed knife; lolly sticks (LS) as spacers; pastry brush; greaseproof paper for icing bags; Ateco (or equivalent) icing nozzles 1, 2, 15 and 22; 255mm (10in.) round silver board.

1. Having left the cakes overnight, trim the rocket as indicated, sloping at one end and with a flat top. Slice the top of the round cake until it is flat, then position it upside down in centre of silver board.

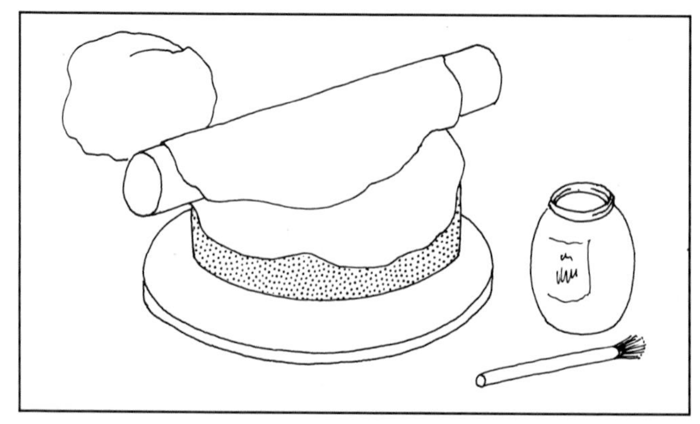

2. Make the fondant, adding flavour if desired. Cut in two, cover one half. (Knead 2 teasp gum tragacanth into remaining half.) Roll out to 2 LS thick, then cut circle to cover top and sides of cake. Brush cake with jam, carefully apply fondant, then trim round bottom edge.

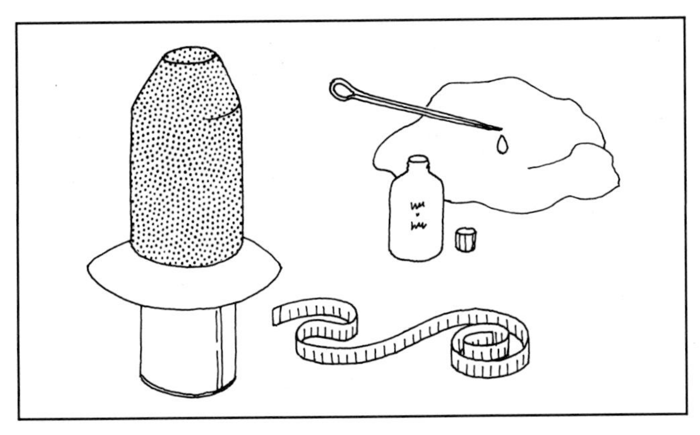

3. Place rocket on an up-turned tea plate, then put the plate on a small jar or tin so that it can swivel round. Colour the remaining half of fondant pale blue. Measure height and circumference of rocket.

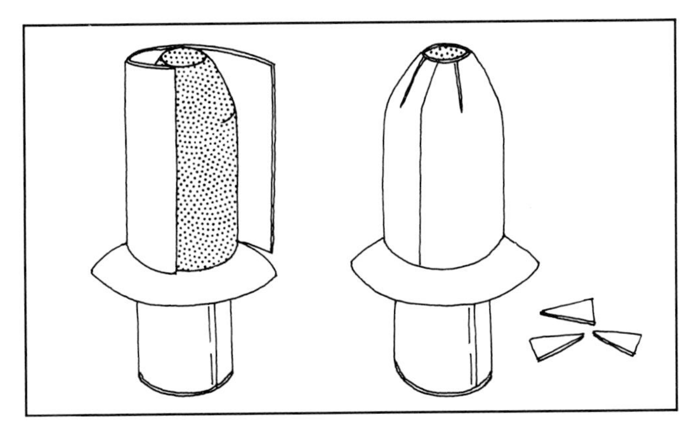

4. Roll fondant to 2 LS thick and cut to size. Brush sponge with jam. Carefully wrap fondant around sponge. Cut out four Vs at top to fit nozzle.

5. Take a little of the blue fondant, add some more blue and model a point for the rocket. Place it on waxed paper. Leave everything to dry overnight.

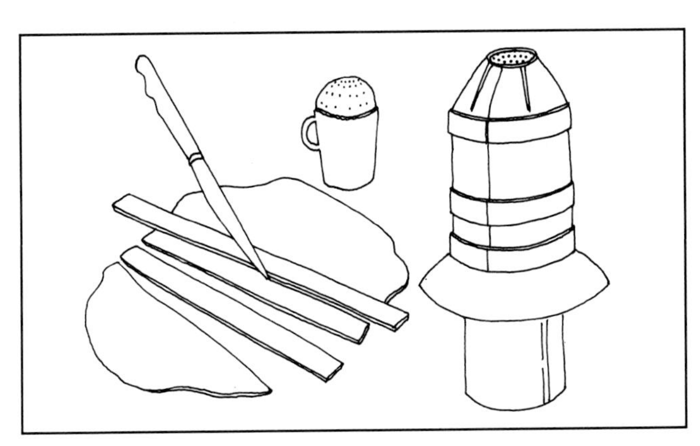

6. Measure circumference of rocket again, roll fondant to 1 LS thick, cut three strips 20mm (¾in.) wide. Brush backs with egg white, then position as indicated.

7. Make up the 110g (4oz) of royal icing and keep in an airtight container. Spread a film of jam on top of the rocket, add dabs of royal icing and press on the point of the rocket.

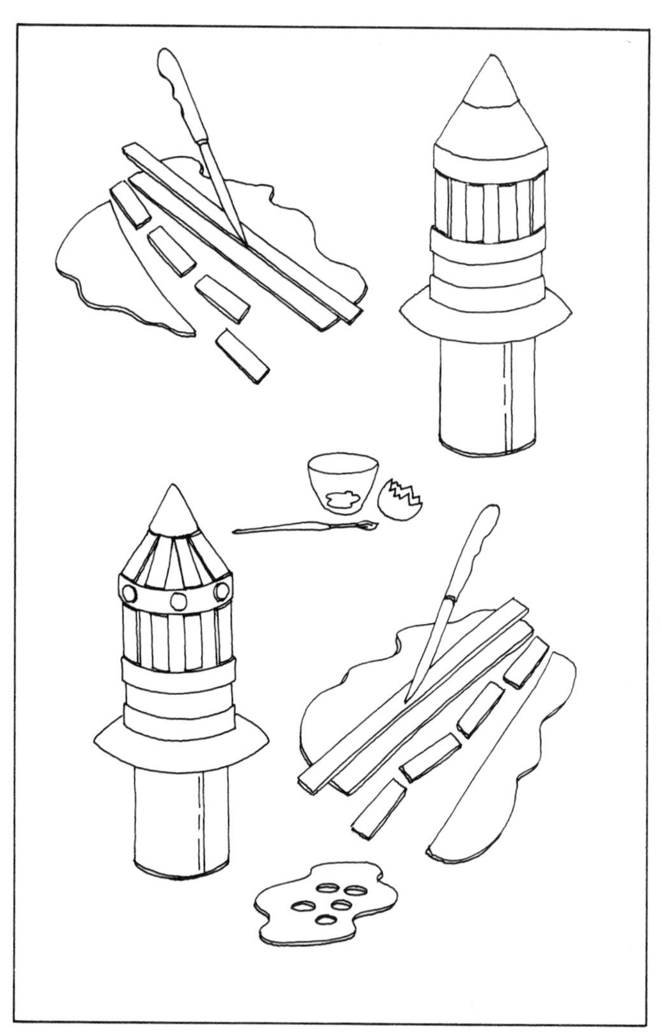

8. Roll blue fondant to 1 LS thick. Cut ten strips 10mm (3/8in.) wide and attach where indicated on rocket. Cut nine strips to fit on nozzle. Position strips with egg white but avoid seam of fondant at back of rocket. Cut out and attach five round, white windows (1 LS thick).

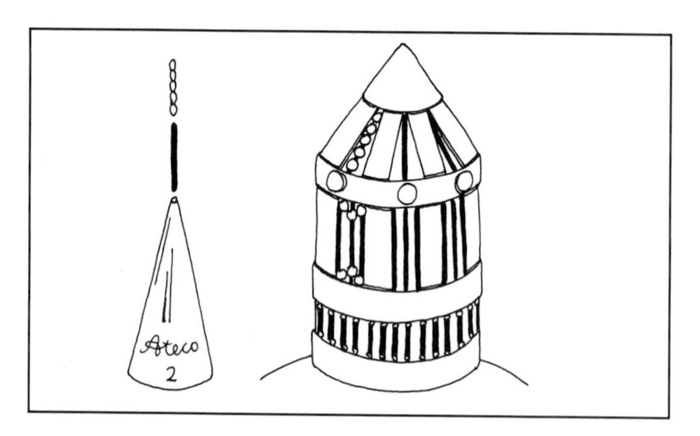

9. Using *No. 2 nozzle* pipe blue lines where indicated. Add silver balls as soon as each line has been piped. Pipe little dots at top and bottom of each line near rocket base. Leave to dry overnight.

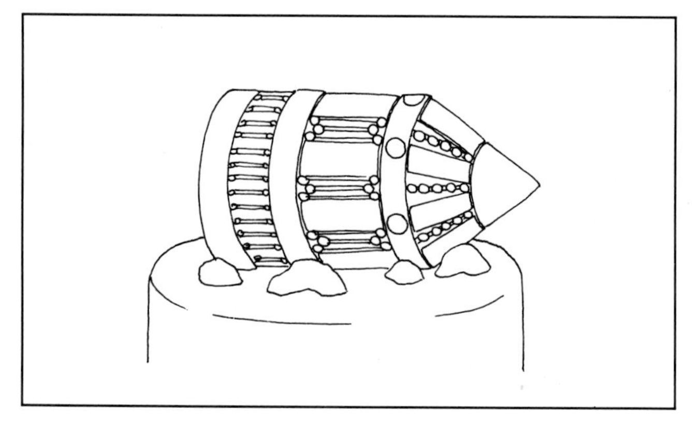

10. Carefully transfer rocket to cake (rocket seam underneath). Secure with lines of royal icing and position rough lumps of white fondant (moon rocks) to support – these are secured with dabs of icing.

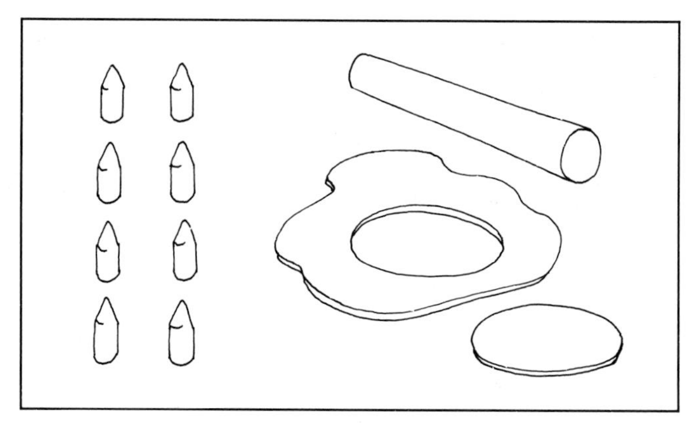

11. Add more blue to blue fondant and model eight small rockets 14mm (½in.) diameter and 55mm (2¼in.) long. Roll fondant to 2 LS thick and cut a circle to fit rocket base. Coat sponge with jam and apply fondant.

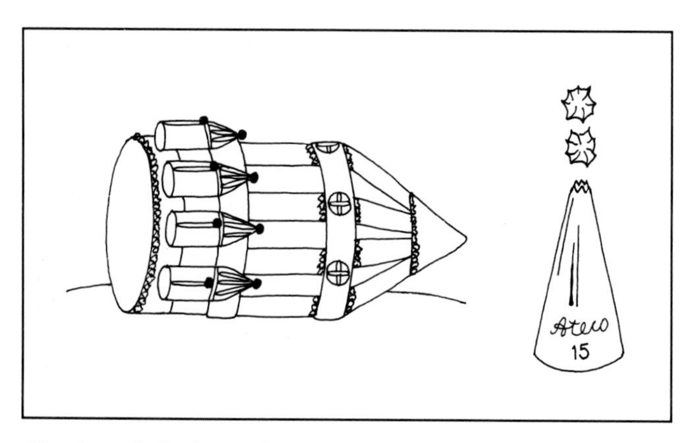

12. Attach little rockets with dabs of icing. Pipe lines where indicated (*No. 2*) and position silver balls. Using *No. 15* small star, pipe stars around base seam, on strip seams and at base of point.

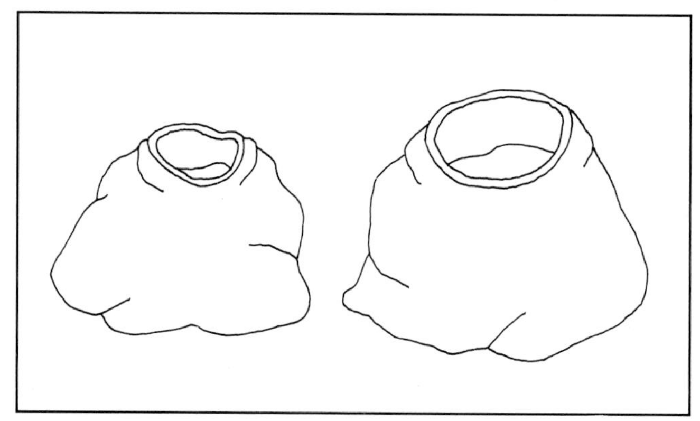

13. Position more moon rocks on surface. Model two craters, as shown, and position in front of rocket using egg white to secure.

14. Add green to remaining white fondant, model two heads with big ears, and two arms. Place inside the craters. Stick a pair of antennae on each head with dabs of icing. Mark mouths with a knife.

15. Using *No. 1 nozzle* pipe green eyes, noses and crinkly hair onto moon-men, then a dot on each antennae. With *No. 15* pipe pale blue stars on moon surface. Using *No. 22* pipe larger stars round base of moon.

Indian tepee

This cake can be decorated in one day. There will be quite a few spare sponge trimmings when the cake has been cut to shape, so perhaps you will find a use for them – there is usually a hungry-looking child around on baking day, lurking near the kitchen table with an eye on the leftovers and offcuts!

If your daughter or son has done project work at school on the American Indians, you may have access to genuine Indian symbols and design work. These could be incorporated into the piping on the tepee.

Please read the General Notes on pages 6 to 9 before starting to decorate the cake. Also read through the step-by-step instructions and check the ingredient and equipment lists.

Ingredients for cake

340g (12oz) butter
250g (9oz) caster sugar
420g (15oz) self-raising flour
250g (9oz) ground rice
250ml (9fl oz) milk beaten with 5 large eggs
filling
Make from this recipe: 3 × 150mm (6in.) round cakes

Ingredients for fondant and royal icing

450g (1lb) icing sugar, plus 170g (6oz)
1 egg white, plus ¾
2 tblsp liquid glucose
flavouring (optional)
Also: warm sieved apricot jam; 50/50 mixture of cornflour and icing sugar in a dusting dredger; brown, yellow, black, red, green and orange food colouring.

Equipment

Basins for mixing icings; sieve; spoons; rolling pin; sharp-pointed knife; lolly sticks (LS) as spacers; pastry brush; small paint brush; greaseproof paper for icing bags; Ateco (or equivalent) nozzles 2, 3 and 41; 230mm (9in.) round silver board.

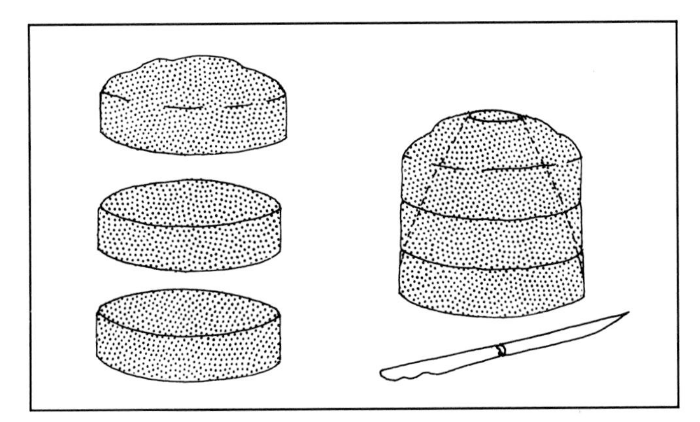

1. Having left the cakes overnight, trim two of the tops until perfectly flat. Stand them on top of one another and cut to a conicle shape, leaving a flat surface at the top about 40mm (1½in.) diameter (very little sponge is sliced from the bottom cake).

2. Carefully take each cake off and fill with jam and/or butter cream. Replace cakes and position them in centre of silver board. Cut a triangle out for opening, as shown.

Make 450g (1lb) of fondant. Brush entire cake with warm sieved jam.

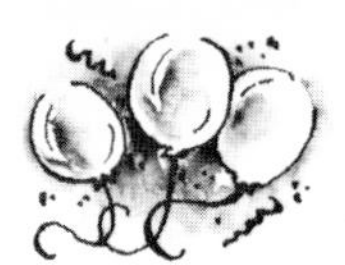

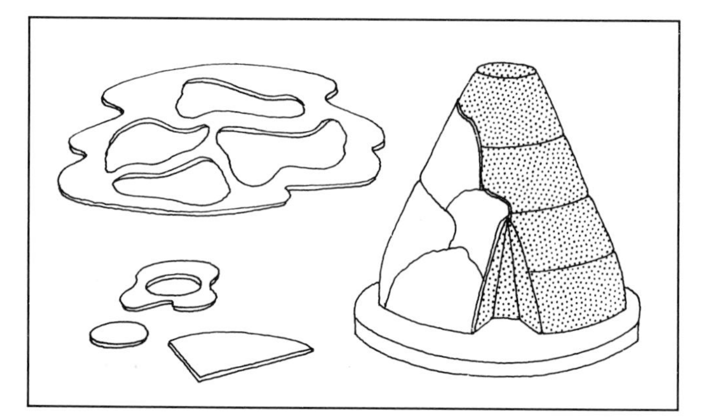

3. Colour the fondant brown. Roll to 2 LS thick and cut into irregular pieces, as shown. Apply to cake (allow some of the fondant to wrinkle, like buffalo hide). Measure door opening and cut a piece of fondant to fit. Roll fondant to 1 LS thick, cut a circle 45mm (1¾in.) diameter.

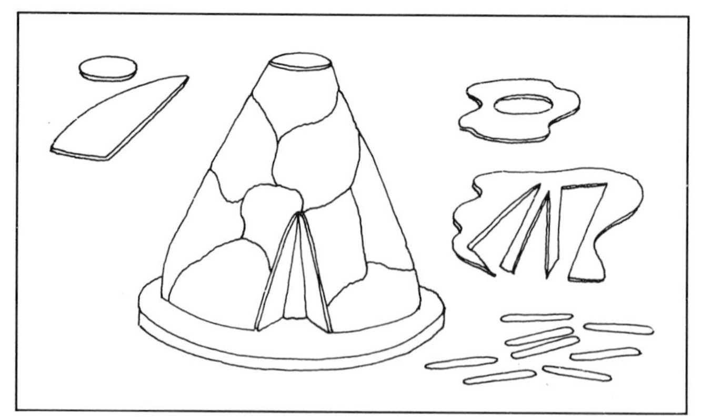

4. Leave door and circle on one side.
Add black to brown trimmings. Roll to 2 LS thick and cut a circle for top. Apply. Cut three pieces to line inside opening. Apply. Roll remaining fondant and cut into eight 45mm (1¾in.) lengths. Leave to dry.

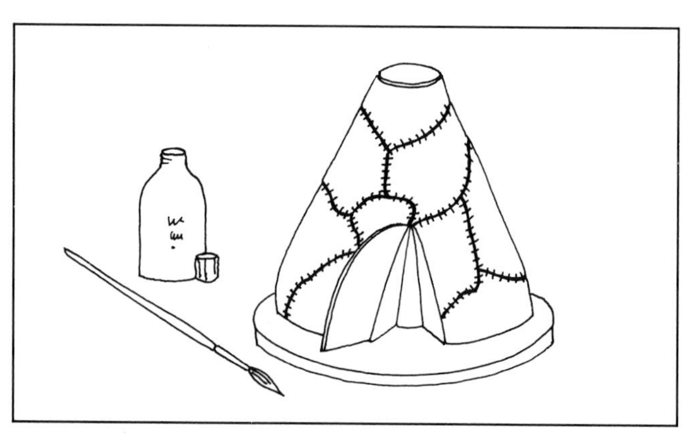

5. Brush one edge of opening with egg white and attach door, slightly away from wall of tepee.
Paint brown lines along seams of fondant on tepee, then paint stitching, as shown.

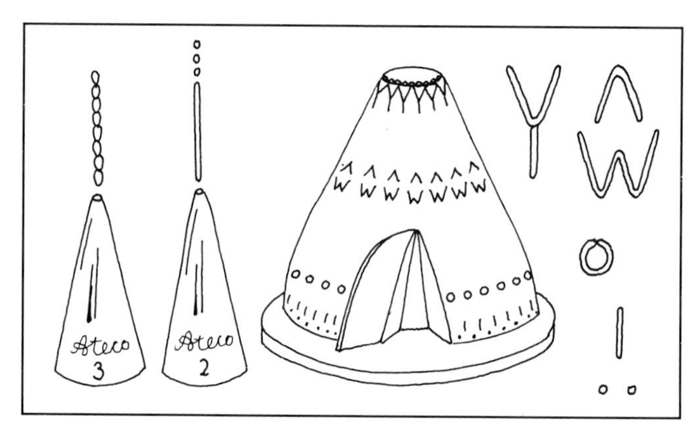

6. Make the 170g (6oz) of royal icing. With *nozzle No. 3* and yellow icing, pipe a line of continuous dots around top of tepee. With *No. 2* and same colour, pipe Ys as shown. Pipe Ws and upturned Vs just above centre. Pipe circles, lines and dots where indicated.

7. Pipe lines on door, and bird symbol on the circle of fondant. With *nozzle 41* and pale orange icing, pipe zig-zag lines where indicated. Using green icing and *No. 3*, pipe Vs and dots as shown, and an eye in the bird symbol. Change to *No. 2 nozzle* and deep orange icing.

8. Pipe Vs, dots and lines where indicated, and around bird's tail. Paint three brown vertical lines on door. Attach poles, indenting top surface slightly and using egg white to secure. Attach symbol with dabs of icing. Using *No. 3 nozzle* and yellow icing, pipe two more lines of continuous dots around top of tepee.

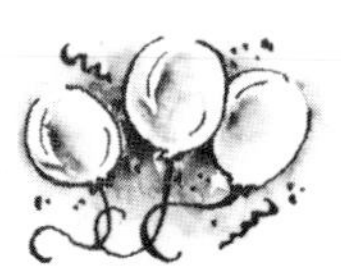

Early settlement fort

Not wishing to introduce violence, I decided to make this a peaceful early settlement fort. Strictly speaking it probably should be a triangular shape, but this would mean less cake to eat! The walls should be much thinner, which would also mean less cake.

The piped lines are easy to manage if you can tip the front of the board up. Gravity will then pull the lines against the wall.

Please read the General Notes on pages 6 to 9 before starting to decorate the cake. It is a good idea also to read through the step-by-step instructions and check the ingredient and equipment lists.

Ingredients for cake

450g (16oz) butter
340g (12oz) caster sugar
560g (20oz) self-raising flour
340g (12oz) ground rice
280ml (10fl oz) milk beaten with 6 large eggs

Make from this recipe:
1 × 280mm (11in.) square cake

Ingredients for fondant and royal icing

670g (1½lb) icing sugar, plus 280g (10oz)
1½ egg whites, plus 1¼
3 tblsp liquid glucose
flavouring (optional)
Also: warm sieved apricot jam; 50/50 mixture of cornflour and icing sugar in a dusting dredger; yellow, brown and black food colouring.

Equipment

Basins for mixing icings; sieve; spoons; rolling pin; steel rule; sharp-pointed knife; lolly sticks (LS) as spacers; pastry brush; greaseproof paper for icing bags; Ateco (or equivalent) icing nozzles 2, 3 and 7; 360mm (14in.) square silver cake board.

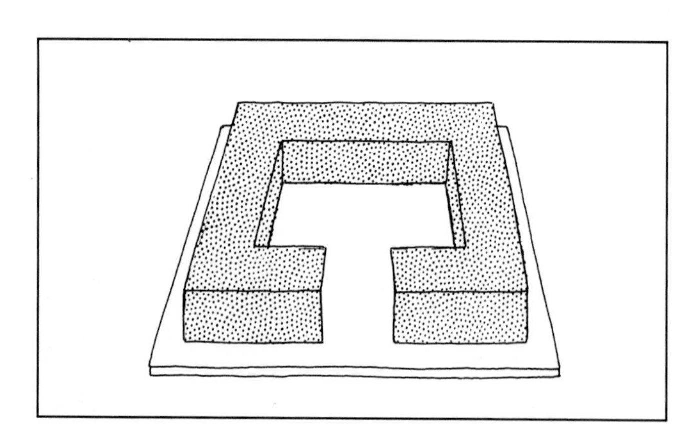

1. Having left the cake overnight, slice the top flat. Cut a 165mm (6½in.) square from the centre and a 50mm (2in.) piece from the front, as shown. Carefully turn cake over and position in centre of board.

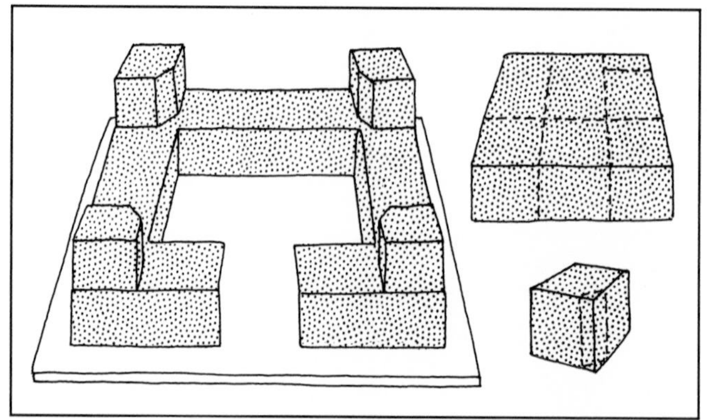

2. Cut the square into three. Cut four pieces to fit at each corner of fort, with a sliver cut from one corner of each, as shown. Smear bases with jam and/or butter cream, and position, slanting side facing inwards.

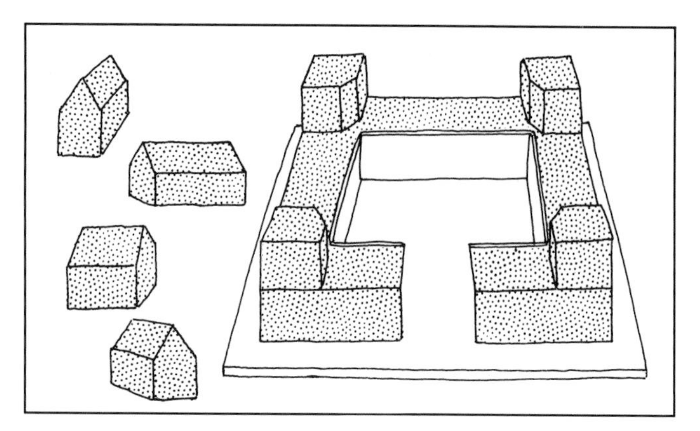

3. Cut part of remaining sponge into four buildings with sloping roofs. Make the 670g (1½lb) of fondant, colour all but a small piece pale brown. Brush inside walls of fort with jam. Measure the walls in turn, roll fondant to 1 LS thick and apply carefully.

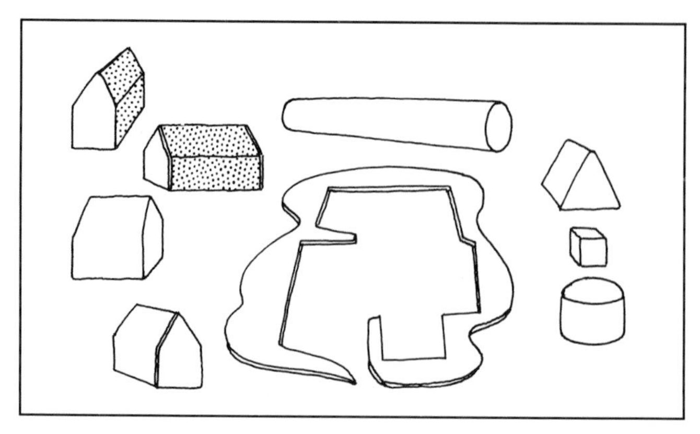

4. Brush little buildings with jam. Roll fondant to 1 LS thick. Cover sides first, then cut front, roof and back in one piece. Model a little well, as shown, but do not assemble.

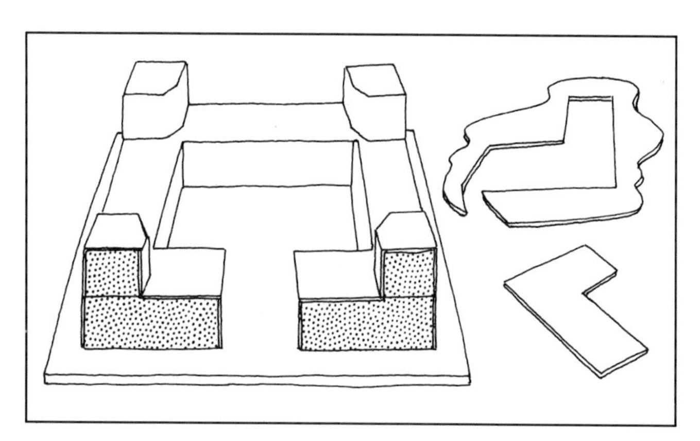

5. Add more brown to fondant. Brush all sponge surfaces of cake with jam. Roll fondant to 1 LS thick. Measure surfaces in turn, cut fondant to fit and carefully apply. Continue until cake is completely covered.

6. Roll fondant to 1 LS thick. Cut five pieces 7mm (¼in.) wide, 60mm (2½in.) long, with a point at one end. Cut three narrow pieces to go across. Leave to dry, then stick cross-pieces on with egg white. Leave on one side.

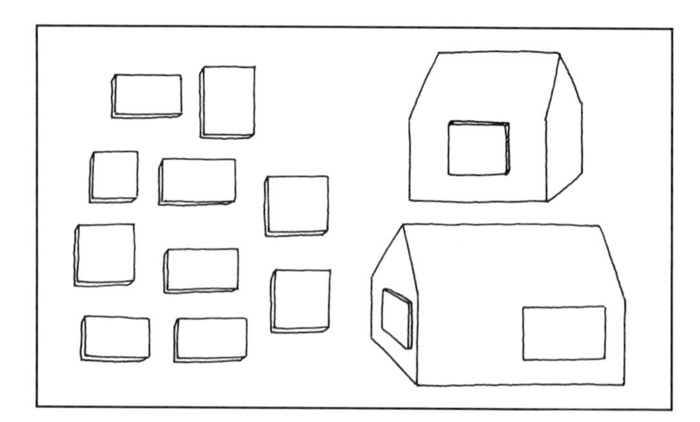

7. Colour the piece of white fondant yellow. Roll to 1 LS thick and cut ten windows of varying size. Brush backs with egg white and apply to buildings and inside walls of fort.

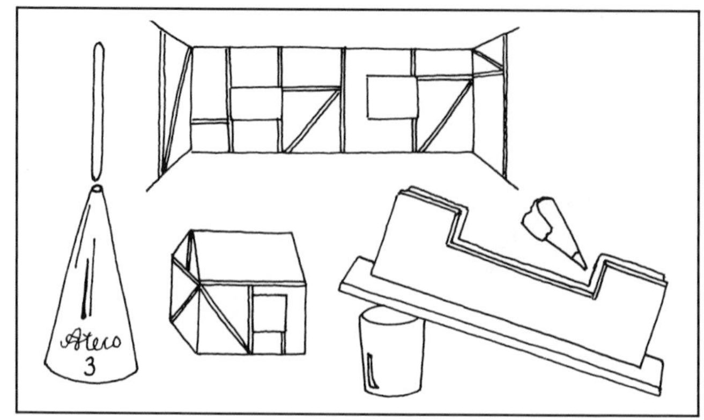

8. Make the 280g (10oz) of royal icing. Leave about three teaspoonsful white and colour remainder brown. With *nozzle No. 3* pipe beams on building and inside fort walls, as shown – tip the board up slightly (supporting with a cup or glass) for each facing side.

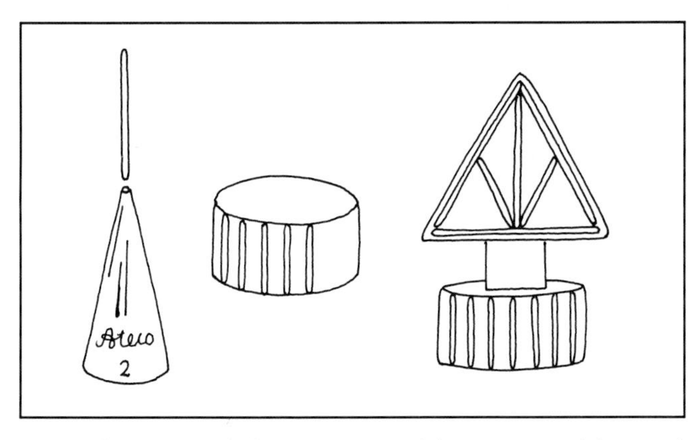

9. With *No. 2 nozzle* pipe vertical lines around base of well. Pipe a dab of icing in centre and attach small support. Dab top of support and attach roof. Pipe beams on both ends of roof.

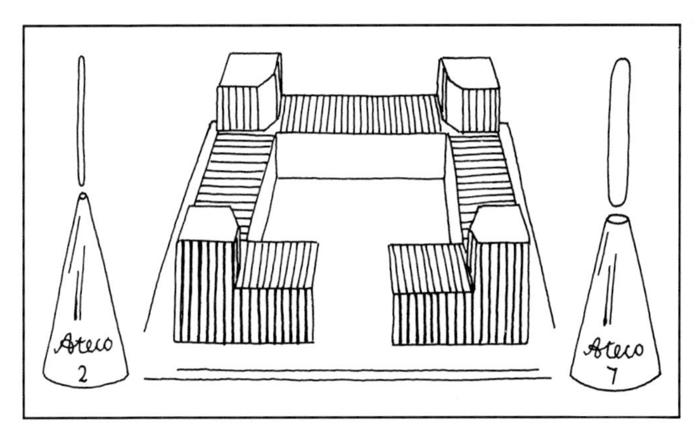

10. Remembering to tilt board, use the same nozzle to pipe lines inside gateway, on flat surface of each wall, and on inside walls of lookout posts (in that order).

With *No. 7 nozzle* pipe lines on outside walls, again tilting board.

11. Colour the remaining white icing ochre (yellow and a drop of brown). With *No. 2 nozzle* pipe irregular lines on roofs of buildings. Finish with a line of continuous dots along ridges.

12. Add black to remaining brown icing. With *No. 2* pipe ladders on sides of lookout towers, as shown. Using *No. 3* pipe continuous dots around top of lookout towers, on edges of walls, down four main corners and around base.

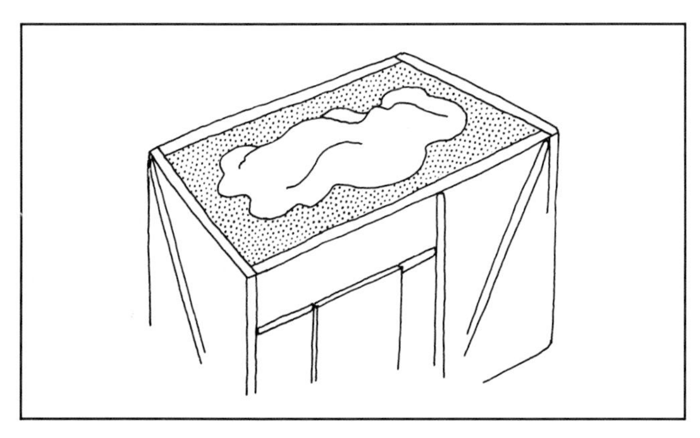

13. Smear the base of each building with icing and carefully position inside the fort.

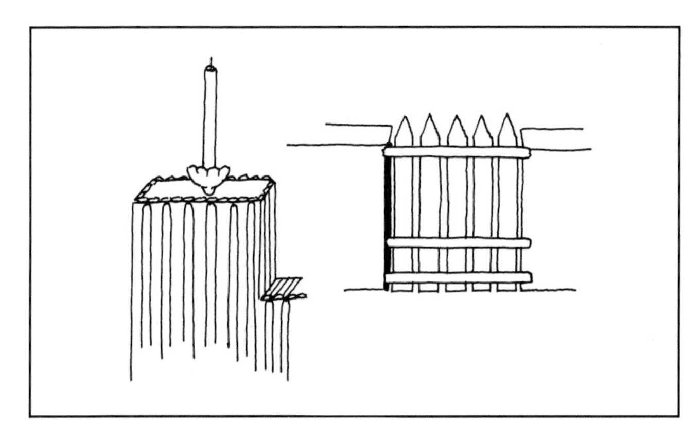

14. Pipe a line of icing down one side of entrance and attach gate. Stick a candle in each tower (or however many are required) and secure them.

Fun Cakes

Fast-food addict

Apart from those who have suddenly become weight-conscious, most young people are happy to have chips with everything. This cake would be ideal for those who will eat nothing but chips and the usual accompanying greasy food. A couple of sausages could also be added.

The cake can be decorated in a day. To add more fun, each item of food could have a different flavour – peppermint chips, vanilla egg, strawberry beans, banana beefburger!

Please read the General Notes on pages 6 to 9 before starting to decorate the cake. Also read through the step-by-step instructions and check the ingredient and equipment lists.

Ingredients for cake

220g (8oz) butter
170g (6oz) caster sugar
280g (10oz) self-raising flour
170g (6oz) ground rice
140ml (5fl oz) milk beaten with 3 large eggs
filling (optional)

Make from this recipe:
1 × 200mm (8in.) round cake

Ingredients for fondant and royal icing

790g (1¾lb) icing sugar, plus 30g (1oz)
1¾ egg whites, plus ⅛
almost 4 tblsp liquid glucose
flavouring (optional)
Also: warm sieved apricot jam; 50/50 mixture of cornflour and icing sugar in a dusting dredger; yellow, blue, green, brown and orange food colouring.

Equipment

Basins for mixing icings; spoons; sieve; rolling pin; steel rule; sharp-pointed knife; lolly sticks (LS) as spacers; pastry brush; small paint brush; crinkled chip cutter; greaseproof paper for icing bag; Ateco (or equivalent) icing nozzle No. 3; 250mm (10in.) round silver board.

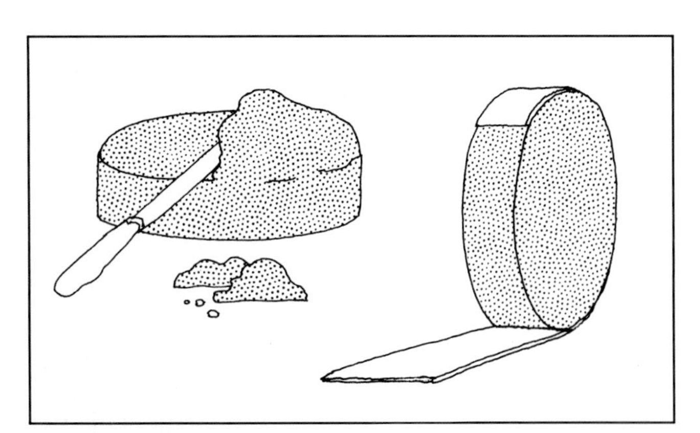

1. Having left the cake overnight, slice the top flat. Turn cake over and place in centre of silver board. Make the fondant. Measure circumference and depth of cake. Roll fondant to 2 LS thick and cut a piece to go around cake. Brush cake sides with warmed jam. Roll cake onto fondant.

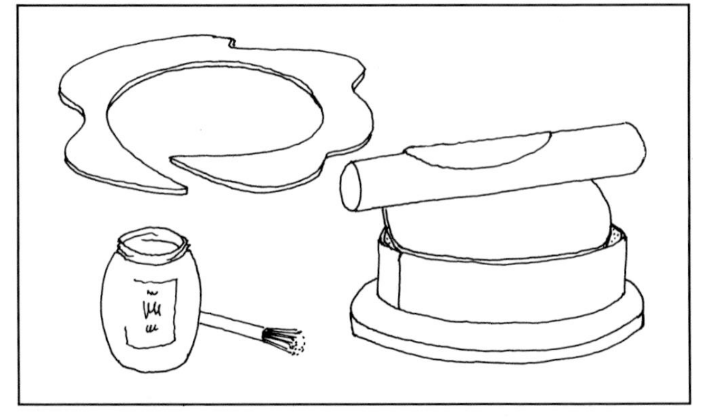

2. Brush top of cake with jam. Roll fondant to 2 LS thick. Cut circle to fit (cut round cake tin). With help of rolling pin apply fondant.

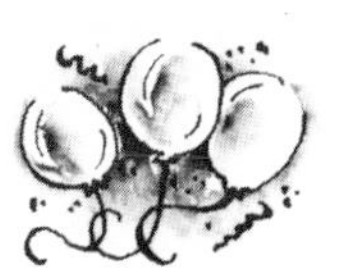

3. When fondant is dry, paint repeating flower design around sides. Make up the royal icing. Pipe a line of continuous dots around top fondant seam.

4. Take 170g (6oz) of fondant. Add brown colouring and a little black. Add more brown and partially mix. Start to shape the beefburger, pinching top to give an uneven surface. Make three grill grooves with paint brush handle, paint some black in the grooves. Leave to dry, then bend a little to make surface cracks.

5. Take 80g (3oz) of fondant. Colour orange with a little brown. Form into baked beans. Flatten some pieces to make bean sauce. Position beefburger on cake, then put dribbling sauce and beans around, using egg white to secure.

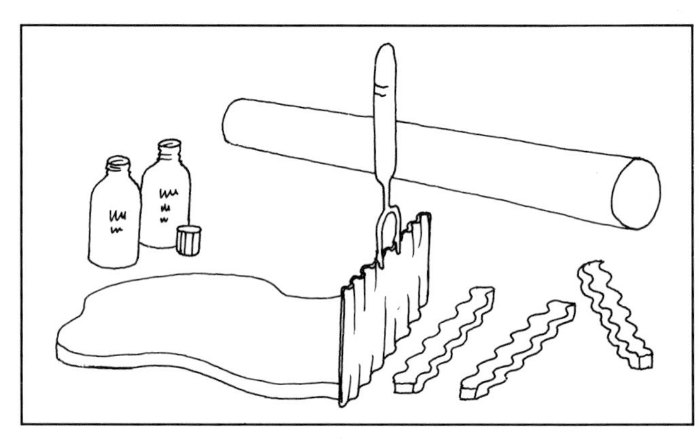

6. Take 140g (5oz) of fondant. Colour it with a little yellow, partially mix in a little brown. Roll to 4 LS thick and cut into chips with crinkled cutter. Arrange around back of beefburger, securing with egg white.

7. Take about 60g (2oz) of fondant. Form white of egg from a ball, flatten and smooth it. Form yellow yolk from a ball, flatten slightly and round off.

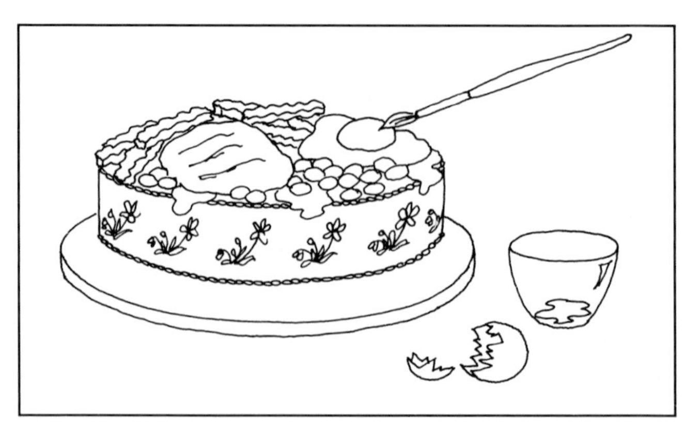

8. Position egg white in remaining space of cake, then secure yolk with egg white. Brush beefburger, chips and egg yolk with egg white to give nice greasy finish.

Soap

This very ornate marble soap dish and smooth bar of soap can be given to the young person who is constantly being told by members of the family not to spend all her/his life in the bathroom – or, it can be given to the young person who is persistently being told by his/her parents to 'get washed!'

(The theme for the cake was not planned. I had intended a wood-grain finish for another cake, but the resulting marble effect was so interesting, I felt it must be put to use.)

The cake can be decorated in one day.

Please read the General Notes on pages 6 to 9 before starting to decorate the cake. Also read through the step-by-step instructions and check the ingredient and equipment lists.

Ingredients for cake

170g (6oz) butter
110g (4oz) caster sugar
220g (8oz) self-raising flour
110g (4oz) ground rice
110ml (4fl oz) milk beaten with 2 large eggs
filling (optional)
Make from this recipe: 1 × 900g (2lb) loaf cake

Ingredients for fondant and royal icing

670g (1½lb) icing sugar, plus 60g (2oz)
1½ egg whites, plus ¼
3 tblsp liquid glucose
flavouring (optional)
Also: warm sieved apricot jam; 50/50 mixture of cornflour and icing sugar in a dusting dredger; brown, red, black, blue and gold food colouring.

Equipment

Basins for mixing icings; sieve; spoons; rolling pin; steel rule; sharp-pointed knife; lolly sticks (LS) as spacers; pastry brush; small paint brush; greaseproof paper for icing bag; Ateco (or equivalent) icing nozzles 3 and 98; 250mm (10in.) square silver board.

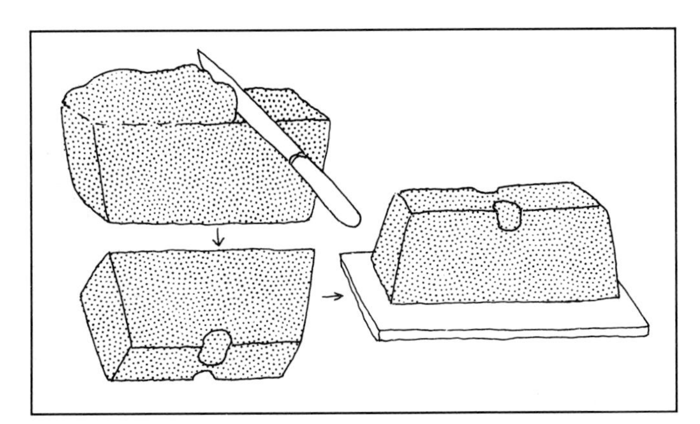

1. Having left the cake overnight, slice the top so that the surface is perfectly flat. Cut small pieces from the centre edges at front and back, as shown. Turn cake upside down and place in centre of silver board.

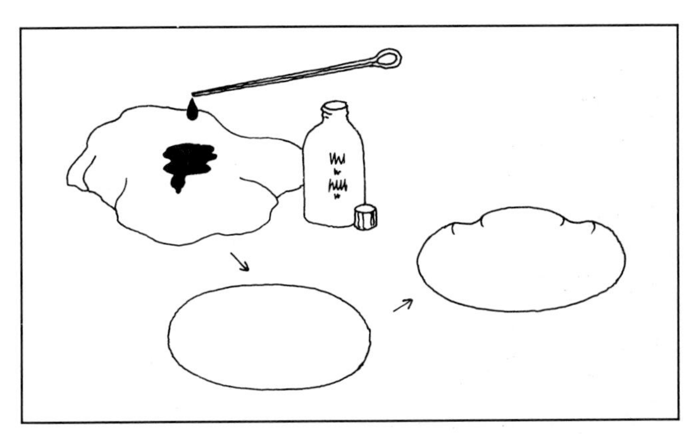

2. Make 670g (1½lb) of fondant. Take about 220g (8oz), colour it pale blue and form a smooth oval – some icing sugar may have to be kneaded into the fondant so that the shape does not flop. Form indent in top of soap with finger when the shape is perfectly smooth. Leave to dry on dusted surface.

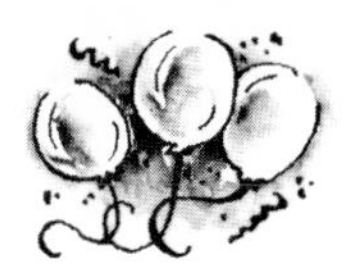

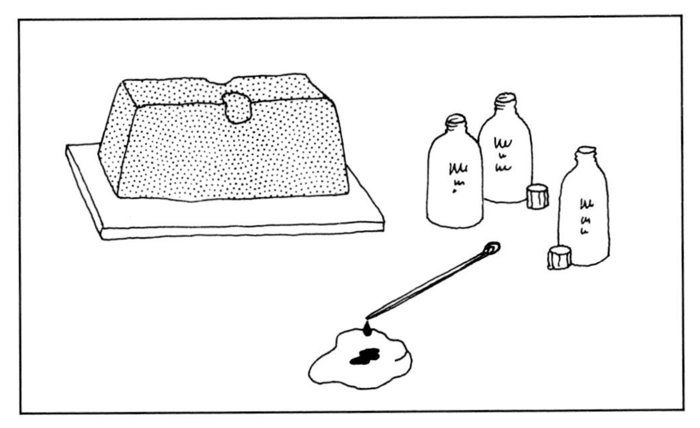

3. Take a small piece of fondant, about 30g (1oz) and colour it rich brown, adding some red and a little black. The five pieces of fondant covering the cake have each to be worked with a fresh piece of white so that the marble effect is not lost.

4. Brush cake with warmed jam. Take a piece of white fondant, form into a flat oblong and dab with small pieces of brown. Knead very lightly then roll to 2 LS thick. Cut to fit front of cake, easing fondant into recess on top edge.

5. Repeat with sides and back, then top, easing fondant into recess and smoothing with finger so that the join cannot be seen. Make the 60g (2oz) of royal icing.

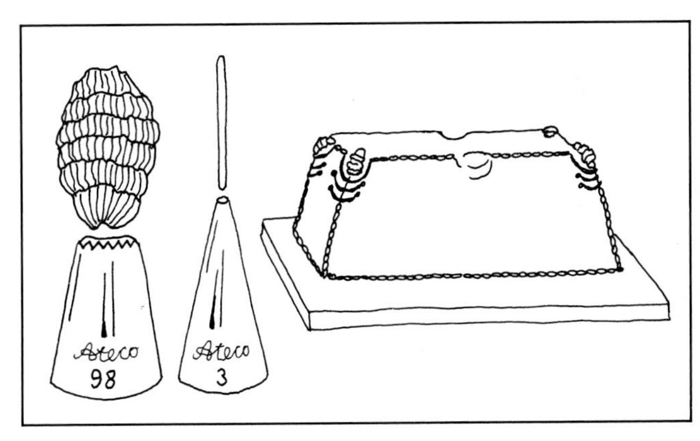

6. With icing *nozzle No. 98* pipe white scrolls on corners of cake. With *No. 3* pipe three curved lines under scrolls on each side. Pipe lines of continuous dots down the corners, along top edges and around base.

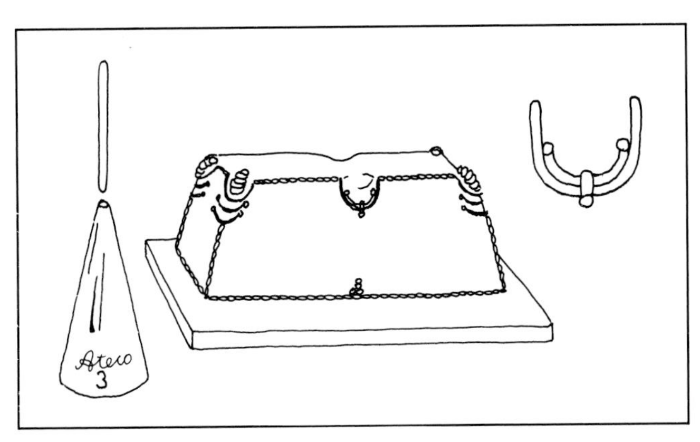

7. Pipe four dots in centre of front and back base lines. Pipe a solid line around recess, then another line inside, as shown, with a dot at each end. Pipe a small line in centre over the two lines, ending with a dot. Repeat with recess at back.

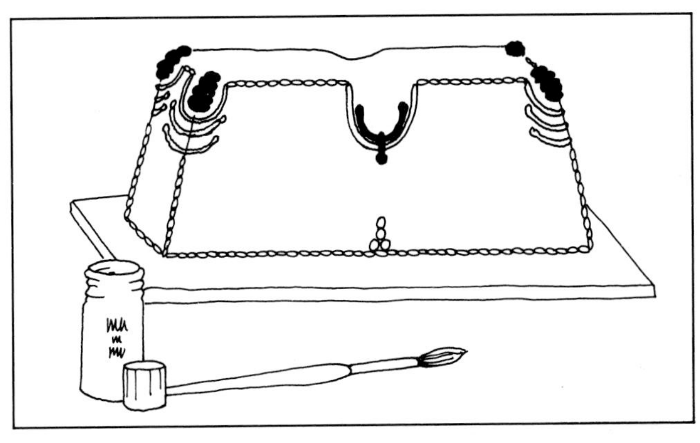

8. When piped icing has dried, paint scrolls and lines on recess, as shown, with gold colouring. Position soap on slab. Secure, if desired, with egg white.

Shoe polishing kit

This is specifically for the child who constantly frowns at the request to polish his (usually boy's) shoes. A very young child might not understand (or might even be a little hurt) by the cake, but an older child of 12 or 13, with a sense of humour, will appreciate the message.

The most time-consuming part of decorating is taken up by piping of the brush bristles. Everything else is quite straightforward and the cake can be completed in two days.

I suggest that dried fruit should not be added to the cake as it has to be cut up and the pieces of fruit may distort the shapes.

Please read the General Notes on pages 6 to 9 before starting to decorate the cake. It is also useful to read through the step-by-step instructions and check the ingredient and equipment lists.

Ingredients for cake

450g (16oz) butter
340g (12oz) caster sugar
560g (20oz) self-raising flour
340g (12oz) ground rice
310ml (11fl oz) milk beaten with 6 large eggs
flavouring, or filling, for main cake
Make from this recipe:
1 × 280mm (11in.) square cake

Ingredients for fondant and royal icing

1.120kg (2½lb) icing sugar, plus 220g (8oz)
2½ egg whites, plus 1
5 tblsp liquid glucose
Also: 220g (8oz) marzipan; warm sieved apricot jam; 50/50 mixture of cornflour and icing sugar in a dusting dredger; red, yellow, green and brown food colouring.

Equipment

Basins for mixing icings; sieve; spoons; rolling pin; steel rule; sharp-pointed knife; lolly sticks (LS) as spacers; pastry brush; greaseproof paper for the icing bags; Ateco (or equivalent) icing nozzles 1, 2 and 3; 280mm (11in.) square silver board.

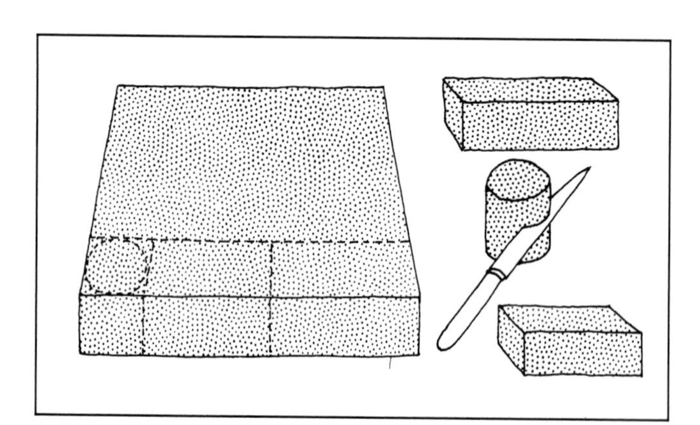

1. Having left the cake overnight, cut off a 56mm (2¼in.) slab – cut from this a 100mm (4in.) piece and a 115mm (4½in.) piece – trim the small remaining square into a circle then slice it in two (see diagram).

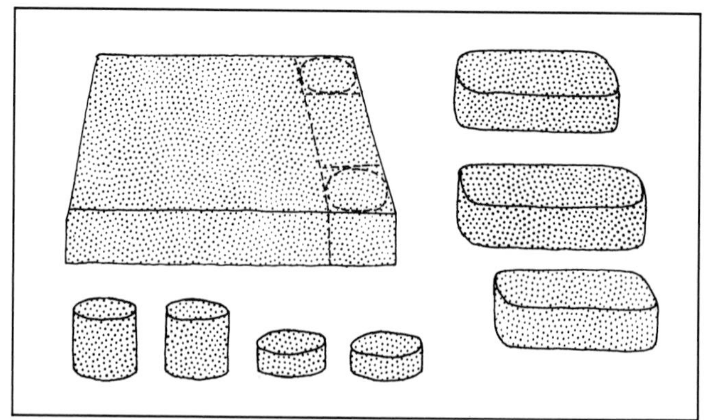

2. Cut another slab 45mm (1¾in.) wide. Cut from this two squares, then trim them into circles. The remainder of the slab will be a brush. Trim all pieces, including the main cake, so that surfaces are flat. Round off the corners of the brushes.

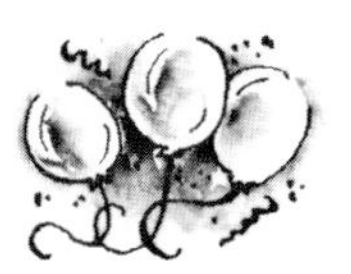

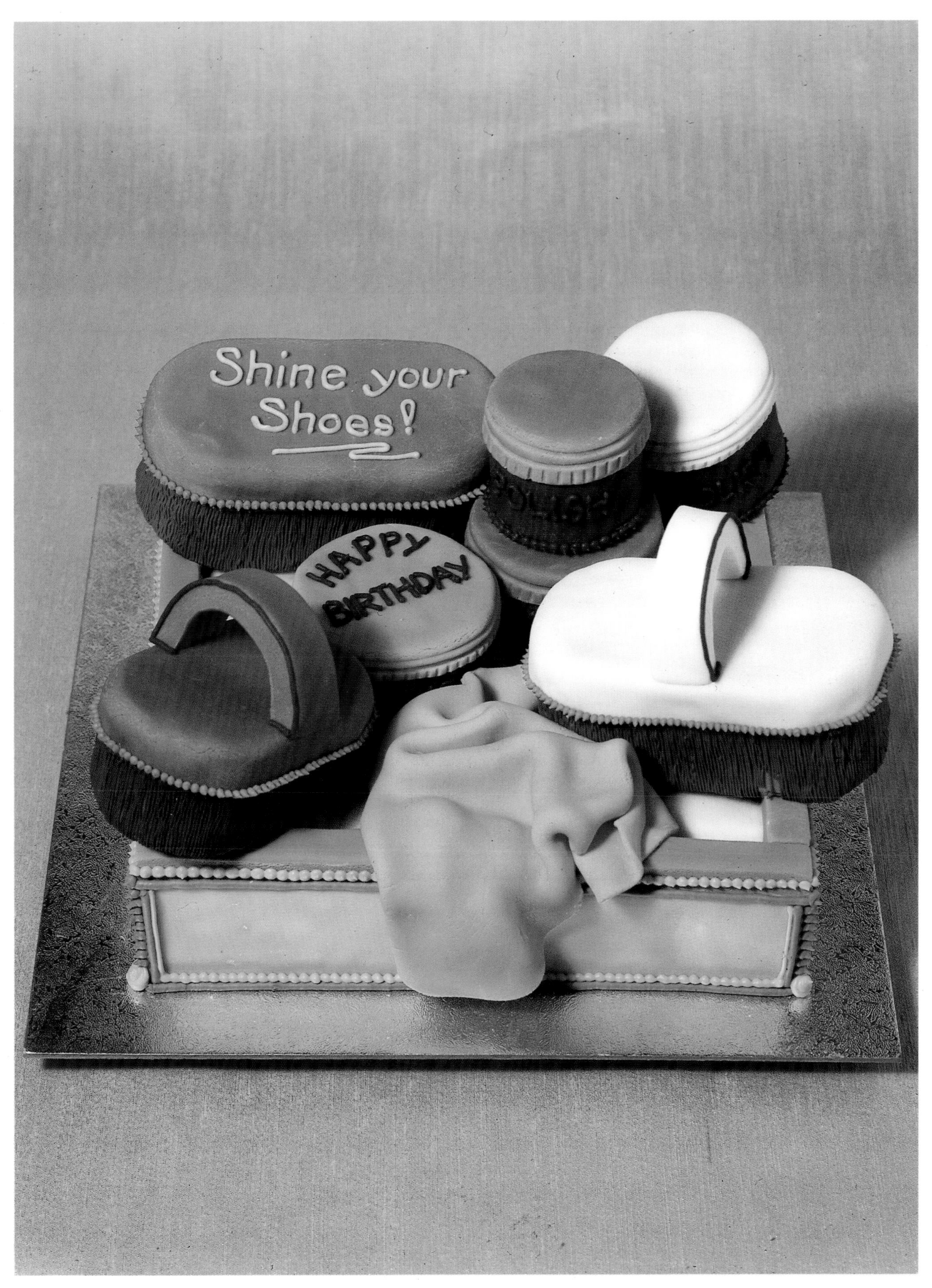
Shine your
Shoes!
HAPPY
BIRTHDAY

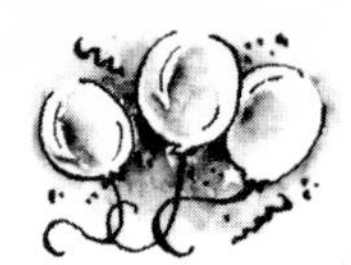

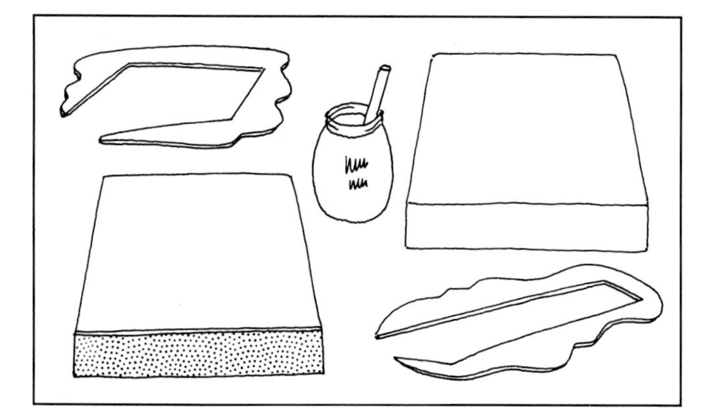

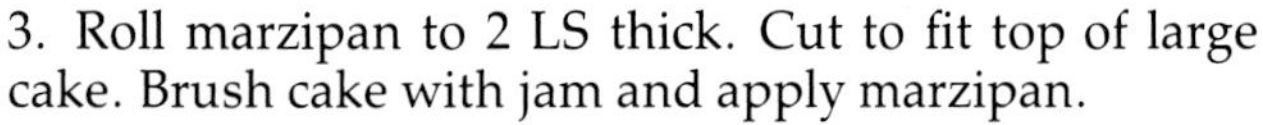

3. Roll marzipan to 2 LS thick. Cut to fit top of large cake. Brush cake with jam and apply marzipan.

Make 670g (1½lb) of fondant. Colour it pale green. Roll to 2 LS thick. Measure cake sides and cut fondant to fit. Brush sides with jam. Carefully apply fondant.

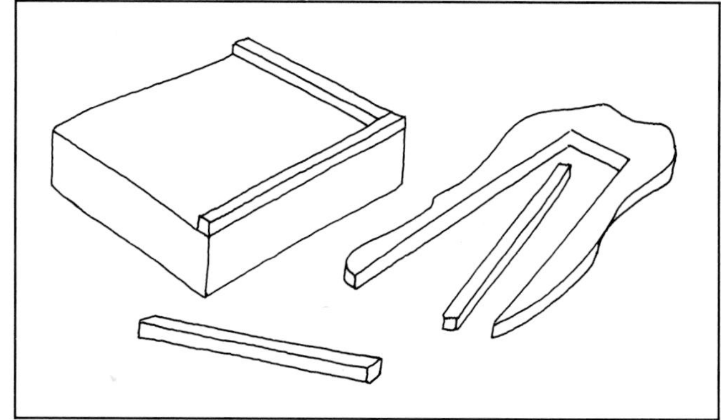

4. Add more green to fondant. Roll to 4 LS thick. Cut into four 15mm (½in.) wide strips. Attach to top edges of cake using egg white to secure.

5. Add brown and a little red to fondant. Roll to 2 LS thick. Cut pieces to fit round cakes (jars of shoe polish). Brush cakes with jam. Apply to tops and bottoms first, then the sides.

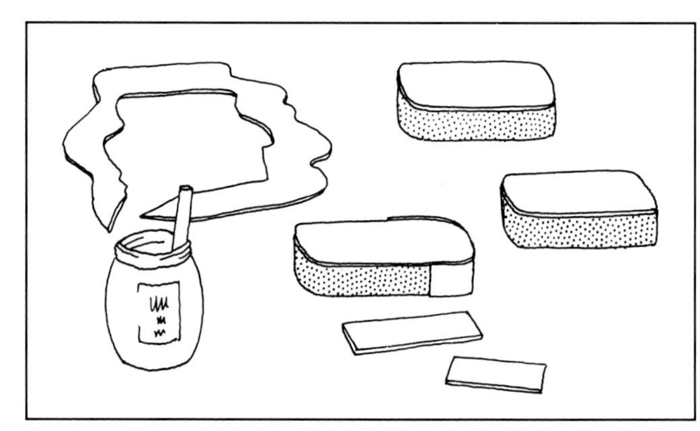

6. Roll fondant to 1 LS thick. Cut three pieces to fit underside of brushes. Brush jam over cake and apply fondant. Cut three pieces to fit round sides of brushes. Brush thin film of jam over sponge and carefully apply fondant.

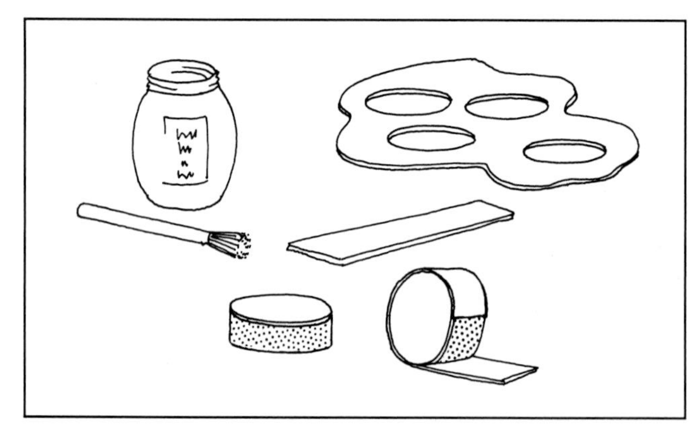

7. Make 450g (1lb) of fondant. Cover 220g (½lb) and colour remainder brown. Roll to 2 LS thick. Cut to fit round cakes. Brush sponge with jam then apply fondant, first the tops, then the bottoms, then sides.

8. Keep back 110g (4oz) white fondant and use remaining, plus trimmings, to make the tops of brushes, handles and lids for polish jars.

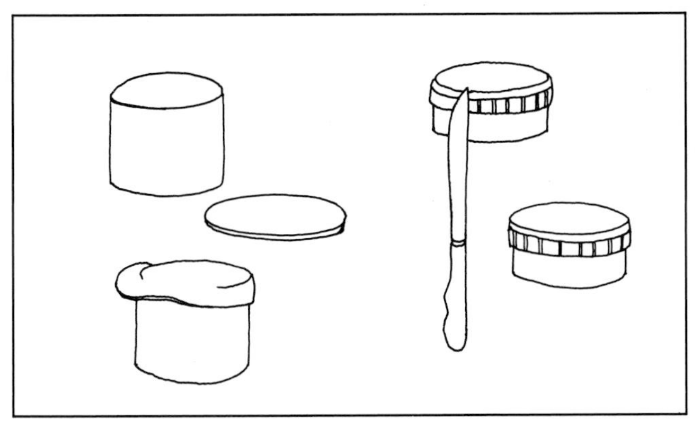

9. Roll to 1 LS thick, cut circles larger than tops of jars. Cut the first top white, then use combinations of colour for remaining three. Secure with egg white. Score lids as shown with blunt edge of a knife.

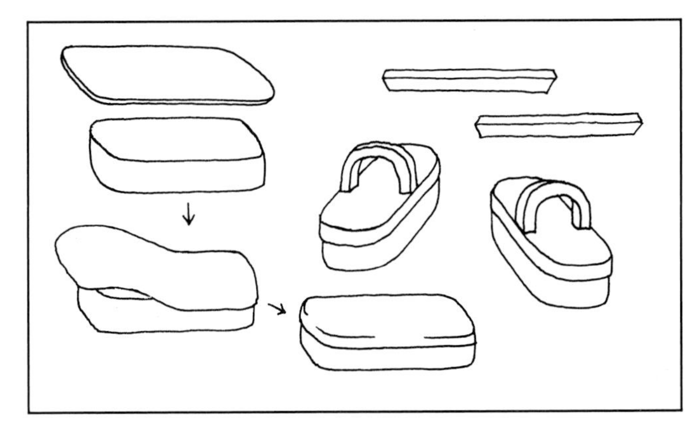

10. Follow No. 9 for colouring. Cut brush tops (1 LS thick) larger than brushes. Secure with egg white. Roll fondant to 4 LS thick, cut handles 20mm (¾in.) wide and 100mm (4in.) long, with each end sloping. Bend round and secure with egg white. Leave all pieces overnight.

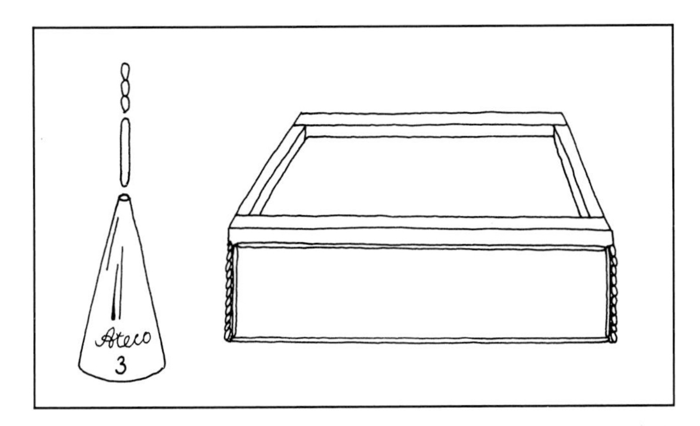

11. Make up the 220g (8oz) of royal icing. Using *No. 3 nozzle* pipe green lines round each side of cake. Pipe dots down each corner.

12. With *No. 2 nozzle* pipe a yellow line of dots and two lines inside green piping, then pipe dots along seams of green edging. Pipe **Shine your Shoes!** on the brush, as shown.

13. With *No. 1* carefully pipe brown bristles around brushes. Pipe green dots with *No. 2* around the tops of bristles. Using brown again and *No. 2* pipe **HAPPY BIRTHDAY** as shown, and **POLISH** on each jar. Pipe dots around the base of each jar. Pipe lines around handles of brushes.

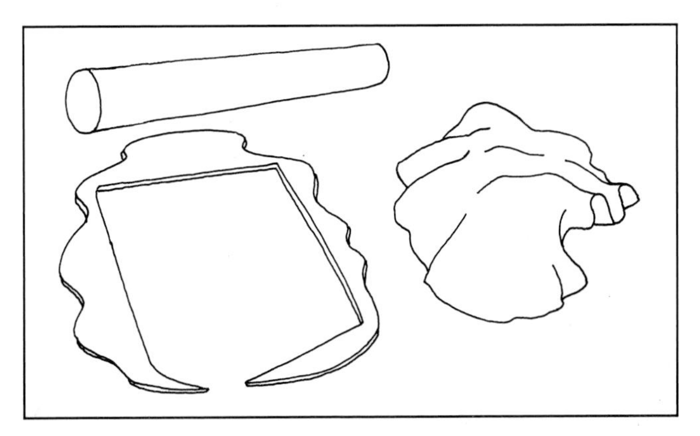

14. Fix everything to main cake using dabs of icing to secure. Colour the remaining 110g (4oz) of fondant with a little yellow and red. Roll to 1 LS thick and place loosely in centre of cake, hanging over the edge, as shown.

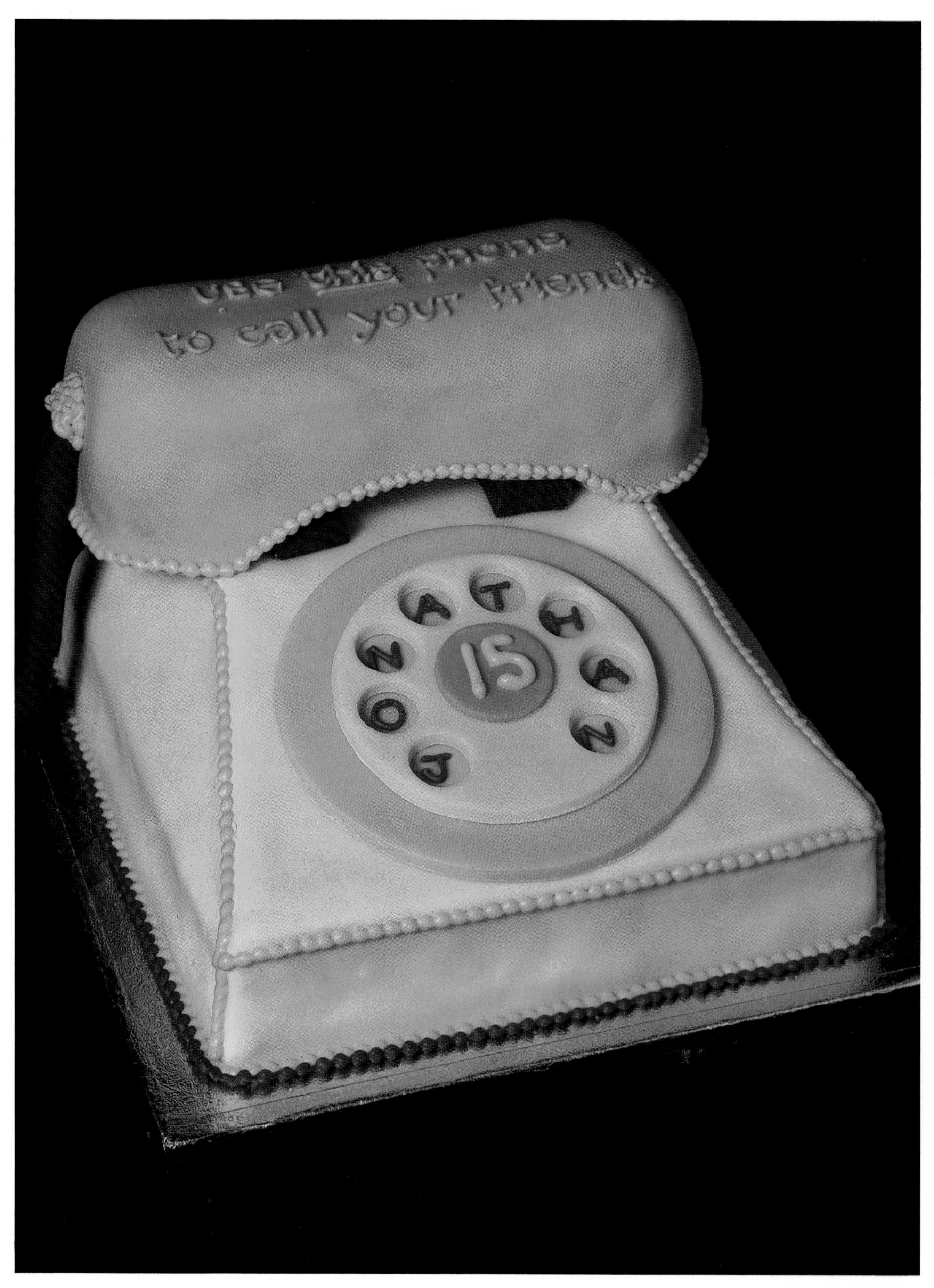
use this phone
to call your friends
JONATHAN
15

Constant telephone user

The rule in our house with regard to children using the telephone is: emergencies only; call at the 'cheap rate' time; do not take longer than two minutes. The rule is constantly abused, so this cake was made with the children in mind.

The cake is simple to make and can be decorated in a day. The three circles of fondant which form the dial can be made by cutting around anything suitable – I used a baking tin for the largest, a beer glass for the next, and the base of an egg cup for the smallest.

Please read the General Notes on pages 6 to 9 before starting to decorate the cake. It is a good idea also to read through the step-by-step instructions and check the ingredient and equipment lists.

Ingredients for cake

340g (12oz) butter
250g (9oz) caster sugar
420g (15oz) self-raising flour
250g (9oz) ground rice
250ml (9 fl oz) milk beaten with 5 large eggs
flavouring (optional)
Make from this recipe: 1 × 180mm (7in.) square cake
1 × 450g (1lb) loaf cake – approx. 190mm (7½in.) long

Ingredients for fondant and royal icing

790g (1¾lb) icing sugar, plus 60g (2oz)
1¾ egg whites, plus ¼
almost 4 tblsp liquid glucose
flavouring (optional)
Also: warm sieved apricot jam; 50/50 mixture of cornflour and icing sugar in a dusting dredger; yellow, orange, and brown food colouring.

Equipment

Basins for mixing icings; spoons; sieve; rolling pin; steel rule; sharp-pointed knife; lolly sticks (LS) as spacers; greaseproof paper for icing bags; pastry brush; Ateco (or equivalent) icing nozzles 2 and 3; 230mm (9in.) square silver board.

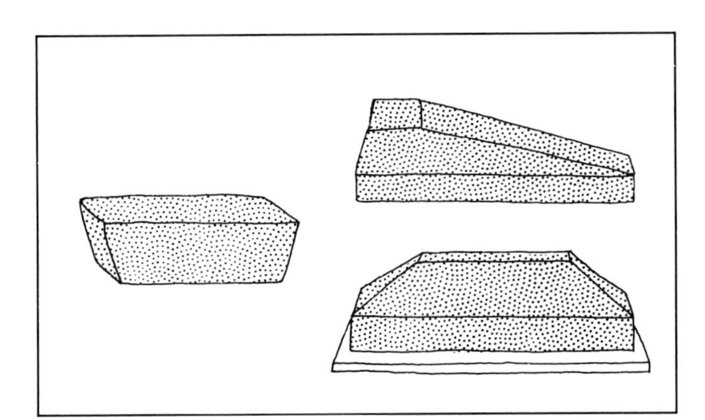

1. Having left the cakes overnight, slice the tops flat. Turn square cake upside down and cut sloping sides as shown. Cut a slope at front, also as shown, leaving enough flat surface for loaf cake to sit on. Position cake in centre of silver board.

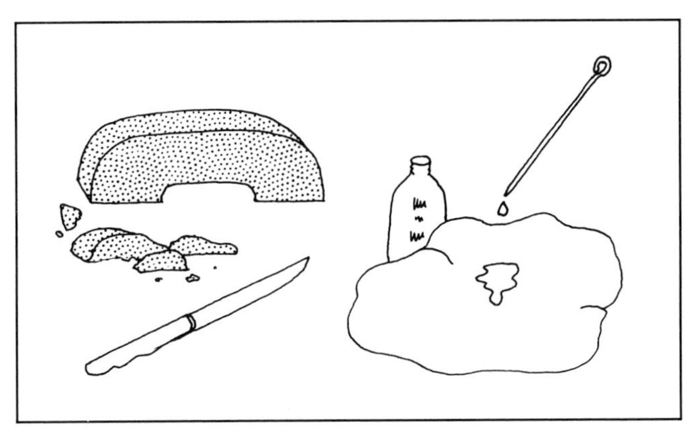

2. Turn loaf cake upside down and round off all corners and edges. Cut piece out of base, as shown.

Make the 780g (1¾lb) of fondant and mix in yellow food colouring.

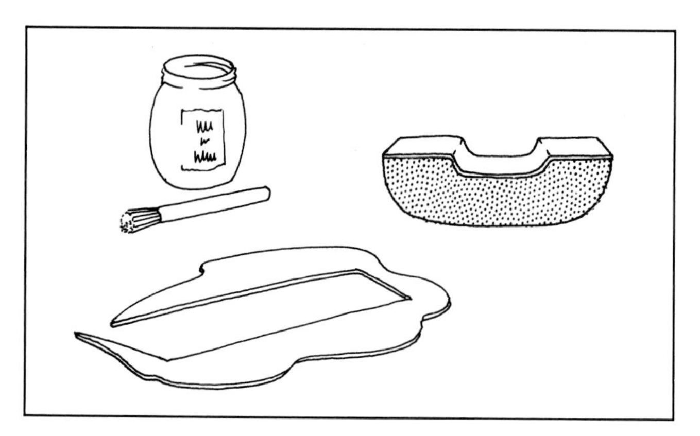

3. Brush base of loaf cake with warm jam. Roll a piece of fondant to 2 LS thick, cut to size, and carefully apply. Leave to dry.

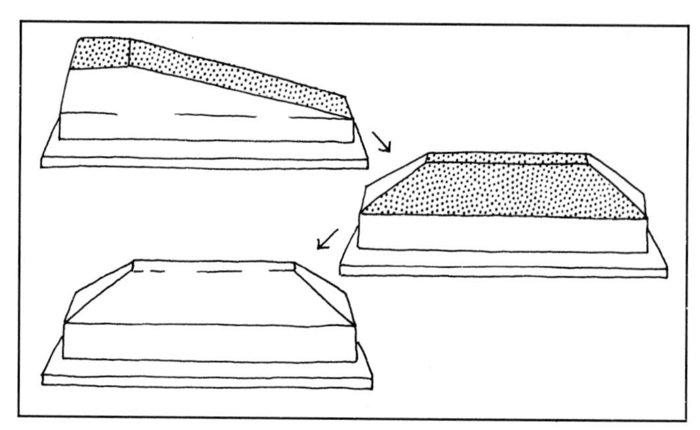

4. Measure dimensions of large cake, then brush with jam. Roll fondant to 2 LS thick, cut to shape, then apply – first back, then sides, front and (in one piece) top and slope.

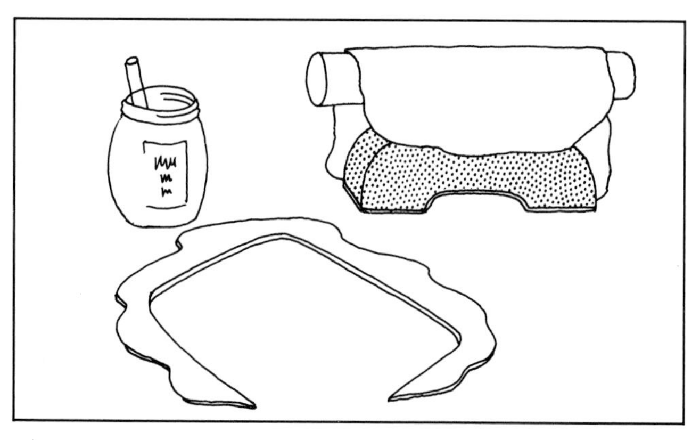

5. Keep a piece of yellow fondant, add orange to remainder. Dust a surface and place loaf cake fondant side down. Brush sponge with jam. Measure cake and roll fondant to 2 LS thick. Cut to shape and with help of rolling pin, apply fondant. Smooth over surface with hands. Leave to dry.

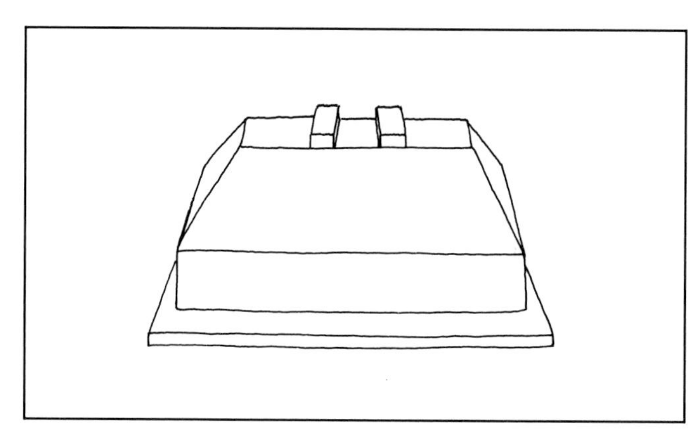

6. Take a piece of orange fondant and add brown. Roll to 4 LS thick and cut out two pieces 20mm (¾in.) wide to support receiver. Position on flat surface of large cake, securing with egg white.

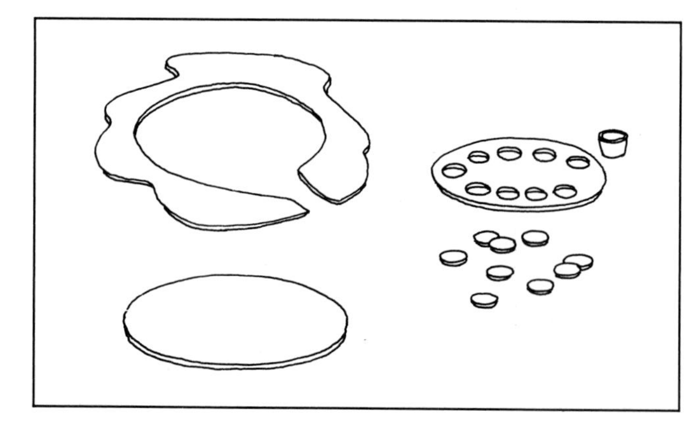

7. Roll orange fondant to 2 LS thick, cut a circle 110mm (4¼in.) diameter. Leave to dry on a dusted surface. Add more yellow to yellow fondant, roll to 2 LS thick and cut a circle 90mm (3½in.) diameter. Cut finger holes with small cutter – as many as number of letters in child's name, if possible.

8. Add more orange to small piece of orange fondant. Roll to 1 LS thick and cut circle to fit in centre of dial. Leave all pieces to dry on a dusted surface for 2–3 hours.

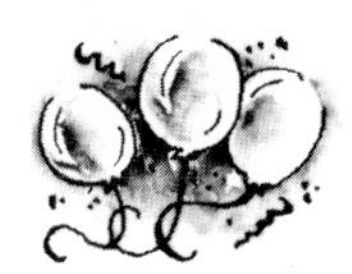

9. When pieces are dry, brush centre back of yellow dial with egg white and attach to large orange circle.
Make up the 60g (2oz) of royal icing.

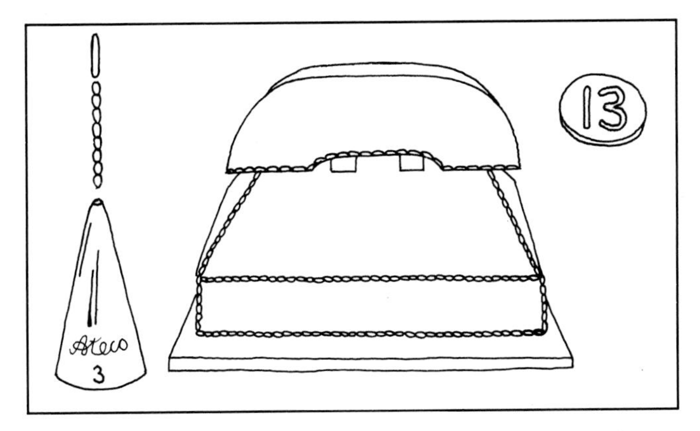

10. With *No. 3 nozzle* and orange icing, pipe lines of continuous dots on all seams of fondant on yellow cake and around base. Brush brown supports with egg white and attach receiver. Pipe continuous dots around bottom edge. Pipe age of child on smallest orange circle.

11. With *No. 2 nozzle* pipe **'use this phone to call your friends'** in bright orange, on top of receiver. (See introductory notes on page 8 for piped writing.)

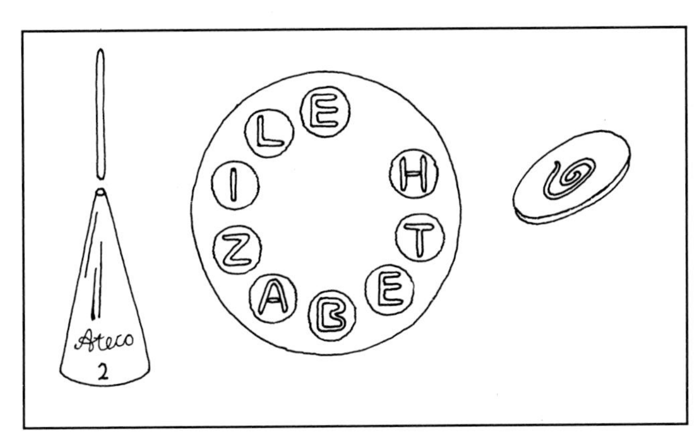

12. Using same nozzle and brown icing, pipe name of child, or something else appropriate, in finger holes. Stick small orange circle on to centre of dial with a swirl of piped icing. Stick completed dial on to telephone, again with piped icing, pressing gently to secure.

13. Using same nozzle and icing, pipe a second line of continuous dots around base of telephone.
Roll fondant trimmings into a ball and add brown.

14. Make a sausage long enough to go from the side of the receiver to back of telephone. Flatten each end a little, then attach with egg white – hold until secure. Pipe three lines of continuous dots, using *nozzle No. 3*, around both joins.

London bus

Apart from the piping (straight lines!) this is one of the simplest cakes to make. It can be completed in an afternoon, although windows etc. are easier to apply if the red fondant has been left overnight to dry.

Piping lines is easy to do once you get used to holding the bag and controlling the flow of icing. Practise on your kitchen table if this cake is your first attempt. The introductory notes for the Shoe Polishing cake may help with the piping of letters and numbers.

Please read the General Notes on pages 6 to 9 before starting to decorate the cake. Also read through the step-by-step instructions and check the ingredient and equipment lists.

Ingredients for cake

220g (8oz) butter
170g (6oz) caster sugar
280g (10oz) self-raising flour
170g (6oz) ground rice
140ml (5fl oz) milk beaten with 3 large eggs
filling

Make from this recipe:
1 × 450g (1lb) loaf cake
1 × 900g (2lb) loaf cake

Ingredients for fondant and royal icing

450g (1lb) icing sugar, plus 110g (4oz)
1 egg white, plus ½
2 tblsp liquid glucose
flavouring (optional)
Also: warm sieved apricot jam; 50/50 mixture of cornflour and icing sugar in a dusting dredger; bright red, yellow and black food colouring.

Equipment

Basins for mixing icings; sieve; spoons; rolling pin; steel rule; sharp-pointed knife; lolly sticks (LS) as spacers; pastry brush; greaseproof paper for icing bags; Ateco (or equivalent) icing nozzles 1, 2 and 3; 230mm (9in.) square silver board.

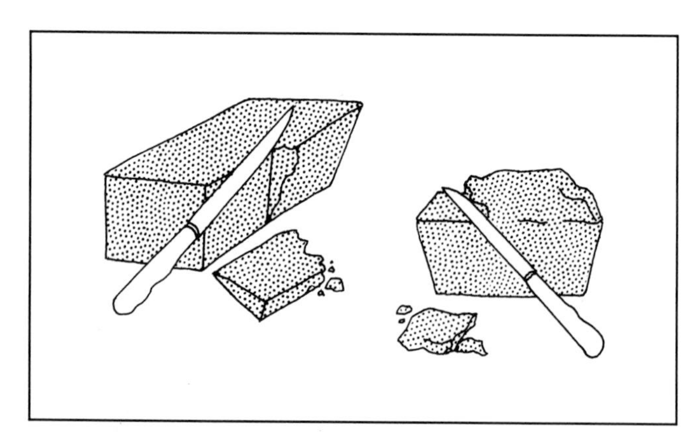

1. Having left the cakes overnight, slice the top and sloping sides of the 900g (2lb) cake so that it becomes a square-sided oblong. Slice the top from the 450g (1lb) cake and neaten the sloping sides.

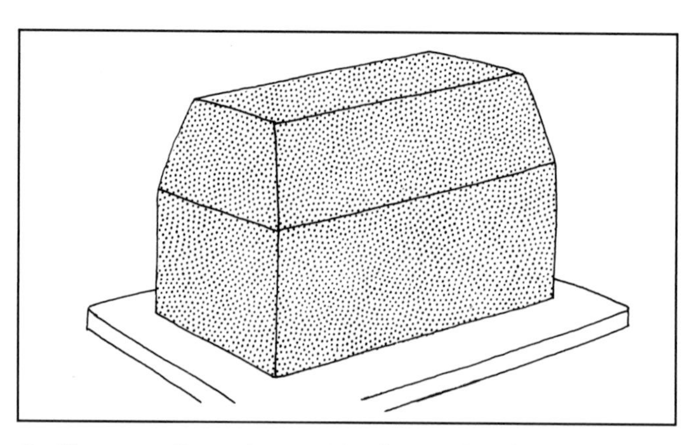

2. Turn smaller cake upside down. Sandwich the two cakes together with butter crean and/or jam. Position in centre of silver board.

3. Make 450g (1lb) fondant. Put 80g (3oz) on one side (covered) and colour remaining fondant bright red. Measure dimensions of cake, then roll fondant to 2 LS thick.

4. Cut front and back pieces first. Brush cake with jam then carefully apply fondant. Cut side pieces, brush cake with jam, apply fondant. Cut top and repeat the above. Trim edges if necessary.

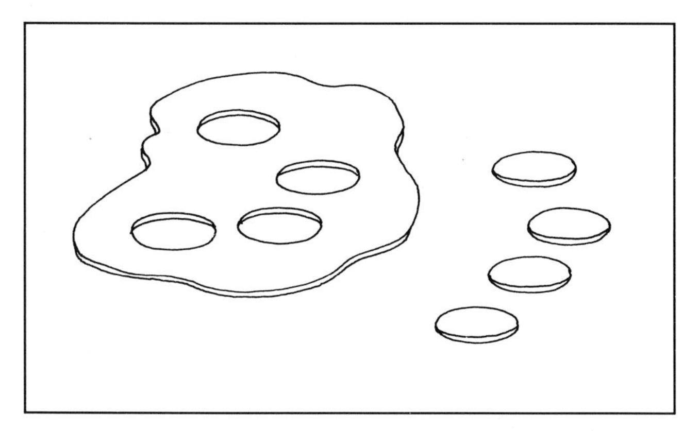

5. Take a little red fondant. Roll to 1 LS thick and cut four circles 15mm (5/8in.) diameter. These go in centre of wheels.

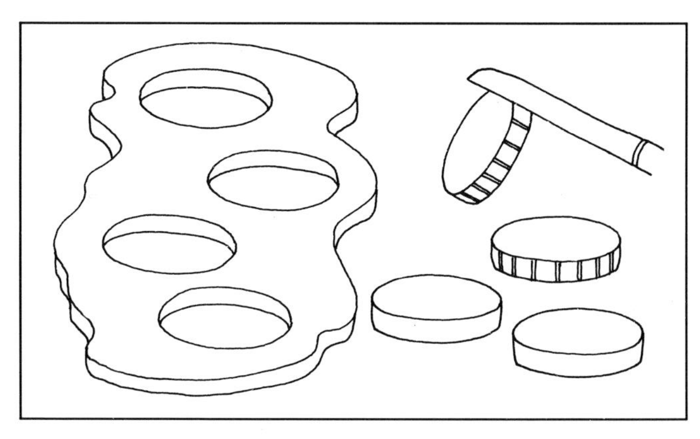

6. Add drops of black colouring to some of red fondant. Roll to 4 LS thick and cut four circles 30mm (1¼in.) diameter. Mark a tread round the edges with blunt side of a knife.

If possible leave everything to dry overnight.

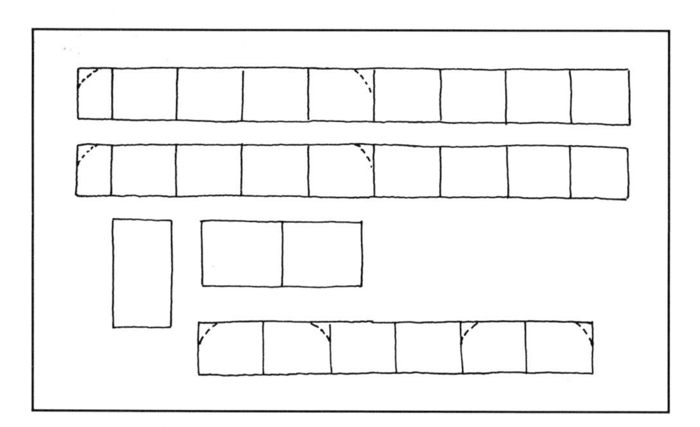

7. Take 60g (2oz) of remaining white fondant, add a little black colouring. Roll to 1 LS thick and cut strips 20mm (¾in.) wide. Cut windows and doors as shown.

8. The two front windows are slightly larger than the others. Round off corners of windows where indicated. Carefully brush backs with egg white and apply to bus. Position wheels using egg white, then apply red circles in centres.

9. Roll white fondant to 1 LS thick and cut two headlights 6mm (¼in.) diameter. Brush backs with egg white and position under large front windows. Cut a 12mm (½in.) square, cut off corners and position above front window.

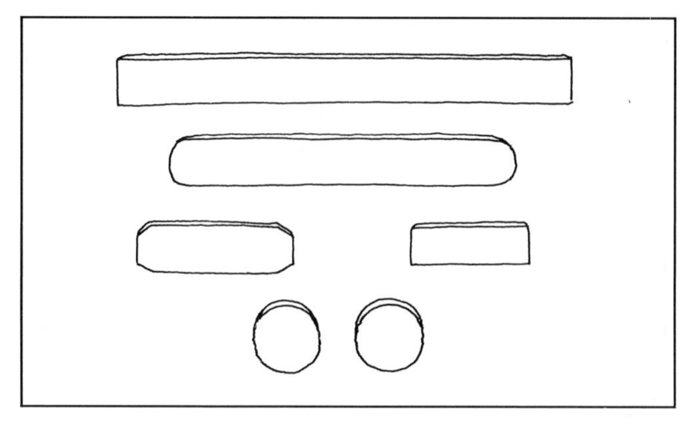

10. Use remaining fondant, adding yellow colouring to some, to make bus signs. Roll the fondant to 1 LS thick. The signs can be applied before or after the lettering has been piped.

11. Make up the 110g (4oz) of royal icing, add enough black colouring to make medium grey. With *No. 2 nozzles* pipe round the edges of windows and door, as shown.

12. Mix some black to the icing to make darker grey. Still using *No. 2* pipe dark grey dots along seams of red fondant – around top edge and down front. Pipe other markings on bus as shown, then pipe number of bus – child's age.

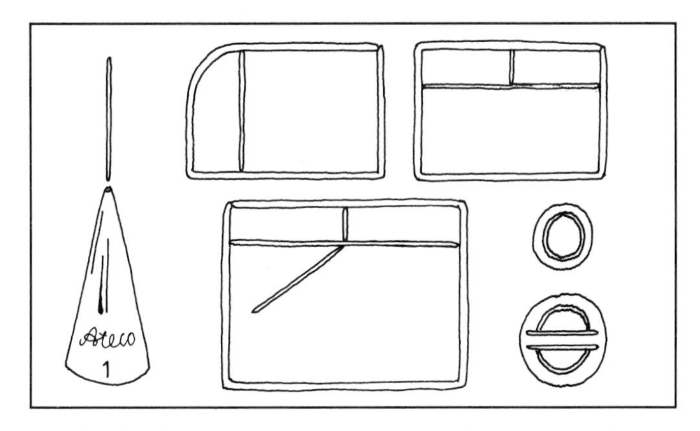

13. With dark grey and *No. 1 nozzle* pipe details on windows, windscreen wipers, circles on head-lights and details on signs.

14. On front sign pipe **London**; on back sign **LONDON**; on one side **HAPPY BIRTHDAY**; on the other side **LONDON SIGHTSEEING TOUR** . Finally, with a *No. 3 nozzle* pipe a line (avoiding wheels) round base of bus.

LONDON SIGHTSEEING TOUR

HAPPY BIRTHDAY

London LONDON

The sample words above can be used to trace from – see the introductory notes on page 8, for piped writing and centering.

Racing track

When this cake was made I was unable to obtain the correct sized silver board: I cellotaped four 200mm (8in.) boards together and the fondant roads were layed to cover up the joins (but they do give the cake a little more interest).

The cars on the track are based on 'Formula Fords', the lowest of the Formula cars in which most racers begin their careers (they are also the easiest to model).

The cake can be decorated in two days. Please read the General Notes on pages 6 to 9 before starting. It is also a good idea to read through the step-by-step instructions and check the ingredient and equipment lists.

Ingredients for cake

340g (12oz) butter
250g (9oz) caster sugar
420g (15oz) self-raising flour
250g (9oz) ground rice
250ml (9fl oz) milk beaten with 5 large eggs
buttercream for filling

Make from this recipe: 1 × 180mm (7in.) round cake
1 × 900g (2lb) loaf cake

Ingredients for fondant and royal icing

1.120kg (2½lb) icing sugar, plus 170g (6oz)
2½ egg whites, plus ¾
5 tblsp liquid glucose
flavouring (optional)
Also: warm sieved apricot jam; 50/50 mixture of cornflour and icing sugar in a dusting dredger; green, black, silver yellow, red and blue food colouring.

Equipment

Basins for mixing icings; sieve; spoons; rolling pin; steel rule; sharp-pointed knife; lolly sticks (LS) as spacers; pastry brush; paint brush; greaseproof paper for icing bags; 55mm (2¼in.) round cutter; 15mm (⅝in.) round cutter; Ateco (or equivalent) icing nozzles 1, 3 and 9; 400mm (16in.) square silver board.

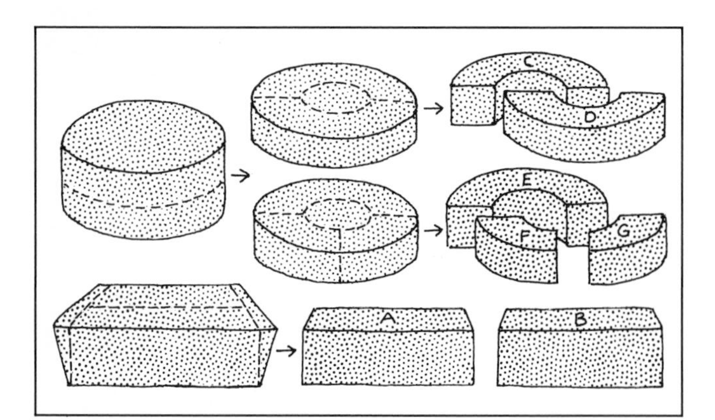

1. Having left the cakes overnight, slice the tops flat. Slice the round cake in half. Cut away sloping sides from loaf cake, then cut in half lengthways. Press large cutter in centre of both round cakes, then cut each cake in half, and one half in half again, as shown.

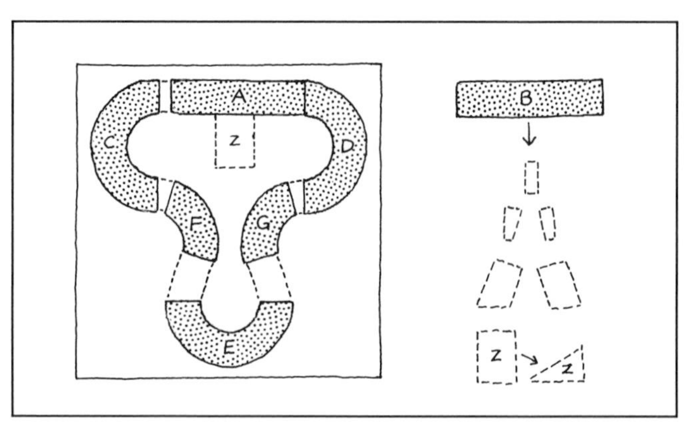

2. Position pieces on board, as shown. Cut remaining half of loaf cake to fit spaces, then cut a sloping piece to go inside track. Go round track with knife, levelling surfaces and neatening joins. Stick all pieces together with buttercream. Make the 1.120kg (2½lb) of fondant. Colour 1kg (2¼lb) green.

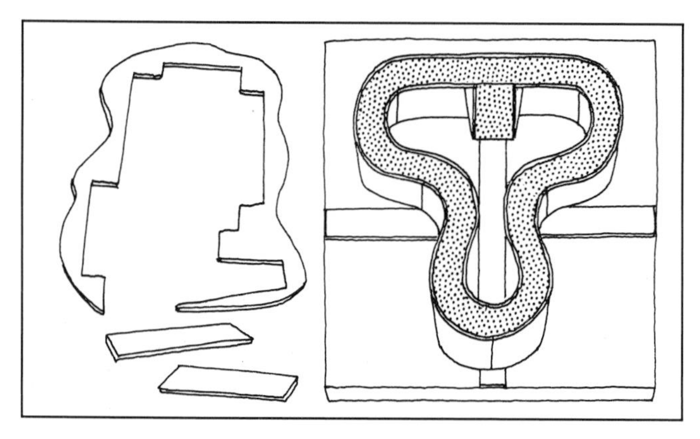

3. Brush inside walls of track with warm jam. Measure depth of wall and then roll fondant to 2 LS thick. Cut into manageable pieces and apply. Repeat with outside walls. Cut roads to fit where indicated, 2 LS thick and 25mm (1in.) wide. Attach to board with egg white.

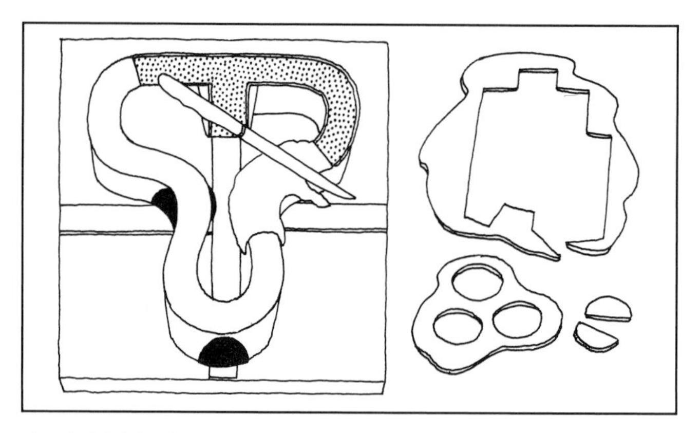

4. Add black to green trimmings, to make grey. Brush top of track with jam. Apply as before, cutting fondant roughly to shape, then trimming after application. Add more black to some of trimmings for tunnels. Roll to 1 LS thick and cut three circles with large cutter. Cut in half and apply where indicated.

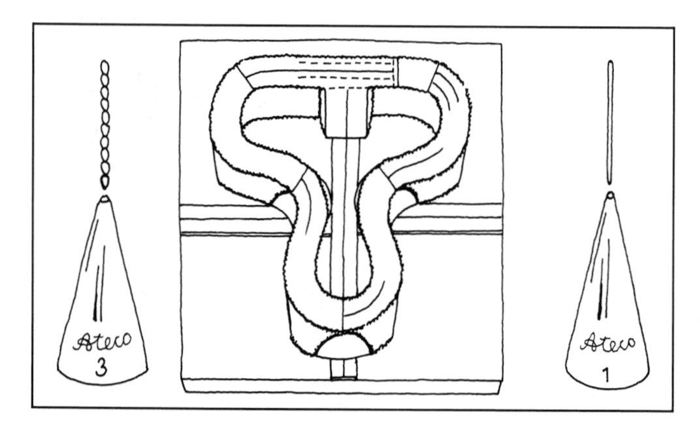

5. Make the 170g (6oz) of royal icing. With *No. 3 nozzle* and green icing, pipe continuous dots along track edges, then around base and tunnels. Pipe black continuous dots along edges of roads on board. With *No. 1* and white icing, pipe markings on track, as shown (pipe a line across fondant joins).

6. Add blue to some grey trimmings and model two cars as shown, 5 LS thick and about 50mm (2in.) long, 12mm (½in.) wide. Add black to remaining trimmings. Roll to 3 LS thick and cut 32 wheels with small cutter. Make indent in each centre with *No. 9 nozzle,* then paint silver. Leave on dusted surface.

7. Using remaining white fondant, model six more cars in different colours (break a little piece from each colour and make six helmets, as shown). Leave to dry for an hour.

8. Attach wheels and helmets to cars, using egg white. With *No. 1 nozzle* and white icing, pipe goggles on helmets. Using different coloured icing, pipe lines on helmets, then numbers and lines on cars. Leave for 30 minutes, then attach to track with egg white.

Train

I thought a tender or truck full of jolly pink pigs would be a change from the usual sweets or chocolates. It would be fun to have the pigs in different flavours, say strawberry, banana, lemon and orange – the flavouring should not make any difference to the colour.

As it is impossible to buy a cake board to fit the train, I had to join two 200mm (8in.) boards together. Tape the boards on top and underneath, using a clear cellotape.

The cake can be decorated in a day, but two days would be better. Please read the General Notes on pages 6 to 9 before you start. Also read through the step-by-step instructions and check the ingredient and equipment lists.

Ingredients for cake

280g (10oz) butter
220g (8oz) caster sugar
360g (13oz) self-raising flour
200g (7oz) ground rice
220ml (8fl oz) milk beaten with 4 large eggs

Make from this recipe: 1 × 200mm (8in.) square cake
2 × 140g (5oz) food-can cakes

Ingredients for fondant and royal icing

1.340kg (3lb) icing sugar, plus 110g (4oz)
3 egg whites, plus ½
6 tblsp liquid glucose
flavouring (optional)
Also: warm sieved apricot jam; 50/50 mixture of cornflour and icing sugar in a dusting dredger; yellow, blue and red food colouring; edible silver balls.

Equipment

Basins for mixing icings; sieve; spoons; rolling pin; steel rule; sharp-pointed knife; lolly sticks (LS) as spacers; pastry brush; paint brush; greaseproof paper for icing bags; Ateco (or equivalent) icing nozzle No. 2; 60mm (2¼in.) round cutter; 2 × 200mm (8in.) square silver cake boards; clear cellotape.

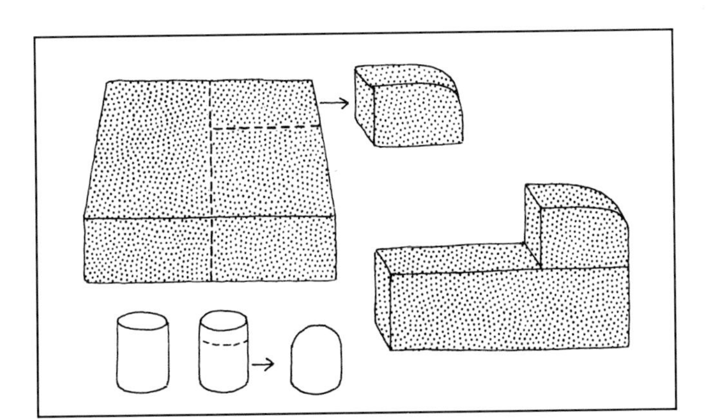

1. Having left the cakes overnight, slice the tops flat. Cut square cake in half. Cut a 60mm (2½in.) piece from one half, rounding off one of top edges, as shown. Cut one of little cakes to 50mm (2in.) high, and round off top. Attach cabin to engine with jam and/or butter-cream.

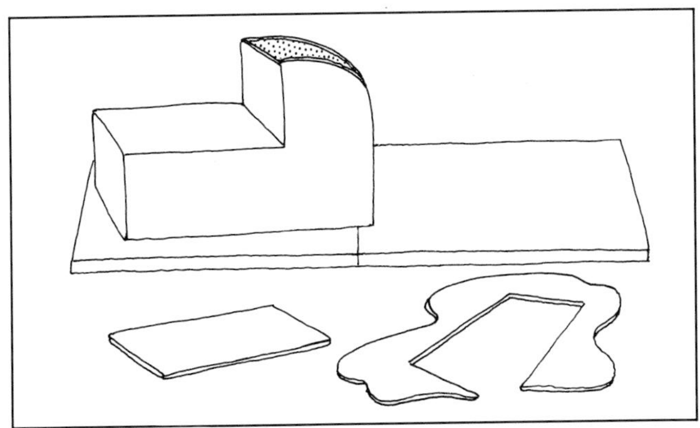

2. Make the 1.340kg (3lb) of fondant (in two batches for ease). Position engine at slight angle on board. Colour 560g (1¼lb) of fondant pale yellow. Measure dimensions, then brush with jam. Roll fondant to 2 LS thick, cut each piece to size and apply: sides, front, top of body and front of cabin.

3. Cut top of cabin and back in one piece. Make a hook, as shown, and attach to back with egg white. Roll trimmings to 2 LS thick and cut four circles with cutter. Leave on a dusted surface. Colour 450g (1lb) of fondant pale blue. Position tender on board. Cover as before: back, front, sides then top.

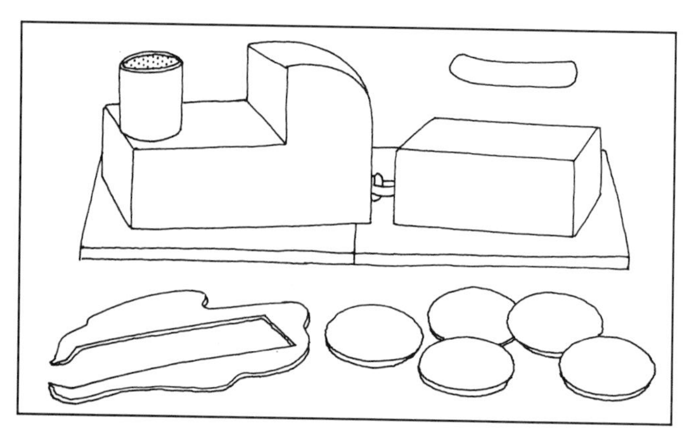

4. Roll fondant to 2 LS thick and cut five more wheels. Roll a small piece, place around hook and attach to front of tender with egg white. Measure circumference of chimney then brush with jam. Cut fondant (2 LS thick) and apply. Position on engine using jam to secure.

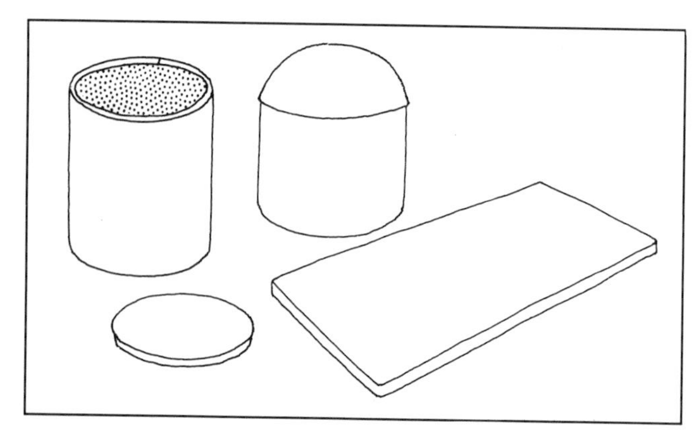

5. Brush top of chimney with jam and apply one of blue wheels. Brush top and sides of dome. Cover top, with newly cut yellow wheel, and sides as for chimney.

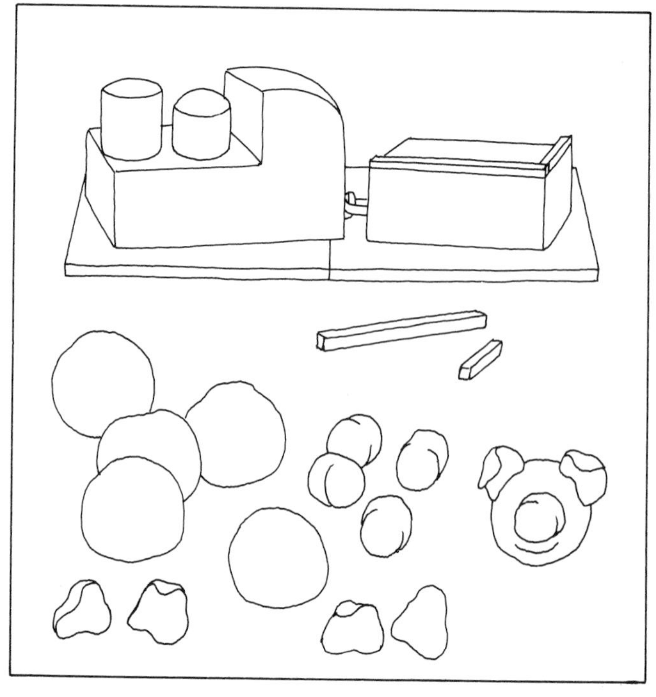

6. Add blue trimmings to about 80g (3oz) of white. Roll to 4 LS thick and cut strips 10mm (⅜in.) wide to go round top of carriage. Attach with egg white. Add a little red to remaining white fondant. Model pigs' heads, as shown. Attach ears and noses with egg white. Mark smile with blunt edge of knife.

7. Position each head in carriage while still soft. Attach silver balls with dabs of egg white. Put a little fondant underneath two heads at front to give impression of bodies. Slice back of seventh head and attach to window

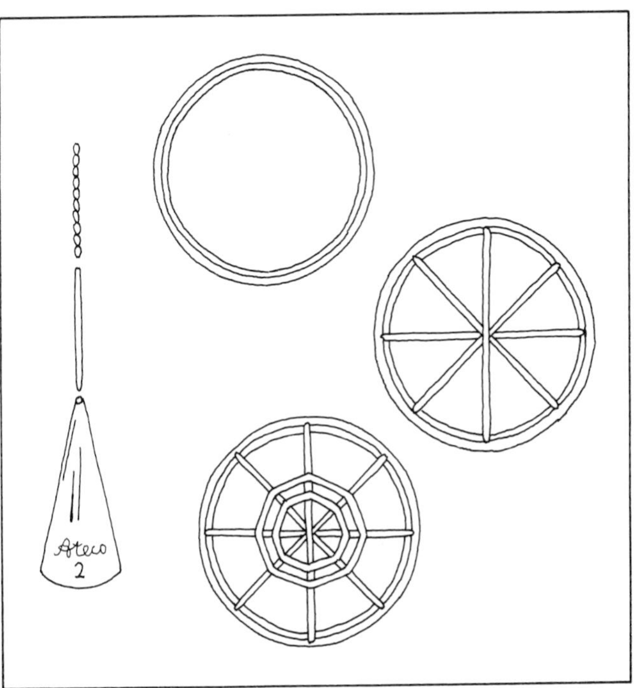

8. Make the 110g (4oz) of royal icing. Colour half blue, half yellow. Pipe continuous dots along all fondant seams and around base of cakes. Pipe lines on cabin top and on wheels, as shown. After 30 minutes, attach wheels to engine and carriage, using egg white to secure.

Seasonal

Halloween

Halloween (All Saints' Eve) was a feast originally celebrated by the Celts as the eve of their new year. Fires were lit to ensure new life after the winter. In later times, ghosts and witches were thought to roam the earth and the fires were built to keep them away. Burning candles in pumpkins is said to come from an Irish legend: a man called Jack was barred from heaven because of his meanness. As he had nowhere to go, he walked the earth (along with the ghosts and goblins) carrying a lantern. 'Trick or Treat' is a fairly recent innovation. Children go from house to house, in costume, asking for a treat – fruit, money or candy. If the treat is forthcoming, they promise not to play a trick.

When all the cake ingredients have been blended, divide the mixture between the two tins, putting rather more in one than the other. The cake can be decorated in one to two days. Please read the General Notes on pages 6 to 9 before starting. Also read through the step-by-step instructions and check the ingredient and equipment lists.

Ingredients for cake

340g (12oz) butter
250g (9oz) caster sugar
420g (15oz) self-raising flour
250g (9oz) ground rice
250ml (9fl oz) milk beaten with 5 large eggs
Make from this recipe: 2 × 180mm (7in.) round cakes

Ingredients for fondant and royal icing

670g (1½lb) icing sugar, plus 110g (4oz)
1½ egg whites, plus ½
3 tblsp liquid glucose
flavouring (optional)
Also: warm sieved apricot jam; 50/50 mixture of cornflour and icing sugar in a dusting dredger; blue, black, flesh, silver and yellow food colouring.

Equipment

Basins for mixing icings; sieve; spoons; rolling pin; sharp-pointed knife; lolly sticks (LS) as spacers; pastry brush; greaseproof paper for icing bags; Ateco (or equivalent) icing nozzles 1, 2, 3, 7 and 15; small star cutter; 55mm (2¼in.) round cutter; 250mm (10in.) round silver cake board.

1. Having left the cakes overnight, slice the tops flat. Cut a 25mm (1in.) piece from the shallower cake and 15mm (⅜in.) from the other, as shown. Make the 670g (1½lb) of fondant. Brush deeper cake with jam and position towards front of silver board. Take 340g (12oz) of fondant and roll to 2 LS thick.

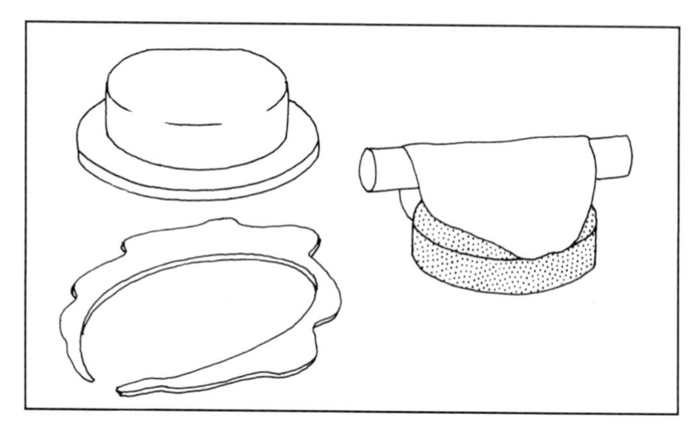

2. With help of a rolling pin, cover cake (apart from cut piece at back). Add 220g (8oz) of fondant to trimmings and colour darkish blue. Apply to shallow cake (apart from cut piece) as before. Leave on dusted surface. Break off two thirds of trimmings, add black, then put to one side.

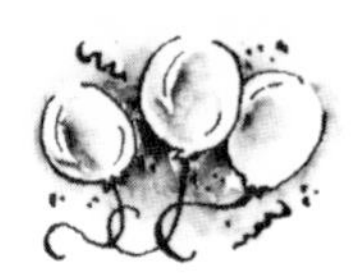

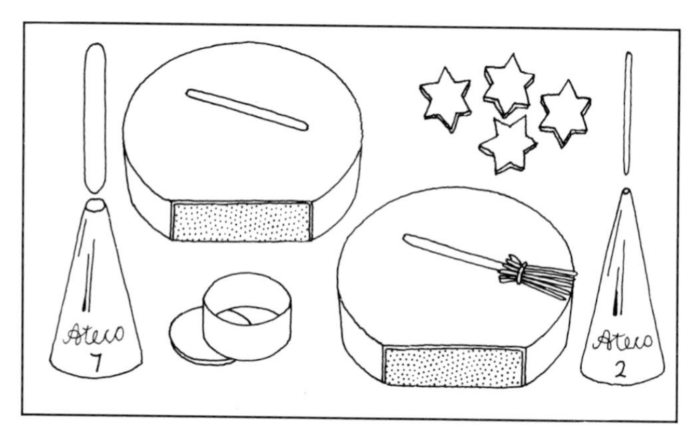

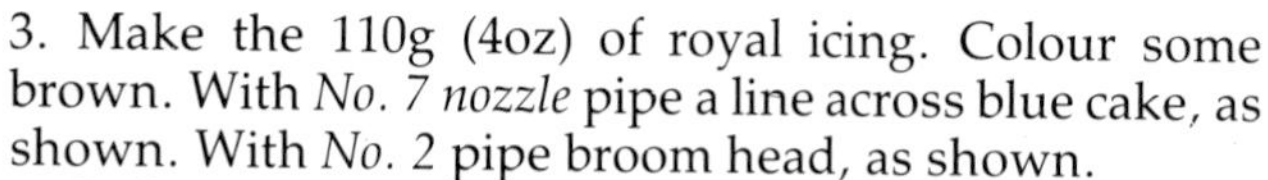

3. Make the 110g (4oz) of royal icing. Colour some brown. With *No. 7 nozzle* pipe a line across blue cake, as shown. With *No. 2* pipe broom head, as shown.

Roll some white fondant to 1 LS thick, cut four stars and a half moon. Leave on dusted surface.

4. Take 110g (4oz) of fondant and colour yellow. Shape into three balls. Make a hole in each centre, then mark grooves with blunt edge of knife. Stick in white candles. Leave on dusted surface.

Take a little fondant and add flesh. Model face and hands of witch (face flat on one side).

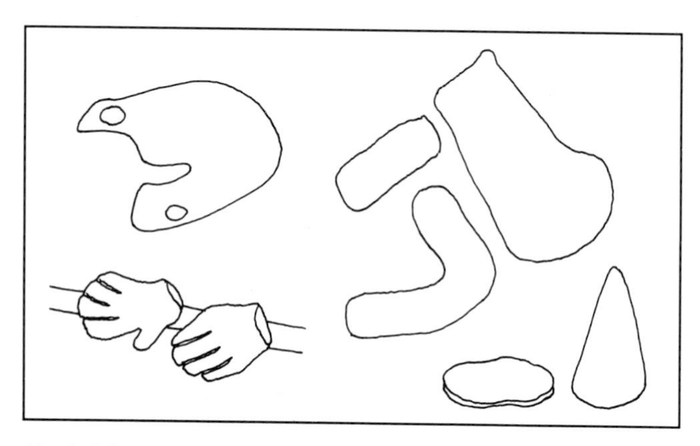

5. Add warts to nose and chin (poor lady!) Attach head to cake and hands to broomstick, using egg white. Mark fingers with knife. With black fondant, model witch pieces, as shown. Attach short arm to cake first, then body, then top arm. Model the hat and brim. Stick together, leave on dusted surface.

6. With *No. 1 nozzle* and dark grey icing, pipe eye, brow and crinkly hair. Position leg and shoe. Roll fondant to 1 1 LS. Cut skirt, as shown, and attach.

Make three large and three smaller balls (for cats). Cut in half and stick to sides of white cake with egg white.

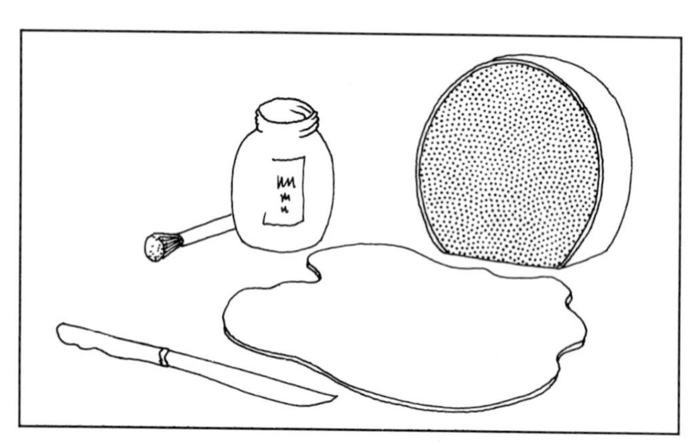

7. Stand blue cake upright and brush back with jam. Roll fondant trimmings to 1 LS thick. Lay cake on fondant. Carefully lift and position, with jam, at back of white cake. Attach pumpkins to cake with egg white.

8. With blue icing and *No. 15 nozzle*, pipe stars around base, and part of top edge, of white cake. Paint stars and moon silver and attach with egg white. With *No. 1* and dark grey icing, pipe eyes, whiskers and ears on cats. Use *No. 3* to pipe tails.

Christmas eve

This is one of my favourite cakes. Having manoeuvred his way down the chimney and safely delivered the seasonal gifts, Father Christmas now finds himself stuck – the mince pies and sherry must have added a few inches to his waistline.

The cake can be decorated in a day, but you may find it easier to do it in two days. Please read General Notes on pages 6 to 9 before starting. Also read through the step-by-step instructions and check the ingredient and equipment lists.

Ingredients for cake

450g (16oz) butter
340g (12oz) caster sugar
560g (20oz) self-raising flour
340g (12oz) ground rice
280ml (10fl oz) milk beaten with 6 large eggs
buttercream for filling
Make from this recipe: 2 × 180mm (7in.)square cakes

Ingredients for fondant and royal icing

1.340kg (3lb) icing sugar, plus 30g (1oz)
3 egg whites, plus ⅛
6 tblsp liquid glucose
flavouring (optional)
Also: warm sieved apricot jam; 50/50 mixture of cornflour and icing sugar in a dusting dredger; black, red, brown, green, yellow and blue food colouring.

Equipment

Basins for mixing icings; sieve; spoons; rolling pin; steel rule; sharp-pointed knife; lolly sticks (LS) as spacers; pastry brush; 15mm (⅝in.) round cutter; greaseproof paper for icing bags; Ateco (or equivalent) icing nozzle No. 1; small paint brush; 250mm (10in.) square silver board.

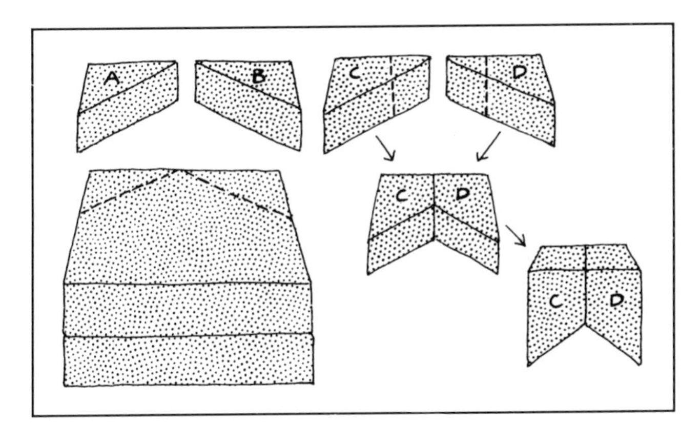

1. Having left the cakes overnight, slice the tops flat. Put one cake on top of other, measure 90mm (3½in.) up each side and cut to top middle point, as shown. Take two of remaining pieces and cut off 40mm (1½in.) as shown (the larger pieces join to make the chimney).

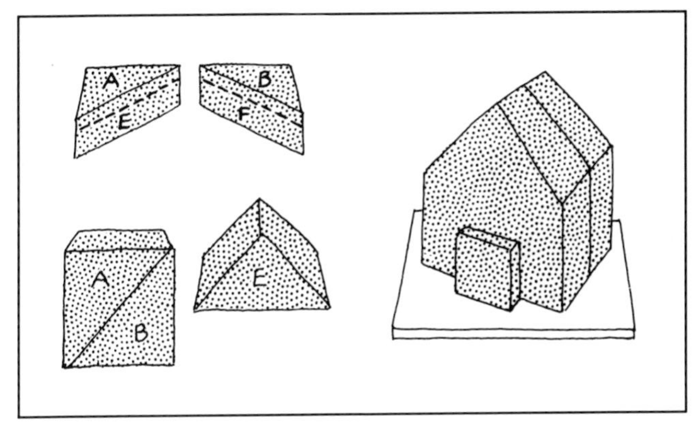

2. Slice a third from the two remaining pieces. The two shallow pieces will join to make porch (trim to make a 75mm (3in.) square). One of the deep pieces will be porch roof. Sandwich main house and porch together with buttercream. Position, at an angle, on silver cake board.

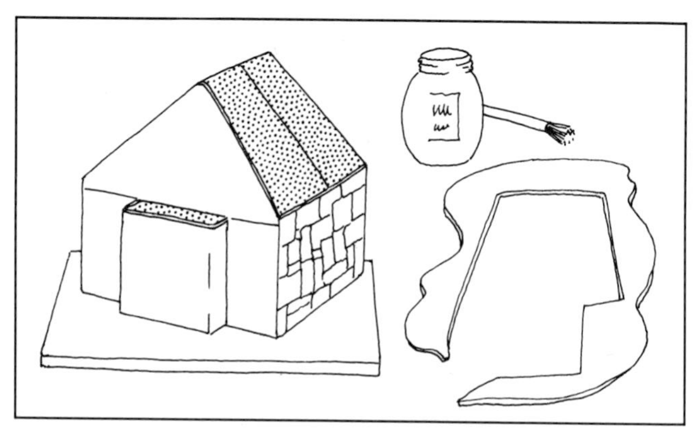

3. Make 900g (2lb) of fondant and colour grey. Measure house back then brush with jam. Roll fondant to 2 LS thick, cut to size and carefully apply. Mark stones with blunt edge of knife. Repeat process of covering for both sides of porch, porch (in one piece) and gable end, marking stones after each application.

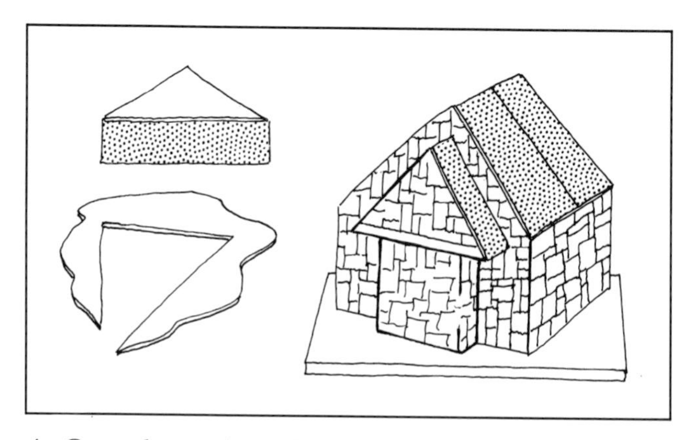

4. Cover base of porch roof with fondant 1 LS thick. Brush back and base with jam and position on top of porch. Roll fondant to 2 LS thick, cut to fit front porch roof, apply and mark stones.

5. Measure dimensions of roofs then brush with jam. Roll fondant to 1 LS thick, cut to size, then carefully apply. Join chimney pieces together with jam and a layer of fondant. Leave to dry (overnight if possible).

6. Make the 30g (1oz) of royal icing. Measure sides of chimney, then brush with jam. Roll fondant to 2 LS thick, cut to fit, then apply. Stand chimney upside down and mark stones. Brush inside sponge with jam, then dab icing along inside join. Carefully position on roof.

7. Make 450g (1lb) of fondant. Brush top of chimney with jam. Take 110g (4oz) of fondant, flatten with hands and apply to chimney, pushing it gently down sides. Colour some fondant pale yellow, roll to 1 LS thick and cut three oblong windows roughly 45mm (1¾in.) long and 30mm (1¼in.) deep; and two round windows.

8. Paint brown leading on windows. Brush backs with egg white, attach round windows to each side of porch, others to each wall of house. Roll some green fondant to 1 LS thick, cut a door and shutters for oblong windows, mark grooves while still soft. Brush backs with egg white, then apply.

9. Make brown fondant, roll to 2 LS thick, cut sills for windows (half circles for round ones) and surround for door. Brush with egg white and apply. Take white fondant, brush tops of windows with egg white and attach snow.

10. Take grey trimmings. Cut in two, add green to half and blue with a little yellow to other half. Roll to 1 LS thick and cut tiles about 15mm ($\frac{5}{8}$in.) diameter. Starting at bottom edge, apply with egg white to both roofs, stopping 20mm ($\frac{3}{4}$in.) from top ridge.

11. Using soft white fondant cover roof ridges and around base of house, as shown. Colour about 170g (6oz) of fondant red and some flesh, for hands and head. Model hands and head as shown. Stick hands to chimney and mark fingers with blunt edge of knife.

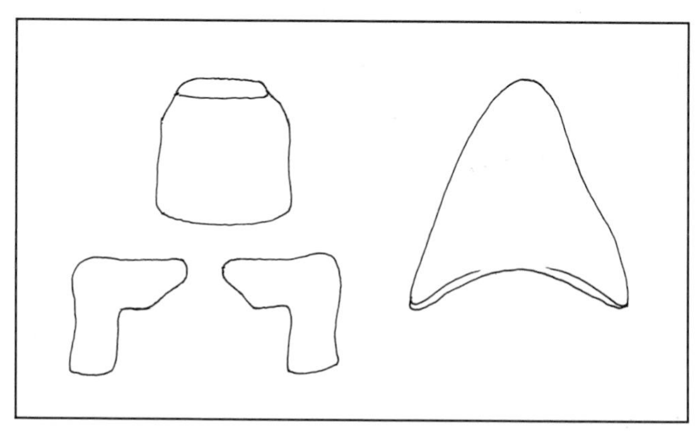

12. Model body and arms as shown. Position, with head, securing with dabs of egg white. Model a hood – a flat triangle – and attach to head. Roll some white fondant and attach around hood and sleeve edges.

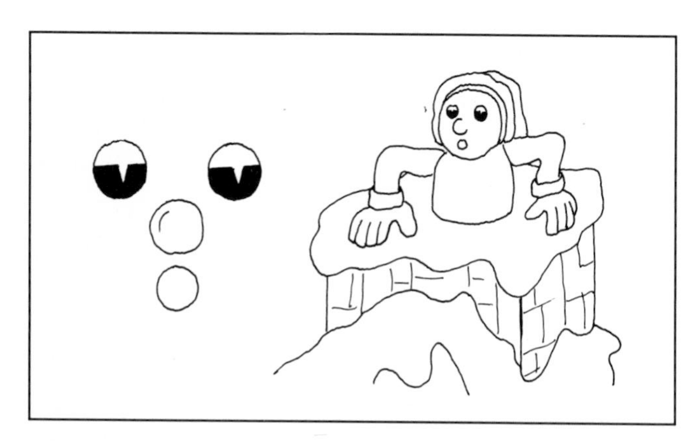

13. Make a little pink nose and attach to face. Press two small white balls flat and attach to face, for eyes. Repeat with red fondant for mouth. Paint eyes with blue colouring, as shown.

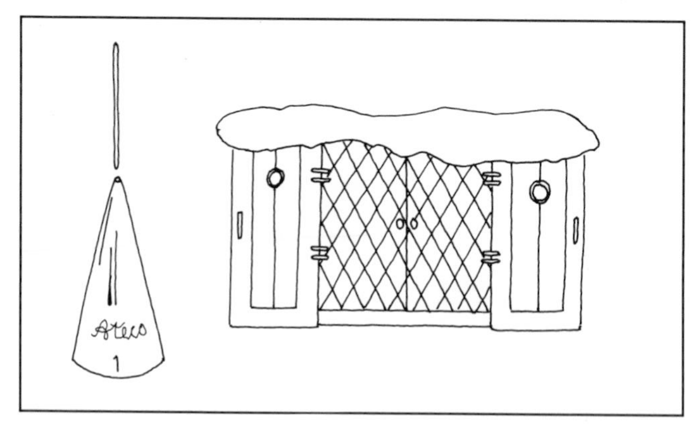

14. With *No. 1 nozzle* and white icing, pipe beard and eye brows. Pipe icicles hanging from some of roof tiles – press nozzle gently into tile, let some icing come, then pull sharply. With brown icing pipe handles on door, windows and shutters, then hinges on shutters.